Process Management to Quality Improvement

Process Management to Quality Improvement

The Way to Design, Document and
Re-engineer Business Systems

Gary Born

JOHN WILEY & SONS

Chichester · New York · Brisbane · Toronto · Singapore

Published 1994 by John Wiley & Sons Ltd,
                    Baffins Lane, Chichester,
                    West Sussex PO19 1UD, England

                    Telephone (+44) 243 779777

Reprinted November 1994, January 1996

Other Wiley Editorial Offices

John Wiley & Sons, Inc., 605 Third Avenue,
New York, NY 10158-0012, USA

Jacaranda Wiley Ltd, 33 Park Road, Milton,
Queensland 4064, Australia

John Wiley & Sons (Canada) Ltd, 22 Worcester Road,
Rexdale, Ontario M9W 1L1, Canada

John Wiley & Sons (SEA) Pte Ltd, 37 Jalan Pemimpin #05-04,
Block B, Union Industrial Building, Singapore 2057

Library of Congress Cataloging-in-Publication Data

Born, Gary.
    Process management to quality improvement : the way to design,
document and re-engineer business systems / Gary Born.
        p.   cm.
    Includes bibliographical references and index.
    ISBN 0-471-94283-9
    1. Production management — Quality control.   2. Process
control.
    I. Title.
    TS156.B655   1994
    658.5'62 — dc20   93–34916
                                                           CIP

British Library Cataloguing in Publication Data

A catalogue record for this book is available from the British Library

ISBN 0-471-94283-9

Typeset in 10/12 pt Ehrhardt from author's disks by
Mathematical Composition Setters Ltd, Salisbury, Wiltshire.
Printed and bound in Great Britain by Bookcraft (Bath) Ltd.

For Pauline, my supporter, critic and wife.

Contents

Preface

In the 1980s, quality surfaced as a key issue for all enterprises in Europe and America, and total quality management summed up a range of different approaches. In the 1990s, business change and process transformation are key issues, and business process re-engineering is the summary phrase for the approaches which help to achieve them. In this book, I have aimed to provide techniques for bridging the many gaps between process-oriented and quality-oriented approaches to managing an enterprise.

The techniques in this book use a common notation for describing business processes: the Quality Process Language. This provides a foundation for analysing and improving those processes. It also enables a business to check that its processes are consistent with its policies and objectives, and that they comply with regulations and standards. The result is a set of effective processes which lead to better performance as well as improved quality.

Business bookshops are full of excellent books describing the principles of business re-engineering and quality management and the benefits which they provide. This book begins where they stop, by providing the methods and detailed examples required to *implement* the approaches. It concentrates on the practical problems which practitioners will encounter, such as how to document processes, how to find areas of improvement and how to implement process changes. In doing so, I have provided many examples and illustrations. If you require more information about the technique, you are welcome to contact me directly: details are provided at the end of this Preface.

This book is the result of ten years' experience in implementing and automating management and quality systems, and many people have helped with support, advice and criticism. Andy Coster, Mike Pilditch and Maurice Resnick provided continuing knowledge and inspiration about quality management. Many of my colleagues at EDS provided moral and sometimes practical support, including Kevin Giles, Jeff Hiscock, Andy Tomiak and Tom Abram.

Several friends and colleagues provided useful advice and comments on drafts of this book, including Penny Daniels, Walter Schwartz, Lawrence Smith, John Souter and Jenny Thornton. I am particularly indebted to the three people who reviewed the book in detail, Alan Jones of Teesside University, David Thomas of EDS UK and Pauline Withers. Diane Taylor and Sarah Stevens at John Wiley & Sons provided useful advice and feedback. Finally, Edna and Franz Hirshler twice provided much-appreciated accommodation and helpful words of support.

Although many of the above have influenced me over the years, I am solely responsible for the contents and opinions of this book.

Finally, I owe many thanks to my family, who helped me to survive the two years it took to write the book. My son Michael inspired me to think more laterally during our long walks. My wife, Pauline Withers, endured endless evenings without me and helped me to experience the joy of writing this book.

Twickenham, England
June 1994

Diagrams and MS-Windows® software to support the methods and techniques in this book are available on computer discs from the author.

The author may be contacted at the following addresses:

Postal: *Gary Born*
           P.O. Box 235
           Twickenham, Middlesex
           TW1 1LJ
           ENGLAND

E-Mail: *100302.21@compuserve.com*

1

Integrating process management and quality management

The art of progress is to preserve order amid change, and to preserve change amid order.

Alfred North Whitehead

1.1 METHOD IN THE MADNESS

Pity the poor manager in the modern enterprise. An era of unprecedented global competition and technological change has led to an apparent contradiction. Costs must be reduced to the minimum, yet constant innovation is also required to retain competitiveness. With continual effort and the cooperation of all workers, both of these may be achieved, but there is a final element in the equation: *quality*. No matter how innovative or inexpensive a product or service, customers are insisting that it be to a high specification with few or no faults. And governments are insisting that more and more regulations be complied with. How can enterprises cut their costs and innovate rapidly, while also maintaining a consistent and high level of quality and compliance with regulations?

Process management is one approach to this problem. Modern management practice recognizes that the old ways of looking at a business—through functional organization charts or isolated departments—are not appropriate for a modern enterprise. Thus, process management focuses on the key processes for the enterprise, which provide value for its customers. There are many other names involved in this discipline: business process design, business process improvement and business process re-engineering (BPR) are some of them.

Another approach to this problem is quality management. This term encompasses various methods, mainly those of total quality and quality systems, such as quality assurance and quality control. Here the emphasis is on understanding and meeting customer requirements and expectations, and on 'getting it right first time'.

Although both process management and total quality management are needed in the highly competitive, global business environment, the two approaches are rarely integrated. Process management usually emphasizes strategic and enterprise-wide improvements, particularly in the BPR school, where radical and rapid improvement is the watchword. Total quality approaches emphasize continuous improvement and tend to have a much longer time period. Given these differences, it is easy to get confused about which direction to take.

This book provides a set of techniques for integrating process management and total quality management. It is based on a graphical notation general enough to represent all processes in an organization, yet it also provides a basis for the main techniques of quality management. This enables the staff of the organization to document and understand their processes, while also providing a set of tools for analysing and improving the quality of those processes.

Here we take the view that quality must never be sacrificed in organizational processes. However, there are some areas where quality management has failed to deliver on its promises. The next section examines some of these areas.

1.2 THE QUALITY REVOLUTION

Quality is here to stay. From the status of a little-known and poorly understood technical discipline, quality is now at the top of the management agenda. It is one of the key issues for competitiveness in the 1990s.

As recently as the 1970s, managers and customers in Europe and the USA still put their emphasis on the simple goals of efficiency and cost reduction. Quality was considered an expendable ideal that could be sacrificed to the 'need' to produce and sell goods cheaply.

That changed in the 1980s. The Japanese challenge demonstrated that it was possible to produce goods efficiently yet with the goal of zero defects. Quality gurus— some of whom, like Deming, had taught the Japanese about quality—were taken seriously in the West for the first time. Management practice changed radically, and Total Quality became a banner for managers to rally behind.

The quality revolution has occurred but, like all revolutions, it is threatened. The threat arises not from foreign competition or lack of willingness by staff, but from the large costs that quality management imposes if it is not done well. When done poorly, quality management can result in increased bureaucracy and can demotivate staff. Quality management succeeds only when the cost of the quality system is less than the cost of defects and poor service which would otherwise result. And often that is not the case.

For large manufacturing companies, the cost of introducing a comprehensive quality system can equate to a substantial part of its yearly profits. For smaller companies, it can be prohibitive. They are fearful of being sandwiched between customers who demand certification to recognized quality standards, and the cost and increased complexity of such a system (*Financial Times*, 1991).

The techniques described in this book will help companies meet the challenge of better quality but with acceptable costs. These costs include the costs of setting up a quality system as well as the cost of running it. For example, in a typical total quality programme, initial costs include that of culture change, training, documentation of processes and staff time. Ongoing costs include further quality awareness campaigns, the staff costs of quality improvement teams (or quality circles), and reorganization costs resulting from quality improvement initiatives. Those costs can be substantially reduced if the efforts on quality management are merged with those on process management. However, as the next section demonstrates, this is not as easy as it sounds.

THREATS TO QUALITY MANAGEMENT

The current emphasis on quality management arises from the demands of customers for ever-increasing standards of high quality, and the need by suppliers to produce quality goods and services consistently, but with reasonable costs. There is no question that quality has improved dramatically as a result of better practices, but there have been some negative trends. In many cases, the employees of organizations suffer from the implementation of badly designed quality management systems, or because they are poorly trained to apply such systems. Sometimes the efficiency of organizations suffers under unnecessary red tape and bureaucracy. And—more often than we would like to admit—quality management hasn't always delivered the results!

A few of the most commonly encountered problem areas are described below.

The tail wags the dog

In a complex and interconnected world, organizations are supplying goods and services to a wide public in many different countries. Each country has laws and regulations which affect those products. The rules continue to multiply, with the European Community's Single Market and the increased number of regulations for ensuring safety, food quality, product liability and dozens of other areas.

As a result, companies need to comply with a baffling variety of requirements merely to stay in business. Unfortunately, many are reacting by introducing management systems that, although complying with the requirements, are poorly tailored to the organization's own needs and culture. The intention behind these systems is good, but the result too often is a mass of unreadable and unusable procedures. They tend to be highly inflexible, and the result is that staff are demotivated (if they are lucky enough to understand the procedures at all).

Organizations need to tailor their quality systems to their own requirements, not to the form of a general standard or regulation. This is not an easy task, as so many companies have found to their cost. The methods described later in the book will show how to analyse an organization and its systems and then how to design a quality system suited to it which also complies with the applicable regulations. They also show how to reduce paperwork and records to the minimum required to satisfy these regulations.

No one really understands the whole process

A quality system is a people system: it is designed by people, it is administered by people, and above all it is there to serve people. It is only as good as the people who carry it out, and they can do so successfully only if they are fully involved in it and understand it. However, this area is often overlooked. If staff receive training in quality, it is at the broad and superficial level, and it does not prepare them for the complexity of procedures in modern organizations. Staff need to understand their own work as well as how their work is connected to that of others.

Take a purchasing officer (PO) as an example. No doubt the organization will have well-defined procedures established for requisition, purchasing and acceptance of goods, all of which are well understood by the PO (assuming that he or she is well trained). But there is also a large amount of interaction with other parts of the organization, and with external suppliers of goods. How will the PO handle a 'slightly' incorrect requisition form—by correcting it or by sending it back? Suppose that there is a delay in receipt of an order—will the PO notify the requisitioner?

This book provides a method to assist in deciding how much to document in procedures, and how to make it clear whose responsibility each activity is. It also provides some techniques for writing procedures which are easy to read and to follow. When procedures are properly described, they are much easier to teach to people, and it is much easier to correct problems when they do arise.

Excessive bureaucracy

Many people think that *all* procedures are bureaucratic by their nature, but this is not the case: it is only poorly written procedures that lead to red tape and unnecessary paperwork. A well-known American writer has described a nightmare scenario:

In New York City there are people called 'expeditors'. They are not government employees, but have been created by the private sector because of the time and complexity of getting government licences and permits. The 'expeditor' is paid to procure the various documents necessary to conduct business legally. Anyone trying to get permits on his own will soon find it cannot be done. *(von Hoffman, 1991)*

Clearly, such regulations are far too complex to be understood and followed by the organizations being regulated, and the results can only be poor quality, unnecessary costs and poorly motivated employees.

Later, we will investigate a number of ways in which red tape and other forms of bureaucracy can be reduced by procedures which are well structured and properly adapted to the needs of suppliers, users and customers.

The cost of quality systems

Small and large organizations spend considerable sums in setting up and maintaining quality systems. Such systems require a considerable investment in staff time and costs, and in the documentation systems required to support them. While some of these costs are inevitable, many are unnecessary and can be avoided with improved management and design techniques. The methods described later show not only which processes and paperwork are required to meet given requirements, but also which are not required. They also provide techniques for measuring and reducing the complexity of paperwork.

The bottom line—has it delivered the results?

Even if the above problems are overcome, management must still confront the key issue: has the quality system delivered the results? Has it improved the quality of products or services, efficiently and with improved satisfaction by customers, users and staff? Very often, the results are not encouraging.

In Britain, more than half of all companies which began a total quality management (TQM) programme in the 1980s, did not meet their objectives—and Price (1992) claims an 80 percent failure rate. What were the reasons for failure? John Oakland (1989) lists four major difficulties:

- management is not fully committed and reverts to meeting short-term gains
- scepticism due to lack of organizational focus on quality
- loss of credibility for TQM, which becomes last month's or last year's flavour
- teams become bogged down in trivia instead of tackling the important problems.

A systematic approach to quality management—such as that in this book—attacks all four difficulties head on. It provides a consistent reference point for management, linking short-term measures with long-term effects. The method provides a focal point and language for addressing quality issues, facilitating communication and direction among staff. It provides a framework for continuous improvement, demonstrating both what has been achieved through the quality programme and what issues remain to be tackled.

1.3 BUSINESS PROCESS RE-ENGINEERING—THE ANSWER?

Improved quality management offers the prospects of savings in both staff costs and in the costs of quality, such as rework costs. The results can be significant, but these days companies are demanding faster and bigger returns than such a programme can give. Typically, a total quality programme will take three or four years before it provides a significant improvement. Costs may not necessarily go down—and may even go up, as more time and effort are spent on quality. As a result, companies have asked themselves if total quality approaches are sufficient for them to remain competitive, and whether there is another approach which can give much faster results and significant cost savings.

Responding to this challenge throughout the 1980s, management thinking evolved a grand concept for radical change in an organization, based upon total redesign of an organization's processes and taking into account the full power of modern technology. It is commonly referred to as business process re-engineering (BPR).

The advocates of BPR speak of an explosion of creativity and productivity which results when we ignore existing processes and redesign them from scratch. Productivity gains of several hundred percent have been reported. With such gains to be made, it is not surprising that total quality and related approaches have tended to recede from the top of the management agenda.

In reality, however, the picture is not as simple as this. First, BPR has not arisen independently from other developments of recent years, and in fact its dual roots are total quality and the just-in-time (JIT) approach to materials flow. Many concepts, including benchmarking, cellular manufacturing, concurrent engineering and flexible manufacturing are common to both BPR and to total quality approaches. Even the one concept of TQM which BPR would seem to reject—continuous improvement—plays a role in most BPR methodologies, since they advocate its use between the occasional periods of radical change.

More significantly from the viewpoint of quality, BPR and quality management are bound together by commercial and other pressures of the global economy. Customers are not just looking for the least expensive item, they also want quality and customer service. A company which radically redesigns its processes without taking the customer, and continuity of service, into account, is doomed to a loss of market share and a fall in revenues in the longer term, no matter what the reduction in costs. It is relatively easy for its competitors to discover the secrets of its processes and they will soon copy them and be able to compete on costs. What they cannot copy are the reputation of the company and the goodwill of its customers, and these are the province of quality management.

So we are left with the inescapable fact that in designing and redesigning processes, we need to provide equally for the design of the quality management component. This calls for a method of integrating the twin approaches of process and quality management.

Chapter 7 deals with many of the ideas of this section in greater detail.

1.4 INTEGRATED PROCESS MANAGEMENT AND QUALITY MANAGEMENT

The examples above illustrate the need for integrated process and quality management, based on well-structured procedures, sensibly applied. For an organization to function effectively, it must have visible and easily understood procedures that assist staff in carrying out their work and provide accountability for all operations. Providing such a system is not trivial, and it cannot be done without considerable thought and hard work. But the results will more than justify the effort.

Modern management must deal with degrees of complexity unheard of only a few decades ago. They must integrate many systems—for example, for purchasing, personnel, accounting, stock control, and computing—when each of these systems is itself highly complex. At the same time, they must ensure that they comply with a baffling variety of legal, safety, regulatory and other requirements relevant to their organization. While struggling with these issues, the manager is under irresistible pressure from global competition to reduce costs to the minimum.

Faced with such pressure, we are obliged to provide structure and organization, which enable us to deal with such complexity. We group similar processes, collect similar information into records and classify the various activities which the organization must deal with. We organize staff and computer systems into units which deal with similar types of problems or situations.

In all disciplines, the provision of structure or classification is dealt with through a systematic method recognized by the practitioners (Born, 1990). In engineering, architecture, medicine and other practical professions, the practitioners learn the relevant methods and then apply them to solve problems. Process and quality management have the same need—to approach the problems with a systematic method, which facilitates structuring of problems and produces practical solutions.

One of the key criteria for a satisfactory method is that it be applicable to a wide range of problems and concerns dealt with by the discipline. Once a method is in place, it provides a language and a framework for doing work; therefore, it must have the scope to deal with all problems which may arise. In quality management, the range of problems centres on 'conformance to requirements' (Crosby, 1979). When this is interpreted most widely, as in TQM, requirements are not just those of the direct customer, but also those in internal departments and the wider requirement of the law and of regulatory agencies. Seen this way, all procedures and operations carried out are the concern of quality management, and compliance issues are at the heart. A method which can deal with all such issues uniformly will provide an efficient and elegant solution to the problem of quality management.

In process management, the problems centre on definition of the objectives of the organization, and the design of processes which support them. Since efficiency and effectiveness are almost always major objectives, the organization will also require that processes (1) make efficient use of resources, including human and material resources; and (2) provide effective results, in terms of meeting the requirements of customers and other stakeholders in the organization. A systematic method must also provide support for these essential process attributes. Finally, the method must support people as they carry out processes. It should enhance their working lives and help them to discover better and more interesting ways of doing their jobs. It should support empowerment and an involvement in decision-making by everyone involved in the process.

1.5   WHAT THIS BOOK PROVIDES TO THE READER

This book provides a systematic method for integrating process management with quality management. It is based on a notation—called the Quality Process Language (QPL)—which is capable of representing and analysing all processes within an organization. It also provides a basis for quality management approaches, such as ownership of processes, improved communication and compliance with requirements and regulations. QPL has been used in many types of organization, large and small, highly structured and loosely structured. It provides a foundation for practical approaches, such as facilitated workshops, process mapping and improvement, and documentation of procedures.

Once you have mastered the notation of QPL (presented in Chapter 2) you will be able to represent the activities and roles, inputs and results of any organization. Later, you will learn how to convert this notation into ordinary text and flow charts, for use in procedures and other documentation about the organization.

The use of QPL provides a common language for process and quality specialists to communicate directly. This offers an opportunity to discuss and design organizational and process changes without ignoring the effects on quality. QPL is a diagrammatic language, and it makes it easier for non-quality specialists to understand how processes affect quality and vice versa.

Some parts of the book offer specific guidance on key areas of process management. In particular, Chapter 5 provides several lists to assist in process analysis—the inspection of a process description to determine errors and weak points. Appendix 2 provides process templates for three common quality models, which are frameworks for redesigning the management approach of an existing organization.

Other parts provide guidance and a general approach to assist you in modifying and improving the processes of your organization. You will learn how to use QPL to check for compliance. You will also find guidance on how to integrate the approach of the book with BPR and common techniques for quality management and industrial engineering.

The method covered by this book is summarized by four statements:

- A systematic method is required to integrate process management and quality management.
- The method should support the controlled and documented design of all organizational processes.
- The method should be applicable to:
  - all aspects of quality management involving procedures and compliance with standards and regulations
  - provision of good communications with other systems within the organization
- The method should provide a framework for monitoring effectiveness and efficiency of all processes and for using the results to improve them.

These principles are the objectives and signposts for the method described in this book. Such a method provides the language needed to communicate, when a management system is designed or improved. Subsequent chapters will develop this method. Examples and case studies will illustrate the wide application of the method on many problems in a range of disciplines.

1.6   READING THIS BOOK

How the book is organized

This book centres on a method for process design and quality management, along with its use in developing and *using* work instructions, procedures and other descriptive documents. An overview and introduction to the method is provided in Chapter 2. The other chapters provide further detail and illustrate use of the method through a number of practical examples and case studies.

The chapters of this book fit into two parts. The first part—Chapters 2 to 4—defines the notation of QPL. It is used to describe organizations and to structure and write accompanying procedures and documentation. The second part—Chapters 5 to 8—shows how to use the method in three key areas of process and quality management: process analysis, compliance checking, and process change and improvement. Chapter 8 provides practical guidance on how to apply the approach of the book in real situations. Emphasis is placed on people issues and how to integrate this approach with standard approaches to management and organization.

Appendix 1 is a summary of the method. It can also be used as a reference manual for the method. Appendix 2 provides templates for applying the method to three common quality management frameworks: ISO 9000, the Malcolm Baldrige National Quality Award, and the European Quality Award. The ISO 9000 is the international quality standard, and provides a formal requirement for quality systems. It is in widespread use throughout Europe and is gaining acceptance in the rest of the world. The Malcolm Baldrige Award is the premier award in the United States. Although it is awarded to only a few organizations every year, thousands in the USA and in other countries are using it as a model for improvement of their quality methods and practices. The third template is for the European Quality Award, which is broadly similar to the Baldrige approach but with modifications for the different culture and approach of European businesses.

Appendix 3 provides additional technical detail for Chapter 4, on structuring and coordinating processes. Appendix 4 is a guide to documentation commonly used in quality management and to the application of process modelling to conventional quality systems, including ISO 9001.

Guidelines for reading

How you approach reading the book depends on what you want from it. If you want only an overview of the basic techniques, a few chapters will do. Alternatively, you may only be interested in a particular subject, such as compliance; in this case, you should read the general chapters and then the specific chapter on that topic.

While you will want to tailor your own approach, there are four 'standard' approaches you may want to consider:

- quick overview
- specific subject area: documenting procedures, process analysis, compliance or change management
- theory and notation
- technical/in-depth.

Quick overview

If you want a sampler of the approach, with some guidance on applying it to real business situations, look at Chapter 2 to get a feel for the notation. Read the summaries that precede each chapter—Appendix 1 provides a summary of all the key points of the book. Chapters 7 and 8 provide guidance on applying the book in practical business situations and BPR.

Specific subject area

The four principal areas of this book are:

- documenting procedures
- process analysis
- compliance
- change management.

A chapter is devoted to each of these, but you will need to read supporting material to make full use of the information. Figure 1.1 shows the connections between chapters of this book (the notation is a simplified version of the full notation of this book, which is described in the next chapter). The solid lines show the main flow of chapters, as

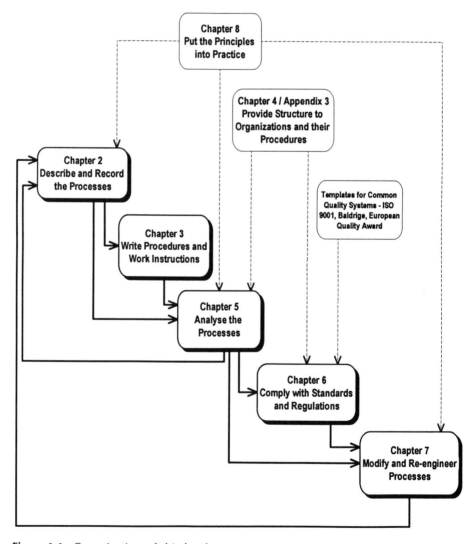

Figure 1.1 Organization of this book

they would be applied in most businesses and other enterprises. The dashed lines show the links between support chapters and appendices and their main applications in the other chapters.

In all cases, you should read Chapter 2 first, to understand the common QPL notation used throughout the book.

Theory and notation

If you are interested only in the theory behind QPL and the general approach to its application, you should read Chapters 2, 4 and 6, as well as Appendices 1 and 3. You should also read some of the examples in other chapters, to obtain an appreciation of how QPL is applied in practice. The process templates in Appendix 2 provide illustrations of some of the more interesting applications of the notation.

Technical/in-depth

To understand the book's approach in full, you should read the chapters sequentially. Each chapter builds upon the previous chapter, and knowledge of the earlier chapters is required for a full understanding. Also, many of the examples build upon examples in earlier chapters.

The only exception to reading the chapters in sequence is Appendix 3, which provides additional technical detail for Chapter 4 and should be read in conjunction with it.

Table 1.1 Conceptual index for this book

Topic	Chapters
Automating the techniques	8
Benchmarking	7
Business process re-engineering	1, 7
Change management	7, 8
Complexity, measures of	7
Compliance	6
Dynamic processes—design and checking	7
Flow charting	2, 3
Inheritance	4
Integration with other techniques	7, 8
People issues	8
Procedures and processes, reviewing and revising	3, 5
Process design	2, 3, 4, 7, 8
Process diagrams	2, 4
QPL values	8
Quality and process improvement	7, 8
Quality management, principles and concepts	1, 2, 7
Static processes	2, 3, 7
Structuring documentation and processes	4, 6
Verifying information in process diagrams	3, 5
Writing procedures and instructions	3, 5, 8

Conceptual index

If none of these suggested approaches suits your needs, you may want to browse through the book to see how it applies to topics of your choice. Table 1.1 provides a high-level index for a quick overview of topics covered in the book. A full index is given at the end of the book.

2

A language for process and quality management

The limits of my language mean the limits of my world.
Ludwig Wittgenstein, Tractatus Logico-Philosophicus, 5.6

OVERVIEW

This chapter presents the Quality Process Language (QPL), a notation for describing the processes in an organization, along with a framework for quality management. It can be called a language, as it provides a consistent basis for the necessary concepts which will be developed throughout the book. QPL is based on two fundamentals—information and processes—and the interactions between them. These interactions take the form of a network, which allows us to structure procedures and operations.

The elements of QPL are introduced. They include process owners—who use the processes to operate on and transform information. Authorities provide rules and guidance on how to process information, and control determines when a process is relevant. Processes are linked by information, which determine which processes are activated and in what order.

To describe problems and procedures, we need to model the real world, and the chapter extends the language to provide the necessary tools. Information is modelled by providing ways of classifying and describing it, and of describing how it flows between processes. Processes are modelled by describing how they may be grouped and classified, how to determine the scope of a process, and the roles and resources it employs.

The chapter discusses some other notations for process modelling and their relationship to QPL. The principal influence is the Structured Analysis and Design Technique/ICAM Definition Method (SADT/IDEF0), which can easily be converted into QPL. There is also a role for flow charting; subsequent chapters will describe how to use this technique to supplement QPL descriptions.

The chapter concludes with a description of QPL's origins and its relationship with other notations.

2.1   INFORMATION, PROCESSES AND NETWORKS

Chapter 1 summarized the need for a systematic method for process and quality management. This chapter develops the notation for this method. The Quality Process Language is so called because it provides a common means for describing all the processes and information involved in a management system, with quality built into it.

All systems can be described in terms of two basic concepts: information and processes. Information provides us with knowledge about things in the world and the way they are organized. It includes printed documentation, verbal communications such as telephone calls, computer databases and descriptions of material objects. Processes operate on information and transform it—either by changing existing information or by creating new information. Processes include all business operations and are described (or prescribed) by procedures and work instructions. As we shall see, processes are linked by information, or more correctly, by the flow of information.

To model information flow, we need some sort of *network*, defined as a collection of nodes (i.e. processes) and links (i.e. information) between the nodes. This will enable us not only to connect processes, but to show explicitly what information must be communicated between them to execute correctly. It will also show the order in which processes are to be executed. In QPL, only information can be used to link processes, and we will see in subsequent chapters that this is a useful discipline for describing systems and then checking them.

QPL uses a particular form of network called a data flow diagram, but there are many others, including flow charts, flow process charts (Oakland, 1989) and PERT (performance/programme evaluation review technique) charts. An example of a flow process chart is provided in Chapter 7.

In constructing a network we draw a kind of roadmap. In terms of analogies, we can look at processes as cities and towns, and information as the roads, air routes and rail links between them. This map tells us how to get from one place to another.

All procedures can be mapped in this way. Take a very simple one—for purchasing within a large company:

Before placing an order, the purchasing officer will evaluate bids and select the least expensive one which meets the requirement. He or she will notify the decision to the

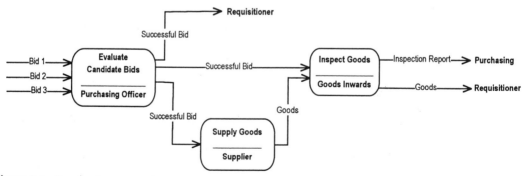

Figure 2.1 Purchasing procedure

requisitioner, goods inwards and the supplier. When the goods are received by goods inwards, they will be checked and an inspection report will be sent to purchasing. The goods will be sent to the requisitioner.

This can be mapped on to the network of processes and information shown in Figure 2.1. The owners of each process—purchasing, supplier and goods inwards—are also shown for clarity.

The rest of this chapter will expand these three basics—processes, information and links between processes—into the QPL language. All concepts in quality management can be described in terms of one of them or as a combination.

2.2 FUNDAMENTALS OF QPL

The previous section discussed process, information and networks as the building blocks for a quality process language. This section will expand these into the basics of QPL. There are six of these:

- process
- information
- process owners
- authorities
- control
- links between processes.

Each is described in turn, with an example of its representation in QPL.

Process

The process is the most basic level of organization in QPL. A process consists of a sequence of steps which transforms information from an initial state (input) to a final state (output). A key characteristic of a process is that it can be broken down into less complicated processes; this makes processes manageable by describing only a limited number of steps at any one stage. Occasionally it is more appropriate to call a process a 'process step', and the terms will be used interchangeably.

The notation for a process is the rounded box shown in Figure 2.2. A name or description of the process is given in the box. In this case, the process—evaluate candidate bids—is one of the process steps of Figure 2.1. The process owner—purchasing officer—is also shown in the box. This is explained later in this section.

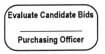

Figure 2.2 Example of a process box in QPL

Information

A process cannot stand alone: it *must* have input or output or both. This information will provide the necessary links between processes and also provide the flow of control which determines the order in which processes are carried out.

QPL does not deal directly with material objects (such as automobiles, components or software), but with information about such objects. This emphasizes the description of these objects and the values that such a description may have. For example, an automobile may be represented by its model or its colour. Alternatively, if the location of the car is relevant, then that attribute will be represented.

The term 'information' is used interchangeably with 'information item' in QPL. Information is also considered the same as data. Strictly speaking, data consists only of values and can provide information only when interpreted by a process. Similarly, knowledge is treated as information only when it is used by, or produced by, a process.

Input

At the point of entry to a process, information is called 'input'. In the QPL notation, input is always shown as a line entering the process from the left, as shown in Figure 2.3, which has been expanded from the previous example. This example shows that two inputs—'list of candidate suppliers' and 'specified requirements'—are needed to evaluate bids as part of the purchasing process.

Note that there may be several information items input to a process. Normally they are represented by separate lines, but we sometimes group them together into a thick line, as shown in Figure 2.4. In this case, 'specified requirements' is a summary term for both types of input.

Output

At the point of exit from a process, information is called 'output'. In QPL, output is always shown exiting the process from the right side. However, there are two forms of output, and they are shown differently in the notation.

Unchanged output

If information is unchanged by a process, then it exits from a process at the right side, as shown by 'list of bids' in Figure 2.5. In this example, evaluate candidate bids needs to make use of the list of bids to select a supplier, but it does not change the list itself. (In some other notations, unchanged output is referred to as 'used' or 'referenced information'.)

Unchanged output is used to coordinate processes. Since it needs to exit from the first process before it can be input to the second, this forces the second process to come

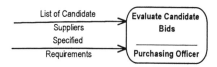

Figure 2.3 Inputs to a process

Figure 2.4 Grouping inputs to a process

Figure 2.5 Outputs from a process

later. This property is useful in ordering processes. In the above example, the list of bids can be passed to the requisitioner after the bids have been evaluated. The use of the list as unchanged output means that the list will not be passed to the requisitioner prematurely.

Changed output

Output that is altered or created by a process is called 'changed output'. In the former case, information may have its values changed by the process—for example, the (value of the) temperature of water will be changed by the process of heating. Alternatively, information may be created by a process, using input (and other) information supplied to the process. In a chemical process such as oil refining, a completely new substance is created by applying heat. (In some other notations, changed output is referred to as 'modified' or 'created information'.)

To show the difference between the two types of output, changed output exits at the bottom of the process, as shown by 'selected supplier' in Figure 2.5. Where possible, the output line is then bent to the right, to make it clear that output has occurred.

QPL distinguishes between changed and unchanged output to help in identifying areas where process descriptions are weak and capable of mistakes. Many mistakes in processes occur at the point where information is transformed or created, and the notation for a changed process makes it easy to spot these points. Other faults occur when process steps are incorrectly coordinated. By identifying unchanged output and using it to coordinate processes, such faults can be spotted and corrected before they do any damage.

Process owners

Process owners are responsible for the execution of processes. They may be people, in the case of most administrative processes, or they may be machines, such as computers for processing data or robot arms for welding automobile parts together. The terms 'role' or 'agent' are also used for this concept. (IDEF0, a related notation for describing processes, uses the term 'mechanism'. This is similar to QPL's use of process owner, although not identical.)

Process owners are closely bound to processes. Each process has exactly one owner, and a process owner has significance only when the process is carried out. To represent this tight binding, QPL represents the owner by naming it in the bottom of the process box, as shown in Figure 2.6A, where the purchasing officer is named as the process owner. If the owner for a process can vary, depending on the circumstances of the process, QPL represents this with an information line which enters from the lower left corner, as shown in Figure 2.6B. In this case, the head of purchasing selects a purchasing officer before the bids are evaluated.

Process owners may have two roles: as well as being *responsible* for the execution of a process, they may also *carry out* the actions which form the process. But the latter is not necessary—the person responsible for an action does not have to participate in any of its steps. An obvious example is the case of the line manager, who is responsible for a process such as purchasing or data processing, but does not actually carry out more than high level managerial and administrative tasks.

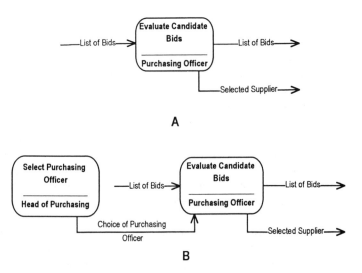

Figure 2.6 Process owners

Less obviously, the process owner may also consist of a named group or organization. Many companies are experimenting with leaderless teams, where members of the team take joint responsibility and rotate the position of team leader. In this case, the team may be the collective process owner. In fact, almost anyone or anything may be a process owner, so long as he, she or it has the principal responsibility for executing the process.

It is not always easy to identify the owner of a process. Many organizations describe their procedures in detailed manuals, but they do not discuss who is responsible for them, assuming that it will be obvious at the time. QPL discourages this, as it violates one of the cardinal principals of quality management: that all responsibilities are clearly defined, and that all people are aware of their responsibilities. The identification of a single agent for each process complements some fundamental management principles. First, it encourages the concept of ownership, where individuals or workgroups are encouraged to take full responsibility for all actions within their control and for their interactions with others. Secondly, it helps to identify genuine processes; if we are genuinely unable to identify an agent for a possible process, then it is most likely that this is not a process at all, and we need to redefine processes and those who have responsibility for them.

Other questions occur when there are multiple or overlapping responsibilities: How do we handle shared responsibility within a workgroup?—By naming the whole workgroup as the process owner. What if a process involves several steps, each of which is the responsibility of a different person?—Then we break the process into its component sub-processes, and name the different owners for each of them. How do we select a single process owner, if a process involves several different departments or functions, all of equal status?—By determining which of these has principal responsibility. This is done by asking questions such as: Who/what do I turn to resolve conflicts? Who is the main supplier for this process? Who is most aware of the needs of the customer? These questions are usually easy to answer in practice. If they cannot be answered, it reveals a weakness in the management system that will require correction anyway.

Authorities

The concept of process owner allows us to specify who or what is responsible for a process. Authorities provide an additional concept which makes clear how the process is specified, and the basis for making decisions.

Authorities take many different forms. In a quality system, we find them most often in documented procedures and instructions, as well as in job descriptions and codes of practice. But an authority can also be 'qualified', as in the case of a person using professional judgement, so long as the person or his/her qualifications are made explicit and documented. When we are ill, we do not ask to see our doctor's written instructions for doing a diagnosis, accepting that authority comes from a combination of qualifications (which, of course, are documented), and experience.

Note that the use of the term 'authority' is not meant to imply authoritarianism or dictatorship in process management. Authorities are needed to clarify the basis for the actions and decisions within a process, not to prescribe a strait-jacket.

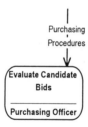

Figure 2.7 Authority for a process

In QPL, the authority for a process is shown entering the process box at the top right, as shown in Figure 2.7. In this case, the purchasing procedures provide the detailed instructions for evaluating bids and clearly act as the authority for this process.

As with process owners, there are situations where there appears to be no authority at all. These include unstructured situations, such as ad hoc meetings or a sudden request to produce a new product urgently. The other extreme may also occur and raise the question of whether the provision of an authority limits the extent of creativity in the situation.

Types of authority in process descriptions

The use of the authority in a process description is a powerful tool for clarifying the objectives of a process and how it is explained or taught to the process owner. Later in this book it will be used as a simple tool for reducing the complexity of process descriptions and managing compliance-related issues.

In some cases, an explicit authority is not appropriate. This usually is the case for qualified personnel, who are able to execute processes correctly by virtue of their qualifications or experience. It is also appropriate where we deliberately need to give staff considerable freedom of action—say, in emergencies, or with unpredictable situations (such as flying a plane). In such cases, the authority can be limited to a framework and, perhaps, a set of guidelines, to specify the basic requirements of the process.

Similarly, the authority is not meant to inhibit creativity. That is why it is fully acceptable to name a responsible, and qualified, person as the authority for a process, who will then apply professional judgement and creativity to solve problems. The formal authority, specifying procedures where appropriate, is provided only as a framework for individual initiative and creativity, where that is appropriate. Where it is not appropriate—i.e. where processes are repetitive, or where any mistake would be dangerous—then the authority must be highly prescriptive and detailed. In this case, it should be designed deliberately *not* to allow creativity and initiative.

Another question occurs when there is more than one authority for a process. Suppose they conflict? We have all experienced the uncomfortable situation where we are producing work for more than one boss, and they have differing expectations and standards. More formally, processes within an organization are subject not only to its own written procedures and work instructions, but also to legal and regulatory requirements. For example, the human resources (personnel) section of a company must comply not only with the company's employee procedures, but also with relevant employment laws. What if the procedures and the laws conflict?

This problem is called 'multiple compliance' and is discussed in Chapter 6, which deals with compliance issues.

Control

Control is a special type of information used to specify the conditions for activating a process. It is specified by showing an information line entering the process box at the top left corner. This is illustrated in Figure 2.8, which specifies that the divisional manager's approval is required before bids can be evaluated.

In QPL, control can be used for the following:

● The condition(s) under which a process is activated.
● The time when a process is activated.
● Synchronizing processes, using either of the above.
● The constraints under which a process operates.

We note that if we specify a time to activate a process, this is the start time. In most cases, there will also be a delay before the process is completed.

Linking processes

Up to this point, processes have been discussed in isolation. However, to be effective within a system, processes need to be linked. In QPL, this is very straightforward, because the only way of linking processes is with information. In the most common situation, these links (or information lines) are direct: the outputs from one process are the inputs to one or more other processes. The information lines show not only the connections between processes, but also the order in which process steps are to be carried out. This is illustrated in Figure 2.1, where the order is shown clearly as: (1) evaluate candidate bids, (2) supply goods, and (3) inspect goods. The mechanism for linking processes is called the 'thread of control'. In QPL, a process cannot be activated until its inputs are available, and they are available only when all processes

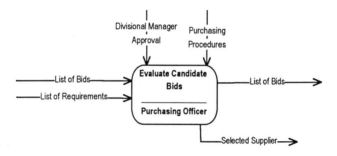

Figure 2.8 Control of a process step

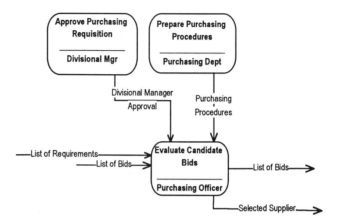

Figure 2.9 Linkages for control and authority

which produced them are completed. This implies that processes are sequenced implicitly.

Information also links process indirectly, through owners, authorities and control. For example, a process may determine which is the most appropriate owner for another process. This information about the owner is then passed to the process via an information line, as shown in Figure 2.6B, where the choice of purchasing officer is made before the officer evaluates bids.

Similarly, a process may produce information which is used as the authority for another process. In fact, this is one of the most important concepts in traditional quality management, where we develop (through a process) written procedures and work instructions, and they are used as authorities for relevant processes.

Finally, information may also be provided to control another process. For example, it may be necessary to check the result of one process before deciding if another process is to be activated. Figure 2.9 provides an example of linkages for both control and authority. This expands the example of Figure 2.8 by showing explicitly the processes which constitute approval by the divisional manager and which prepare the purchasing procedures.

THE ELEMENTS OF QPL—A SUMMARY

The five elements of QPL are defined as:

(1) *Process:* A series of steps or actions.
(2) *Information:* Description of things in the real world, including printed descriptions and verbal communications. Called input when it enters a process and output when it exits. (Changed output is modified or created by a process, while unchanged output is identical to an input.)
(3) *Process owner:* The person or other agent responsible for execution of a process.

(4) *Authority:* The description, specification or justification of a process.

(5) *Control:* The conditions or constraints for activating a process.

The basic QPL notation is summarized in Figure 2.10, which shows a process box and each of the possible components which describe the process and its links to other processes.

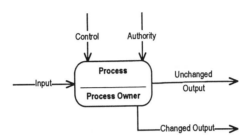

Figure 2.10 Summary of the basic QPL notation

2.3   MODELLING INFORMATION

The previous section described the elements at the heart of QPL. These provide a foundation for describing the activities and documentation of an organization. We now focus on the use of information in QPL. How frequently is information accessed, and how long should it be retained? How does QPL describe the content of information? What about the paths that information takes, enabling processes to communicate? Answers to these questions will enable us to apply QPL to a wider range of problems in management.

Types of information

In QPL, information is the only way in which processes are linked. Since information may change frequently, we need to specify which version of information is used by processes, and how long to retain information. This provides a basis for classifying information items into useful categories, based on persistence—'the attribute of information that regulates how long it needs to exist for the processes which require it'—of useful information: channel, information store and archive. These are explained below, with examples from ISO 9001 (1994) (author's italics):

Channel: Temporary information (or material) needed only for a limited amount of time and not retained. 'The supplier shall arrange for the protection of the quality of product after final inspection and test. Where contractually specified, this protection shall be extended to include *delivery to destination.*' (4.15.5: Delivery)

Information store: Information which is retained, but where only the current version is needed. 'This control shall ensure that ... *obsolete documents are promptly removed from all points of issue or use.*' (4.5.2: Document and data approval and issue)

Archive: Information which is retained and where previous versions are also needed. '[Quality records] shall be stored and retained in such a way that they are readily retrievable in facilities that provide a suitable environment to prevent damage or deterioration and to prevent loss. *Retention times of quality records shall be established and recorded.*' (4.16: Quality records)

In the first example, permanent retention of the product is not an issue, as the process is responsible only for storing and delivering it safely. In Example 2, the standard specifies that *only* the latest issues of documents are relevant. In the last example, the standard specifies that earlier issues of records will be retained, for a specified period.

QPL has a symbol for each of these three types of information, which distinguishes between the way in which each is used. Figure 2.11 shows an example of each symbol.

Channels

Channels are used to convey information which is temporary. Like other information lines, they connect processes, but as the information is not needed after it is used by a process, it is not stored as documentation. When relevant, channelled information is illustrated by drawing a I symbol across the information line. In Figure 2.11, the batch and the delivery slip are treated as channels, as they do not need to be retained after the process is completed.

Information stores

When only the latest version of information is required, it is represented as an information store. This is shown as a rectangle (with squared corners, to distinguish it from a process box). In Figure 2.11, the fault report is treated as an information store, since the process needs to retain a list of the latest faults found.

In quality management, the information store is probably the most common form of information, as only the latest version tends to be needed. Examples include:

● standards, regulations, procedures and work instructions (since in almost all cases, only in the latest version of these documents is relevant)
● user manuals (since only a single release of a product is of interest—the one we are using).

Archives

There are many instances when it is important to retain information for a period of time. Unlike its common usage, QPL's use of the term 'archive' does not refer to the length of time information is stored, only whether previous versions of information are

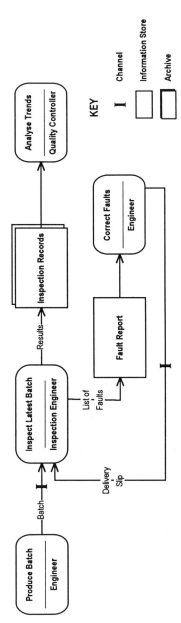

Figure 2.11 Information types

required. If we retain the latest version only, then it is an information store (even if it is retained for a very long time). In Figure 2.11, inspection records are treated as an archive, as previous versions of the records are also relevant for determining trends and monitoring production quality.

The concept of an archive is used extensively in quality management. The most common example is retention of records relating to batches of a product, to facilitate recall of the product if faults should be revealed. In this situation, it would be of no use only to retain information about the latest batch of a food product, or of the latest shipment of automobiles. Other common examples are retention of quality data for trend analysis and computer disks for computer back-ups.

The symbol of an archive, like that of an information store, is a rectangle. However, to indicate the retention of previous versions, QPL also shows a 'shadow' rectangle behind it (as in Figure 2.11— inspection records). An alternative symbol uses just a single rectangle, with a diagonal line across the lower right corner.

Some information can be classified either as an information store or as an archive. A good example is that of working procedures. In most cases, we are interested only in the latest version, and thus it is most appropriate to classify them as information stores. However, in certain cases it is important to retain previous versions of these documents—for example, if in the future we might need to investigate how certain 'obsolete' processes were carried out. A common example of this is the maintenance manual for an old car model. Such a manual is, of course, no longer relevant for newer models of the car, but it is indispensable for maintaining the older model.

Attributes of information

QPL diagrams do not refer to material objects directly, but only to the descriptions which are held within information items. The processes transform these descriptions, providing changed information which may be used by other processes. We call these descriptions the attributes of the information.

For example, consider a quality control system for paint mixing. The person regulating this process is directly concerned not with the material substance itself— namely the paint batch—but in the attributes of that batch—its colour, consistency, composition etc. Each of these attributes can be documented—on paper or in a computer system—and then used to determine whether requirements have been met. In other words, only the attributes of the paint batch can be documented, not the batch itself.

One can object to the use of attributes as a 'replacement' for material objects, noting that there are an infinite number of ways of looking at a thing and describing it! While this is quite true, it ignores the power of processes to determine attributes. When compiling a QPL description, we decide on the *relevant* characteristics, and this is provided by the processes which operate on the information. When we choose the attributes which form a description, we ask what processes will operate on the information, and what information they will need to complete their operations successfully.

While this way of looking at information may seem awkward at first, it provides a common language for describing processes. This is particularly useful in checking compliance of a procedure with a standard or regulation. The latter are usually written in an impersonal style, with passive voice, as in: 'Back-ups of all records must be stored in a fireproof safe.' The procedure which complies with this might be written more directly: 'Now take a back-up and store it in a fireproof safe.'

To reconcile these different expressions and make it easier to compare the two, QPL uses a common means of expression, based on the use of attributes. In this example, the key attribute is location, i.e. where the back-up is stored. Therefore, QPL translates both documents into the common phrase: 'The location of the back-up is to be changed to the fireproof safe.' While this is formalized language, it is clear what the meaning is. It also clarifies the key process: the movement of the back-up into the safe. In this case, the process transforms the location attribute of the back-up. Figure 2.12 shows the QPL description of this process.

Flow of information

Usually, information flows directly from one process step to another, as shown in Figure 2.1. But there are situations where this flow needs to be refined. The most common is where the information needs to be categorized, so that it can be directed to the appropriate process, and this is called a 'case' (or decision point). In the other common situation, the same information is needed by several process steps, which may be activated independently. This is called a 'split'.

Case

In the case construct, a single information line enters the case symbol, but several information lines exit from it. Each of these lines corresponds to a different value (or set of values) of the information. As noted above, this is also called a decision point, as it will decide which process is the next to be activated. The case construct is used to categorize information, which is then used to decide the most appropriate process

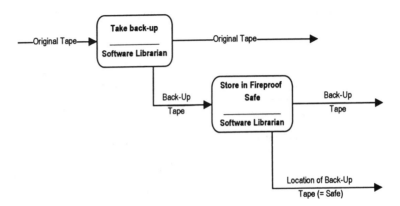

Figure 2.12 QPL description using location as an information item

step to carry out. An example of a case construct is shown in Figure 2.13. In this example, the case divides the result of the check into three categories: reject, rework or agree modifications.

The case construct is used as an alternative and equivalent form of some types of control conditions on processes. But the preference is the case construct, since it emphasizes the classification of information and helps to determine the correct set of attributes. Note that a case construct is actually just a shorthand for a process which classifies information. However, if such a process would only do this classification, and it is unnecessary to specify the other elements (namely, control, authority, owner and other inputs), then the case construct is much simpler to use.

Split

Sometimes an item of information is used by more than one process at the same time. For example, the same instructions may be issued to all workers on an assembly line. To cater for this instance, QPL splits an information line into two or more lines, which will connect to the processes requiring it. Note that this does not necessarily refer to copying the information physically, say with a photocopier, although that might be the way of doing it. The split only implies that the information can be used by those processes in any order. Figure 2.14 provides an illustration of the split symbol, which is a black dot where the information lines separate. In this example, the instructions need to be carried out by two secretaries; the split implies that they are copied or circulated to both.

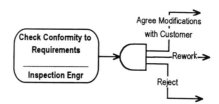

Figure 2.13 Example of a case construct

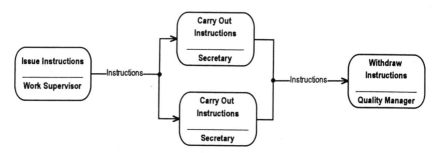

Figure 2.14 Example of a split and rejoin

If there are several splits on a diagram, it will soon become unreadable. Therefore, QPL allows information, after it is used by processes, to rejoin, by reversing the split symbol, as shown on Figure 2.14. However, note that this can be done only if the information has not been modified since it was split. If any of the processes has modified the information in any way, then such a join is no longer possible, and the information must be modelled either as an information store or as an archive, since a new version has been produced.

MODELLING INFORMATION—A SUMMARY

Information is modelled as one of three types, depending on its persistence—how long it needs to be retained and whether earlier versions are required:

Channel: Temporary information (or material) needed only for a
                     limited amount of time and not retained
Information store: Information which is retained, but where only the current
                     version is needed
Archive: Information which is retained and where previous versions
                     are also needed

QPL does not model material objects directly. It models descriptions of objects, in the form of attributes.

QPL provides two constructs for the flow of information. The case construct splits information by category. In controlling process sequences, it provides a decision point for which process is to be activated next. The split construct allows for information to be copied. It can also be used to describe processes where the sequence of activation is not important.

The QPL symbols for each construct are shown in Figure 2.15.

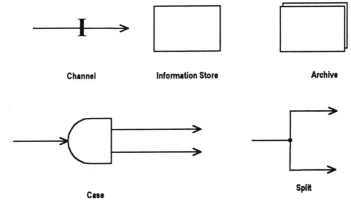

Channel   Information Store   Archive

Case   Split

Figure 2.15 QPL symbols for information

2.4 MODELLING PROCESSES

Up to now, we have seen how a process can be modelled as a single process step, with links to other processes through information lines. There are a number of other issues which must be resolved before we can use processes to model real organizations and activities. What goes on inside a process step, and how do we model it? How do we limit the amount of information shown on a single page? What is the scope of a process? What resources does a process consume? This section addresses these questions.

Process hierarchies

To make a process manageable, it is broken down into smaller sub-processes. Each of these can, in turn, be divided into even smaller sub-processes. This process can be carried out until reaching process steps where there is either just one action, or there is no need to describe the contents of the step in further detail.

This hierarchy of processes provides three main advantages:

- We need to concentrate only on a limited amount of detail at any one time.
- In designing and analysing processes, we can fit all required information for individual sub-processes on to a single page.
- We can view processes at different levels of detail and importance; this helps to decide priorities and to separate 'the wood from the trees'.

The procedure for constructing sub-processes is the same as the process itself. Take the example of Figure 2.8, with a process which evaluates bids. To decompose this process into its sub-processes, we just determine the series of process steps and their connections. The use of information, process owners, and other concepts is the same as before. The result is shown in Figure 2.16, where the 'evaluate candidate bids' process of earlier figures has been decomposed into three sub-processes.

There is an important constraint on this decomposition: it must be consistent with the higher level process. This means that, taken as a whole, inputs, outputs and control must agree with the higher level process. None of the process steps may require an external input, or produce an external output, that the higher level process did not require.

It is, however, possible for these process steps to use information that does not enter or exit from the higher level process. This internal information will appear as information lines (and possibly as stored information) on the more detailed process description, but not on the higher level process box, of course. In Figure 2.16, compliant bids is an example of internal information and does not appear in the higher level process.

Scoping a process

The scope of a process describes its limit of use: the circumstances under which it is appropriate, and what it requires to carry out its actions. In QPL, the scope of a

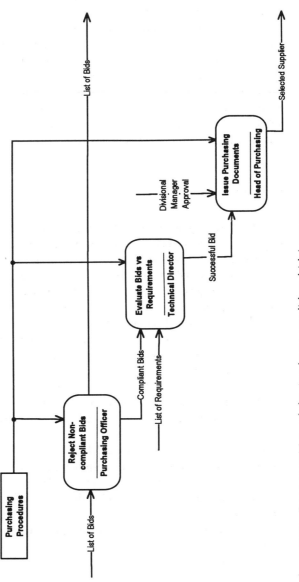

Figure 2.16 Decomposition of the 'evaluate candidate bids' process

process is simply the external view of the process: the information it requires and uses, the owners responsible for it, the authority which gives it jurisdiction, and the control which determines when and if it is appropriate. All sub-processes are within this scope, but they also have their own scopes which must, of course, be more restrictive than the overall scope. For example, for a sub-process to be activated, both its own conditions and those of the higher level process must be met.

Scoping a process enables us to encapsulate it: to hide all details that do not contribute to the external view of the process. (Appendix 3 elaborates on the concept of encapsulation.) This enables us to view only the information required: if we need to know only about the interaction of the process with other processes, then the external view is adequate. However, if we need to know further details about the process, then the internal view is available by breaking down the process into its sub-processes. As later chapters will show, this management of complexity is essential for building and improving complex enterprises in the real world.

Roles and resources

In modelling a process, we often need to know the resources which the process consumes in its execution. Examples of such resources are the time to execute the process, the effort (person-hours) spent in executing the process, the cost of purchases for the process and the amount of physical resources expended. In the case of a manufacturing process, we speak of it taking, say, three hours, requiring six person-hours (two people, full time), with a cost of materials (say the parts to be put together) of $25, and requiring heating, lighting and space costs of $2 (the last category can be treated as a material cost, but it is more common to treat such costs as overheads—or costs to the whole company—since it is difficult to isolate them).

How does QPL model such resources? Earlier we noted that we are interested only in the description of information—its attributes—not directly in physical or material objects. This provides the method for modelling resources: we introduce information to a process which contains the desired values, and note how it has changed after the process.

An example is shown in Figure 2.17, which models resources. The overall process has been broken down into two sub-processes, one to manufacture the parts, and the other to calculate costs. Elapsed time needs only a record of the times when the manufacturing process begins and ends. The staff effort resource is modelled with timesheets or other work records. Material costs are included in the attributes for each raw material input to the process. Finally, overhead costs are part of the information of the environment for the process—we assume that the factory has decided how these costs will be allocated.

Why model resources as information?

Unlike some other approaches—for example, flow process techniques (Ishiwata, 1991)—QPL models resources as information, rather than as part of the process.

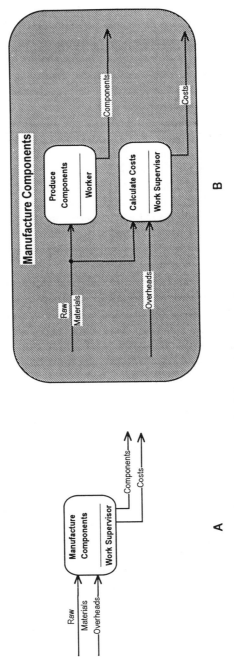

Figure 2.17 Breakdown of a process to calculate resources used

In QPL, it is preferable to keep these separate, for the following reasons:

- Resources consumed by a process are rarely fixed; they vary depending on the exact information used and its values (an infamous example is in software development, where programmer productivity rates vary by up to ten to one. In practice, this means that the programming effort to complete a programming task (i.e. a process) can vary enormously, depending upon the 'value' of the programmer's skill, and to estimate this effort in advance, we must have this information about the programmer.

- The resources attached to a process are not absolute, but vary with the context of that process. For a professional tennis player at a major tournament, energy exerted in a match is absolutely vital if the next game is scheduled for only a few hours later, and there is little time to recover. For a casual player, the energy exerted is of little value (unless one is on a diet). The rise of the Green Movement provides another example. Before the 1970s, renewable physical and energy resources were of little interest; only the money cost of these resources was calculated in a process. Now, in these environmentally sensitive times, the renewability of a resource is a key attribute that companies and governments ignore at their peril (Schumacher, 1973).

- To keep maximum generality and objectivity, we want to treat resources as just another item of information. Different contexts place different value on the same resources. In the financial markets, the time spent by a broker is crucial and can make the difference between a major loss or a gain. When that same broker is relaxing at the weekend, the importance placed on time may change radically. While cooking a barbecue, the broker may even take the view that the more time spent, the greater the value!

2.5   A NOTE ON NOTATIONS

QPL was developed particularly to integrate process and quality management, and the notation reflects this emphasis. However, it has its origins in other modelling notations and retains many similarities.

The basis of QPL is the SADT notation (Ross, 1977), which was developed in the USA in the 1970s (see Figure 2.18). Later refinements of this notation include IDEF0 (Ross *et al*, 1979) and Quality Improvement Methods Analysis (QIMA) (Marsh, 1988).

QPL is compatible with SADT/IDEF0, but it expands some of the elements. For example, IDEF0 includes process definitions within its concept of 'control', while QPL treats this as a separate element. However, to remain compatible with IDEF0, it has retained the convention of entry from the top of the process box. IDEF0 incorporates roles and resources within the 'mechanism'; QPL modifies this somewhat to concentrate on ownership of the process. As shown in the previous section, resources are usually modelled as information—inputs and outputs—in QPL. IDEF0 provides only

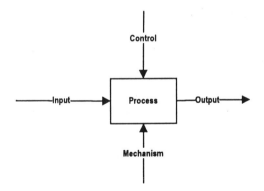

Figure 2.18 SADT/IDEF0 process notation

for one type of output, while QPL distinguishes between changed and unchanged output, i.e. whether the process transforms input or not.

If you are used to using the SADT/IDEF0 notation, you should have no trouble converting to the QPL form, as the notations are quite similar. You should be careful to place the locations of lines entering and leaving process boxes, as this determines which type of element the line represents. In particular, lines entering at the top-left represent control, while those at the top-right represent authorities. A line exiting at the right is an unchanged output, while one exiting at the bottom-right is a changed output.

Other notations which have influenced the QPL notation are MASCOT, Yourdon (Yourdon, 1989), CORE (SD-Scicon, 1989) and Ward and Mellor (Ward and Mellor, 1985) notations.

Why not use a flow chart?

You are probably familiar with flow charts and their use for representing processes. If so, you may be asking whether there is any need to flow chart when the QPL approach is followed.

QPL complements flow charting in many ways. Flow charting is a simple technique, easy to communicate to others. But, there are many instances when the rich notation of QPL is required to capture business and quality processes. QPL provides the depth of notation needed to understand, analyse and structure the processes and information which impact on a quality system, but it is not always appropriate for presenting the results to others. In particular, a simplified form of QPL should be used when facilitating work teams on process description and improvement—Chapter 8 provides more guidance on this subject.

Flow charting is also more appropriate for describing processes to a general audience. The next chapter looks at how to transform QPL diagrams into procedure flow charts.

2.6   SUMMARY OF QPL IN ACTION

Figure 2.19 extends the description of the QPL notation to show how processes may be linked by the different types of information items. It represents a complete summary of the basic QPL notation.

The notation is illustrated by the translation of the purchasing process of Figure 2.1, which is translated into QPL in Figure 2.20.

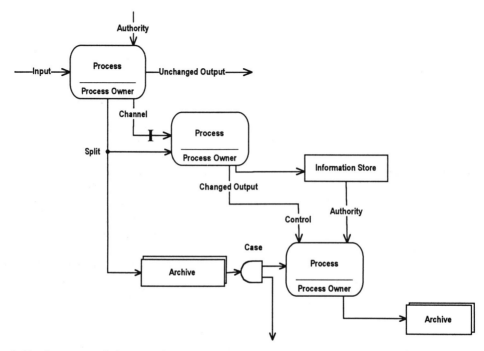

Figure 2.19   Summary of the complete QPL notation

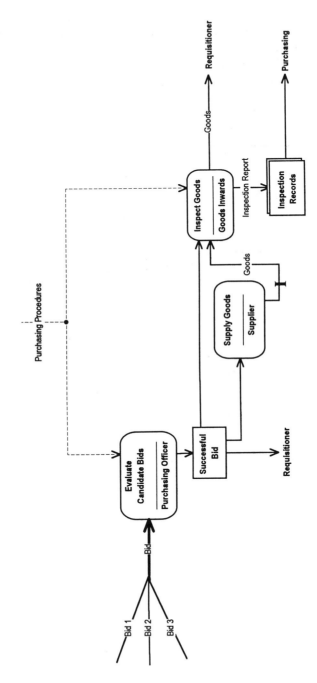

Figure 2.20 The QPL version of the purchasing procedure of Figure 2.1

3

Writing procedures and instructions

In the opinion of many people in industry, there is nothing more important for transaction of business than use of operational definitions. It could also be said that no requirement of industry is so much neglected.

W. Edwards Deming (Deming, 1982)

OVERVIEW

This chapter explains the basics of writing procedures and other documents which provide guidance and instruction. It is based on seven steps:

(1) Provide a description of the document to be produced—the statement of requirements.
(2) Collect and document all activities and information.
(3) Annotate the written description with the elements of QPL.
(4) Draw QPL diagrams.
(5) Verify the contents of the QPL diagrams.
(6) Write the procedure.
(7) Review and revise the procedure.

The statement of requirements for the document provides an essential reference point, and QPL can be used to derive its contents. Following construction of the statement, information is collected about the processes, information and roles to be described, and QPL is used to organize and classify them.

Before writing, the QPL diagram is used to check and revise the information. At that stage, the author is ready to write a draft of the procedure, and several examples will be illustrated.

As QPL represents the content of instructional documents as a diagram, it also can be used to produce procedures in a flow chart format, which is more 'user-friendly'. The chapter concludes with an example of a procedure where the QPL has been translated into a flow chart. This is easier to read than text and thus more likely to be used.

3.1   EVERYTHING YOU WANTED TO KNOW ABOUT PROCEDURES ... BUT WERE AFRAID TO ASK

Chapter 2 provided a description of QPL. QPL is a tool used to analyse and understand systems and their effect on quality. To put those systems into effect, however, we need to express the QPL concepts in a useful and accessible way, in the form which people are most used to: ordinary language. This chapter provides a bridge from the QPL description to such a written description. It specifies a series of steps, starting with the objectives of the document to be written, then writing descriptions in QPL and, finally, converting those descriptions into a written document. As flow charts and other graphical notations are also useful for conveying instructions, it also illustrates the conversion of QPL into these forms.

Since QPL is a language for describing processes and information, it is necessary first to gather information. Part of the chapter is devoted to the collection, organization and verification of this information, which will be incorporated in documents later.

In this chapter, the term 'instructional documents' denotes all documents which give instructions to people. In most organizations, these include standards, procedures, work instructions, codes of practice, standard operating procedures and many other types of document.

Why are procedures and instructions so hard to write?

Of all documents, procedures and instructions are among the most difficult to write. At each step of the production process, new difficulties are encountered. At the end of the process, when they are used to guide activities and to produce results, they can then be difficult to apply. What are some of the reasons?

What problems do we encounter while writing procedures and instructions?

- *Lack of accessible information:* The first problem is that there may be little documentation about what people actually do! It is often compounded by differences in viewpoints between participants: each will have a different view, depending on their roles and functions.
- *Structure clashes:* It is very common for instructional documents to be written by organizations or individuals who have little responsibility for using them. For example, the purchasing department probably will write the purchasing procedures, but most of the users will be departmental and project managers. Different user groups may use the same procedure in very different ways: managers will concentrate on purchasing required goods with a minimum of fuss and time, while the purchasing department has an interest in ensuring that paperwork is completed correctly.
- *Organizational complexity:* Modern organizations have very complex structures, with hierarchical lines of command and multifunctional work groups. People have many roles in a modern organization, and the procedures must reflect this complexity, as well as complying with all applicable laws and regulations. Decision making and lines of communication can be difficult to understand, verify and then to document.
- *Key information:* Instructional documents have only one purpose: to convey instructions accurately and efficiently. To do so, the reader must be able to grasp

the most important information first; details can be filled in only after the reader/user has the necessary understanding of the important points. A major task is to highlight the most important information, while also including less urgent details in the right place.

What problems do we encounter while using procedures and instructions?

Once the document is written, a new set of problems occur, as it passes into active use:

● Procedures and instructions are used by different people in different ways and with different objectives. (In the purchasing example of Chapter 2, staff in the purchasing department have a principal interest in obtaining goods cost-effectively and maintaining lists of acceptable suppliers. The requisitioner's interest is more short term: obtaining the goods rapidly, with as little paperwork as possible.)

● Users of a procedure often have very different training, experience and levels of skill.

● It is very difficult to provide overall guidance, while also catering for the large number of unusual situations which could require individual solutions.

● Modern procedures must comply with many levels of requirements, including international and national standards, local legal requirements, company standards and industry codes of practice. Users of the document can be held accountable if they breach these requirements.

Steps in writing procedures and instructions

This chapter provides a systematic approach to the above problems, based on QPL and its ability to structure processes and information.

The key to writing any good document—whether instructional or not—is structure. People can understand only a limited number of concepts at any time—seven is usually cited as the maximum. Yet a document may need to deal with hundreds, perhaps thousands, of separate ideas, which need to be absorbed and related by the reader. By providing a clear structure in the document, the author assists the reader in navigating through the document. After structure, the second key to good documentation lies in good classification—determining how concepts are related, and using them to characterize all relevant information.

This chapter shows how to use QPL for determining the structure and classification underlying the document. It illustrates how to divide the task into a small number of easy to follow steps. QPL is used to help organize and classify the information, and to provide a 'roadmap' for the author. We'll also see how much information to provide at any one time, and the order of presenting it.

The seven steps of this process are:

(1) Provide a description of the document to be produced—the statement of requirements.
(2) Collect and document all activities and information.
(3) Annotate the written description with the elements of QPL.
(4) Draw QPL diagrams.

(5) Verify the contents of the QPL diagrams.
(6) Write the procedure, using the QPL diagrams.
(7) Review and revise the procedure.

The first six steps are described in the rest of this chapter. The final step—review and revise—is a major process in its own right. It is covered, as part of process analysis techniques, in Chapter 5.

3.2 STEP 1: THE STATEMENT OF REQUIREMENTS

The first step in writing any document is to write a clear statement of what is required. In the case of a procedure or instruction, this includes the scope of the document, the responsible authority, and how it is to be evaluated. It will also include all other details needed by the author for a clear understanding of the processes and information to be described.

QPL provides a concise description of the requirements of any process. By checking that all process descriptions conform to the format of QPL, we ensure that it is a complete and sufficient description of that process (see the checklist).

QPL-BASED CHECKLIST FOR A STATEMENT OF REQUIREMENTS

Process:

● What is the scope of the process(es) covered by the document?
● What processes will these interact with?
● How will the document be evaluated when it is produced?

Information items:

● What information is needed by the process?
● What information is produced by the process?
● What information is updated by the process?

Process owner:

● Who is/are responsible for the processes described in the document?

Authority:

● Who is responsible for the content of the document and its accuracy?
● What other standards or procedures must the document comply with?
● What are the parties that have an interest in the document and the processes that it regulates?

Control:

● Under which conditions and constraints is this document applicable?

The QPL checklist for a statement of requirements suggests a standard contents list, as follows:

Title page, control pages and contents list

1.	*Scope of the procedure*
1.1	Processes covered by the procedure
1.2	Users of the procedure
1.3	Inputs to the procedure
1.4	Outputs from the procedure
1.5	Conditions of use for the procedure
2.	*Responsible authorities*
2.1	Person or position responsible for this procedure
2.2	Others with a stake in the operation of this procedure
3.	*Compliance*
3.1	Standards and procedures which this procedure will comply with
3.2	Procedures and work instructions which will comply with this procedure
4.	*Evaluation of this procedure*
4.1	Criteria for evaluation
4.2	When the evaluation will be carried out
4.3	Persons responsible for the evaluation

Control pages are placed at the beginning of all formal documents and contain information controlling the issue and distribution of the document. They usually include version control information as well.

An example of a statement of requirements, using this standard contents list, is detailed below. The example is based on the earlier example of part of a purchasing procedure shown in Figures 2.1 and 2.20.

Statement of requirements for purchasing procedure

1.   SCOPE OF THE PROCEDURE
1.1   Processes covered by the procedure
This procedure specifies the processes and documentation required to:

(a)   issue a purchase requisition for goods.
(b)   process the purchase requisition.
(c)   issue purchase orders.
(d)   receive and check purchased goods.
(e)   issue the purchased goods to the requisitioner.

1.2   Users of the procedure
The people who will use this procedure are:

(a)   project managers, project staff and their line managers
(b)   purchasing department staff
(c)   accounts department staff
(d)   goods inward staff.

The procedure also applies to the conduct of and relationships with suppliers.
1.3   Inputs to the procedure
The items required as input to this procedure are:

(a)   quotations from potential suppliers
(b)   invoice from successful supplier
(c)   goods or services delivered as part of the purchase.

continued

Statement of requirements for purchasing procedure (*continued*)

1.4   Outputs from the procedure
The items which will be output from this procedure are:

(a)   purchase order
(b)   goods received slip.

1.5   Conditions of use for the procedure
The procedure will be mandatory whenever an item exceeding $500 is purchased.
When under this value, the divisional float may be used as an alternative,
although the procedure can still be used, if the requisitioner desires.

2.   RESPONSIBLE AUTHORITIES
2.1   Person responsible for this procedure
The head of purchasing is responsible for the content and execution of this
procedure.
2.2   Others with a stake in the operation of this procedure
Other roles with a stake in this procedure are:

(a)   the purchasing department, represented by the head of purchasing
(b)   the goods inward department, represented by the head of department
(c)   the accounts department, represented by the head of department
(d)   project managers holding budgets for purchasing
(e)   staff requesting purchases
(f)   suppliers of goods and services requested through the purchasing
       procedure.

3.   COMPLIANCE
3.1   Standards and procedures which this procedure will comply with:

(a)   ISO 9002 Purchasing Requirements
(b)   company accounting procedures
(c)   company personnel procedures
(d)   company contracts procedures.

3.2   Other procedures which will comply with this procedure
All project management and accounts payable procedures will comply with this
procedure.

4.   EVALUATION OF THIS PROCEDURE
4.1   Criteria for evaluation
The criteria which will be used to evaluate this procedure are:

(a)   clarity and unambiguity
(b)   ease of use for all users
(c)   absence of bottlenecks and minimal red tape in the processes
(d)   accuracy and completeness
(e)   provision for collection of information for process improvement.

4.2   When the evaluation will be carried out
The evaluation will be carried out after issue of the draft procedure, and on
subsequent major revisions.
4.3   Persons responsible for the evaluation
The persons responsible for the evaluation are:

(a)   head of purchasing
(b)   nominated project manager
(c)   head of contracts.

These positions may be delegated by the person in the named role.

3.3   STEP 2: COLLECTING AND DOCUMENTING INFORMATION ABOUT THE PROCEDURE

Collecting information

The chosen author of the procedure has written the statement of requirements and agreed it with the responsible authority. Then the panic sets in: 'What information do I need to collect?' The moment of truth has occurred, and the author suddenly realizes what is probably the most difficult area of all. Gathering information is extremely hard to organize and to do successfully.

As is shown in the next section, QPL provides a simple way of annotating textual information. This enables us to concentrate initially only on information gathering, since the structure and classification provided by QPL can be added later. With this advantage, a good way to proceed is simply to ask the responsible authorities—those with a stake in the processes, like departmental staff and users—to write down as much as they can about what is done or what they would like done.

It is not important at this stage to list the concepts in any particular order. However, there is one qualification: if possible, information should be gathered top-down. Initially, the wider picture should be obtained; details can be filled in once this picture is understood. This will make it easier to structure the information later, since an initial framework is available. However, if other reasons make it easier to gather details first, then that is an acceptable alternative.

As a supplementary approach, which is structured around those with a stake in the system, we can also do an initial identification of key processes. The author should gather as much written information as possible about these processes, including:

- existing instructional documentation, including standards, procedures and work instructions
- internal reports and memos
- organization charts
- forms and pro forma
- contents of records, such as database reports.

Existing instructional documents obviously will provide useful information for new instructional documents. The other documents provide further facts, particularly about the information items to be documented in the procedure.

The author may encounter a situation where, for various reasons, the 'stakeholders' are unwilling or unable to provide the necessary information in a written form. In this situation, the author may need to conduct a fact-finding exercise. In addition to the sources suggested above, it will be necessary to conduct interviews (for techniques, see Flanagan, 1954; Kelly, 1955; Sidney and Brown, 1961; Wood-Harper, Antill and Avison, 1985). The interviews may be transcribed into an unstructured written format, as suggested above.

Documenting information

The previous section suggests unstructured text and other documents as media for collecting information. While this is usually a good basis for later QPL analysis, it can be useful to supplement it with more structured information. This section provides some examples of structured documentation techniques.

As noted in Chapter 2, information items provide the necessary links between processes and determine the order in which processes are carried out. For this reason, it is very useful to document the processes in a format that also includes the information passing between them. There are two simple ways of recording this: tabular collection (SD-Scicon, 1989), and the information life history. The first shows the input to and output from a process, indirectly linking different processes. An example of a tabular collection form is shown in Table 3.1.

In this form of data collection, the five columns represent the following:

- Source   —The person, organization or object which provides the input.
- Input   —The input to the process.
- Process   —The process which is being described.
- Output   —The output from the process.
- Destination—The person, organization or object which uses the output.

The tabular collection form of data collection emphasizes processes and their inputs and outputs. This is obviously suited to the QPL notation, but it may not be suited to situations structured around information items. In this case, a second form—the life history—provides a better way of documenting the data. This format allows us to describe each information item with a complete view of its history, from the moment it is created to the time when it either is sent to a final user, is stored, or is destroyed. By concentrating on information, its transformations and its states, such a diagram can point to processes that otherwise might be ignored.

To create a life history diagram, use the notation of QPL to describe the path followed by the information item, noting each process which either uses the information (as control or as an authority, or possibly as unchanged output), or which transforms the information (as changed output). Figure 3.1 provides an example of this format.

In this format, only limited detail about processes and other information items is provided, to allow the author to concentrate on the information item of interest, and the changes it undergoes. The author also notes additional relevant details about the information, including attributes which affect its processing, its initial state and its final state.

Table 3.1 Tabular collection

Source	Input	Process	Output	Destination
Suppliers	Bids	Evaluate candidate bids	Successful bids	Purchasing department
Requisitioners	Purchase requisition	Telephone candidate suppliers	Quotations	Purchasing department

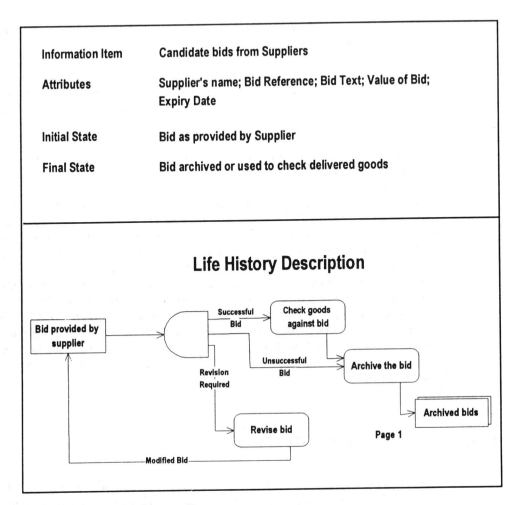

Figure 3.1 Information life-history diagram

By the end of the data collection step, the procedure's author will have gathered information in at least one of the three formats: written descriptions, tabular collections and information life histories. The next step in the process is to collate all this information and to translate it into a common QPL format. This is discussed in the next section.

3.4 STEP 3: ANNOTATING THE WRITTEN DESCRIPTION WITH THE ELEMENTS OF QPL

After gathering the necessary information to be embodied in the procedure, we need to restructure it into a series of QPL diagrams. The information required is contained in the assembled documentation, but it will be very difficult to manage this transition without an additional, organizational step. This consists of a QPL annotation of the documentation, which has two objectives:

(1) it enables the author to classify each part of the document into one of the five elements of QPL—the process, information, authority, owner or control; and
(2) it highlights the connections—information links—between parts of the document.

When we understand how the document is composed of QPL elements and their connections, then it is quite straightforward to draw QPL diagrams, as the next section will illustrate.

This process is illustrated in Table 3.2, where a high-level description of an imaginary language school is provided. This text could be provided either by the head of the school, or it could have been written by the procedure's author after interviewing the head of the school. The QPL annotations in the right-hand column reflect the author's interpretation of the text, in terms of QPL elements.

The previous section discussed structured ways of documenting information, namely tabular collection and information life histories. Note that these are already in a QPL-based format, so that it is unnecessary to provide QPL annotations. The annotation method described here is necessary only for unstructured written text. (Chapter 8 describes another QPL annotation method, using coloured marking pens.) The next section shows how to convert all these forms of QPL-structured information into QPL diagrams.

3.5   STEP 4: DRAWING QPL DIAGRAMS

Now we come to the heart of the process for designing procedures: drawing QPL diagrams. The three previous steps have prepared the information in a suitable format. The statement of requirements includes the QPL elements for the external view of the procedure. Data collection obtains the necessary information. And the annotation step extracts the essential QPL elements. This step restructures this information into a 'pure' QPL form which can be used, not only to write the procedure, but to review and revise it later.

The process of drawing the QPL is expressed in a few guidelines, as outlined below.

Analyse the information by working top-down

Start with the most general and widely applicable processes, and gradually expand the content to the more specific by adding more detail. It is not always easy to spot the more general concepts, and a common mistake in QPL analysis is to provide a description which has all information at a single level. Such a diagram is extremely hard to read and interpret, and it obscures the structure and classification which is inherent in all instructional documentation.

Table 3.2 QPL annotated description of an organization

High level description—Eurolingua (UK) Ltd	Annotation
(1) Eurolingua (UK) Ltd (Eurolingua UK) is the only organization licensed in the United Kingdom by Eurolingua Inc. to teach foreign languages according to the principles of the Eurolingua method.	Process authority
(2) Eurolingua Inc is managed by the president, who is authorized to make decisions regarding its structure, authority and actions.	Process owner Authority
Eurolingua UK will be managed by a managing director with similar authority, reporting to a UK board of directors appointed by, and responsible to, the president of Eurolingua Inc.	Process owner Authority
(3) The UK board of directors ensures that the affairs of Eurolingua UK are run efficiently and in accordance with the objectives and practices of the worldwide Eurolingua organization.	Authority
(4) The president of Eurolingua UK will appoint officers to carry out the functions of the organization in the United Kingdom. These officers report to the president, who also has the authority to remove them from their positions. Both the appointment and removal of officers are subject to ratification by the UK board of directors. Officers will include a head of finance, who is responsible for all financial affairs of Eurolingua UK, the dean, who is responsible for the welfare of all students attending Eurolingua UK courses and workshops, and the marketing director, who is responsible for promoting the courses of Eurolingua UK in other countries.	Process Process Owners/ Authority Authority Process owner Process owner Process owner Process
(5) The curriculum and teaching programme of Eurolingua UK are the responsibility of the head of instruction, who reports to the managing director of Eurolingua UK. The head of instruction is also a member of the Eurolingua Instructors Council, which consists of the other heads of instruction from all national Eurolingua organizations.	Information Item/Process owner Process owners
(6) The UK Teachers Council consists of all recognized Eurolingua instructors in the UK who are currently licensed to teach foreign languages with the Eurolingua method. The function of this Council is to ensure the effective teaching, through correct application of the Eurolingua method, on courses and workshops. The UK head of instruction will act as adviser and chairperson of the Council.	Process Authority Process owner
(7) Licensing examinations for Eurolingua instructors are held quarterly, in accordance with international Eurolingua regulations.	Process/ Authority
(8) Twice a year, all Eurolingua instructors will be appraised to ensure that the quality of their teaching is adequate. Feedback from this process will be sent to the head of instruction, who will compile a report for the board of directors and for Eurolingua Inc. This report will be used to note trends in the quality of Eurolingua teaching, and corrective action will be taken if the trend is negative.	Process Information Item/Process Information Item/Process

Identify the five QPL elements

All collected information should now be analysed and classified into one of the five elements. This should have been done in the previous step, but it is possible that some elements may have been overlooked and can be corrected now.

CHECKLIST FOR IDENTIFYING THE FIVE QPL ELEMENTS

QPL element	Check
Process	Have all activities been identified and classified within a process?
Information item	Have all information items been identified, along with the processes which they are input to and output from? Has the persistence of each information item been specified?
Process owner	Is an individual or operator named as responsible for each identified process?
Authority	For each identified process, is there a named authority which specifies the steps of the process or is formally qualified to carry out the process?
Control	Are the conditions or constraints for each identified process stated explicitly?

Draw QPL diagrams which represent the information collected

As noted above, these should be structured top-down, from general concepts to specifics and details.

Identify weaknesses or missing elements

QPL is fully structured: the elements can relate to each other only in well-defined ways. This raises questions which can be asked of any QPL diagram to check its information:

- Does each process have a thread of information (input or control) which causes it to be initiated? Does it have an owner? An authority? Does it produce some output?
- Are all processes linked to other processes?
- Are processes only linked to other processes at the same level of detail?

Questions such as these help us to refine the QPL logic and ensure that documents which are finally produced are well structured and consistent. Chapter 5 contains many further suggestions for analysing QPL diagrams.

Drawing QPL diagrams is something of an art and requires practice before it can be accomplished smoothly. It is rarely effortless, because at each step new questions arise which must be answered before proceeding. Even an experienced QPL practitioner does not expect to draw perfect diagrams the first time: each attempt to draw them raises new questions. The answers provide additional information, which improves the next drawing. When all such questions are answered successfully, the result is a rigorous description of the processes, structured in a way which can be expressed easily on the printed page or with other graphical aids.

3.6 STEP 5: VERIFYING THE CONTENTS OF THE QPL DIAGRAMS

Before the QPL diagrams drawn in the previous step are used in writing the procedure, it is good practice to verify the information they contain. This provides a check that the author has understood the information correctly, and it confirms that the provider of the information agrees with the author's interpretation. Verification is carried out with the people listed in the authorities section of the statement of requirements. The principal responsibility for verification is with the person named as responsible for the content of the procedure. Other parties named in the authorities section also have an interest in the document, and a sample of them should be used to verify the QPL.

The previous section described some simple checks, arising from the definitions of QPL elements and constraints on their use. The following questions may aid verification:

- Does the QPL structure match that of the organization and its processes?
- Are all information items reflected by actual entities such as standards, procedures, forms, letters, memos and reports? If not, are they represented by material objects or other means of communication, such as telephone calls or other verbal channels?
- Where the QPL diagram represents an information item as one of the three types (channel, information store and archive), is that type reflected in the way that the information is actually used or stored? For example: if information is represented as an archive, have we defined processes which can access and store a specific version of the information?
- Do the owners named on the QPL diagrams represent actual roles, people or groups of people?
- Do the authorities named on the QPL diagrams represent actual documents or qualified personnel?
- Are the communication links on the QPL diagrams (the information lines which connect processes) correctly drawn? Does the specified information actually flow along those lines?

The author should aim to identify all processes in a procedure by the time the QPL diagrams are drawn and revised, and before the procedure is actually written. If possible, attributes of information items should also be identified by this stage: that is, the essential characteristics which the processes will need in order to perform their operations successfully.

3.7 STEP 6: WRITING THE PROCEDURE

By preparing a QPL description of all processes in advance, the author already has done most of the work involved in writing a procedure. Most importantly, a structure now exists both for the description and for the final document. While the words and figures actually used will affect the readability of the document, they will be of little value if they are embedded in a weak or confused structure. People are easily alienated by any instructional document which does not state the steps clearly and in a well-organized fashion.

So the author already is well on the way towards the final document. The next steps involve the translation from two-dimensional diagrams to the more limited format of a written procedure.

The steps are:

(1) Restructure the QPL diagrams into a form suitable for the audience.
(2) Structure the steps into a nested hierarchy.
(3) Write the procedure.
(4) Verify that the procedure reflects the QPL diagram accurately.
(5) Check the readability and usability of the procedure.

These steps are explained below.

(1) Restructure the QPL diagrams into a form suitable for the audience

This mainly entails consideration of the users; it creates a structure which is as close as possible to their functional roles. If there is only a single type of user, this step is relatively easy, as a single restructuring will do. A standard reference on procedure writing (Zimmerman and Campbell 1988: 28–9) provides contents lists for three types of document (see also Tebeaux, 1990: 350–67):

Administrative procedure:
1 Purpose
2 Scope
3 Definitions
4 References
5 Responsibilities
6 Instructions
7 Records
8 Attachments

Mechanical maintenance procedure:
1   Purpose
2   References
3   Personnel requirements
4   Precautions
5   Prerequisites
6   Special Tools
7   Procedure
8   Acceptance requirements
9   Restoration
10 Attachments

System operating procedure:
1   Purpose
2   References
3   System description
4   Precautions
5   System startup
    5.1 Prerequisites
    5.2 Instructions
6   Normal operation
    6.1 Prerequisites
    6.2 Instructions
7   System shutdown
    7.1 Prerequisites
    7.2 Instructions
8   Attachments

These lists are adequate if only a single type of user will read a particular procedure. However, if there are several types of user, then a single restructuring will not be sufficient. It may be possible to provide a compromise structure which is adequate. However, if a single structure is not sufficient, then the author can try several different overlapping structures, and repeat information in the procedure which is written from them.

Typically, this situation occurs when there are several functional roles using the same procedure. We can take the purchasing procedure discussed earlier in this chapter as an example. Many different types of functional staff use this procedure— project managers, purchasing department staff, accounts department staff, goods inward staff and even suppliers—and each type has its own preferred way of working. Generally it is not possible to write a single sequence of steps which all these roles would relate to, and it is preferable to provide several sequences, one for each role.

(2) Structure the steps into a nested hierarchy

This corresponds to a top-down structure of processes. For a process which is to be broken down into sub-processes, it is important to give a strong statement which summarizes the sub-processes. For example, 'Purchasing involves an authorized request by a member of staff, the request for quotes by the purchasing department, the issuing of tenders by candidate suppliers and an award of contract, and the completion of the order by a successful delivery of goods or services.'

(3) Write the procedure

This involves the correspondence between QPL elements and ordinary language, as shown in Table 3.3.

(4) Verify that the procedure reflects the QPL diagram accurately

After the procedure has been written, the author must check that it is an accurate representation of the QPL diagram. This normally is quite straightforward, since the written text has been based directly on the diagram. Looking once more at the elements of QPL, the sorts of questions to ask are shown in Table 3.4. These questions are explored in greater detail in Chapter 5, where the general issue of analysing and reviewing processes is discussed.

(5) Check the readability and usability of the procedure

After checking that the written text agrees with the QPL, the final step is a check that the document is usable by the audience for which it is intended. The reviewer of a written procedure should go through two principal steps in using it: first, reading (or skimming) it to obtain a general understanding of its contents—here the document is used as a description of the relevant processes. Second, the document is used for

Table 3.3 Correspondence between QPL and ordinary language

QPL Element	Textual equivalent
Process	The steps of the procedure at a given level of the hierarchy.
Information item	The information input to an activity or step of the procedure. Information transformed or created by a step. Links with other steps. Persistence of information: retention and access requirements, version control, etc.
Owner	Responsibility for carrying out the procedure or part of it.
Authority	Standards or other procedures which are to be complied with. Qualified staff who may carry out this procedure (when it is not fully explicit and their judgement is required).
Control	Under what conditions or constraints is this step to be carried out?

Table 3.4 Verification questions to ask

QPL Element	Verification questions
Process	Have all processes on the QPL diagram been represented in the text? When a process is broken down into sub-processes, is this relationship clear from the text? Is the scope of each process clear from the text?
Information item	Are all information items in the diagram included in the text? Are the attributes of that information, necessary for the processes, stated in the text? Does the text correctly show the information links between processes?
Owner	Does the text make the ownership of each process explicit? Does it show the correct person or other role responsible for the process?
Authority	Does each process have the correct authority? Where an authority, such as a standard, is created or maintained within the organization's system, is this shown explicitly within the text?
Control	Does the text clearly indicate the conditions and constraints for each process?

reference, after the reader has a general understanding—here the emphasis is on ease of use. Each of these steps involves at least two criteria:

Is the document readable?
First the reviewer must check if the intended audience is able to read the document. Obviously this will involve questions on its readability and whether it has been structured into sections which are easy to read and which fit together well. It also involves an appreciation of the background knowledge and skills of the reader.

Looking more widely, the reviewer should check into other features affecting readability. If any other documents must be read first, is this stated near the beginning of this document? Are external documents clearly cross-referenced, with information repeated when it would be inconvenient to search for the other document?

Is the document easy to apply?
To check that the procedure is easy to apply, the reviewer must look into the kinds of work where it will be used. As the procedure's primary use now is as a reference document, the paramount consideration must be the ease of looking up information: What kind of paperwork do I fill in? Which paperwork is mandatory, and which is only recommended? What do I do if a standard step is not applicable or not relevant in these circumstances?

Examples 1 and 2 in the next section provide a style of writing which reflects this two-fold use of procedures, first as descriptive, then as reference documents.

A list of further questions for procedural documents is contained in Tebeaux (1990: 379–80).

3.8   EXAMPLES

The examples which follow illustrate the use of QPL for three widely differing types of procedures. Each case includes a QPL diagram and an fragment of a procedure based on the diagram.

The first example builds on the Eurolingua language school, looked at in step 3 above. Table 3.2 is a high-level description of the Eurolingua organization, annotated with QPL. The procedure for this example provides a straightforward example of a procedure with an organizational orientation.

The second example is based on the purchasing instructions discussed in several previous examples, and in particular the statement of requirements for the purchasing procedure looked at earlier in this chapter. This example shows a part of the finished procedure which complies with this statement of requirements, along with the QPL diagram on which it is based.

The final example is a new procedure at a much more detailed level. Based on an actual procedure in the computer industry and compliant with the ISO 9000 series of standards, it provides the instructions for raising a goods received form when a purchased item is received. This example illustrates the use of QPL to describe a step-by-step process when little structure is involved.

Examples 1 and 2 are written in two columns. The left column contains high-level information and can be used to get a quick overview of the stages to be followed. The right column contains more detailed information suggested by the QPL lower-level diagrams. This reflects the twofold way in which procedures are used: first as a description of the steps to be followed, then as a reference for the details of the steps. Example 3 requires only a single column, as the information is straightforward and does not need further elaboration.

Example 1: A procedure based on organization

This example is based on the earlier example of Eurolingua (see Table 3.2). That provided an outline of the organization which Eurolingua intend for their UK subsidiary. Now suppose that we wish to formalize this organization by writing a procedure which describes it. Following the steps outlined in this chapter, we produce a QPL diagram (Figure 3.2) based on the annotated description of Eurolingua UK (Table 3.5). This is refined, following the verification procedures presented earlier. In this example, most of the work is spent on clarifying and improving the communication links between parts of the Eurolingua organization.

This example highlights an important principle of organizational procedures: that they do not just describe the organization and functions of its parts. That is a rather obsolete model, based on a rigid hierarchy, where 'everyone knows his or her place'! The modern view concentrates on communication between the parts as much as on their functional organization. People need to understand how they communicate with others, not just their place or function in the hierarchy. The final Eurolingua procedure, which integrates communication elements with the functional structure, will provide staff with the basics of how their organization works and how they fit into it. A comparison with the original description in Table 3.2 illustrates this improvement.

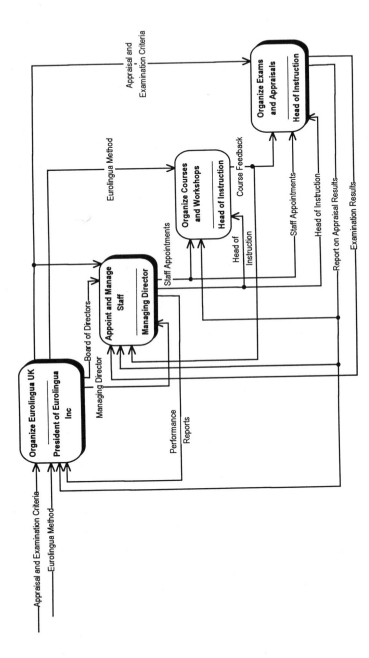

Figure 3.2   Eurolingua UK organization
Eurolingua UK organization (high-level chart)

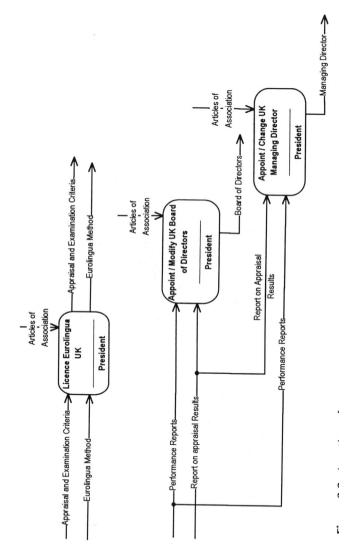

Figure 3.2 (continued)
Detail of 'Organize Eurolingua UK'

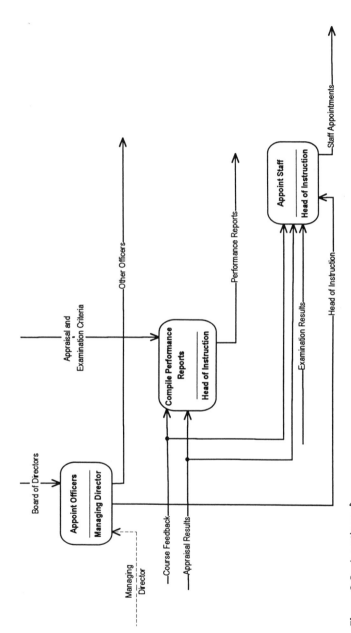

Figure 3.2 *(continued)*
Detail of 'Appoint and manage staff'

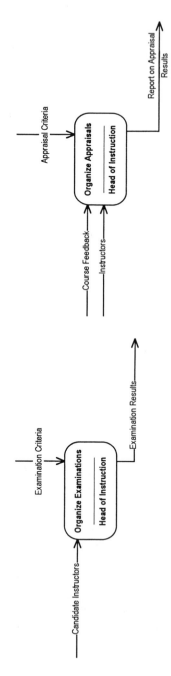

Figure 3.2 (continued)
Detail of 'Organize exams and appraisals'

Table 3.5 Eurolingua UK Organization

Eurolingua UK is a commercial organization, based in the UK, which specializes in the teaching of languages as a foreign language. It is the only organization licensed in the United Kingdom by Eurolingua Inc to teach foreign languages according to the principles of the Eurolingua method. It is managed according to the following organization and rules:

Overview	Notes
1. The president of Eurolingua Inc. appoints the board of directors and managing director of Eurolingua UK Ltd, who in turn report to the president. The president monitors performance of Eurolingua Ltd through performance reports and reports on appraisals of teaching staff.	The president will base his decisions upon the Eurolingua Articles of Association, which acts as the constitution of the worldwide Eurolingua organization. The president will review, at least quarterly, the performance reports and appraisal results from Eurolingua UK and change the managing director and/or board of directors if their performance is not satisfactory.
2. The UK board of directors ensures that the affairs of Eurolingua UK are run efficiently and in accordance with the objectives and practices of the worldwide Eurolingua organization.	
3. The managing director of Eurolingua UK is responsible for the operations and management of the organization. He or she produces performance reports, which are sent to the president of Eurolingua Inc. monthly. He or she also appoints and manages the officers and staff who are part of the Eurolingua UK organization.	Subject to ratification by the board of directors, the managing director appoints the officers and other staff of Eurolingua UK.
4. The head of instruction, appointed by the managing director, is responsible for organizing courses and workshops within the United Kingdom. These shall be run according to the principles of the Eurolingua method. Each of these will be evaluated by students, and some will also be assessed by other Eurolingua instructors. The results of these evaluations will be sent to the managing director.	Course feedback and evaluation results will be used by the head of instruction to compile a quarterly performance report, which is copied to the president of Eurolingua Inc.
5. The head of instruction is also responsible for the organization of examinations and appraisals, which select qualified staff and ensure that their performance is up to the performance expected.	Course feedback will be used as part of these appraisals, and the results will be sent to the managing director, as well as the president of Eurolingua Inc. Examination results will be sent to the managing director to assist in the selection of permanent staff of Eurolingua UK.

Example 2: An administration procedure

This example expands on the earlier purchasing procedures presented in this and the previous chapter. It is typical of administrative procedures in a large organization, where staff process paperwork and need to coordinate several roles. The example also shows a top-down hierarchy of processes—with the top-level chart showing the overall flow of information and the connections between main processes. Two processes—'select a supplier' and 'complete a purchase order'—are broken down into more detailed processes.

Table 3.6 Purchasing procedure

Overview	Notes
1. The person requesting the goods or services, known as the requisitioner, completes a purchase requisition.	If the purchase requisition is found to be incorrect (step 2), it is corrected in this step.
2. The purchase requisition is submitted to the purchasing department, which checks that it has been completed correctly. If not, it is returned to the requisitioner for correction (step 1).	
3. The purchasing department then selects a supplier meeting the needs identified on the purchase requisition.	The purchasing department identifies suppliers on the Approved Suppliers List who have the capability of meeting the order. They are telephoned and asked for prices and conditions (unless a similar order has been placed within the previous month, when new telephoning is unnecessary). Based on the replies, a supplier is chosen.
4. If the selected supplier company confirms that it can fulfil the order in the required time, then the purchasing department completes a purchase order and sends it to the supplier.	Copies of the purchase order are also sent to the requisitioner, the budget holder of the account which will pay for the order, and the goods inward department.
5. When the goods are received or the services ordered completed, the purchasing department records that the order has been completed successfully.	
6. If the goods or services have not been received or completed by the date agreed with the supplier, then the order may be cancelled and the supplier removed from the Approved Suppliers List.	If the goods or services have not been received or completed by the date agreed with the supplier, then the purchasing department checks with the supplier. If a new date is feasible, then it is recorded, and this action is repeated on that date. If a new date is not feasible, and the supplier cannot provide a reasonable explanation, then the supplier is to be removed from the Approved Suppliers List. The order is cancelled, and a new supplier selected (step 3).

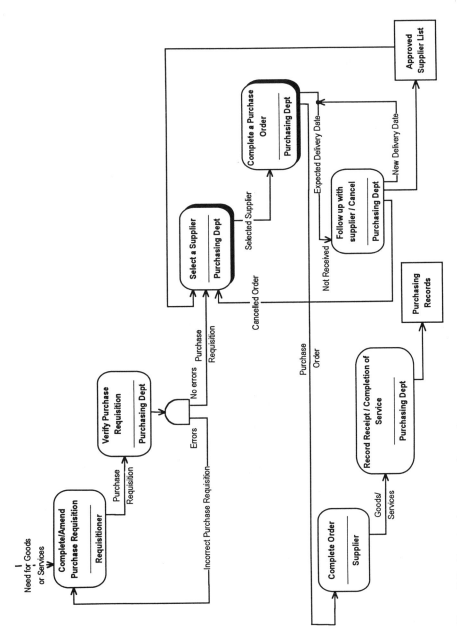

Figure 3.3 Purchasing procedure
Purchasing procedure (high-level chart)

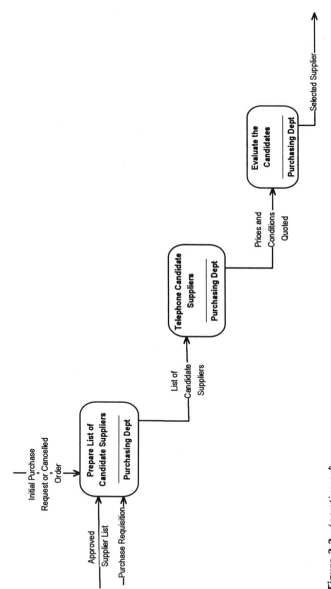

Figure 3.3 (continued)
Detail of 'Select a supplier'

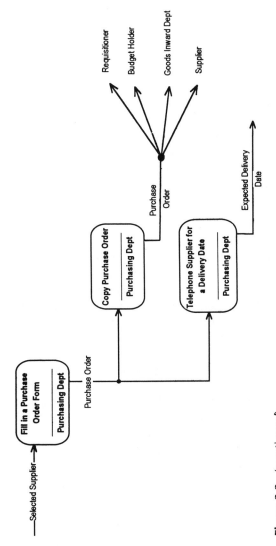

Figure 3.3 (continued)
Detail of 'Complete a purchase order'

Example 3: Technical instructions

This example is a straightforward set of instructions for completing a standard form—in this case the goods and services received note (GSRN). It consists of a series of steps, directly linked by information (see below and Figure 3.4). There are no lower-level processes, so the QPL diagram is at a single level only. The authorities for each step correspond to the letters used to identify each step in the written procedure.

This example illustrates the use of QPL to structure and document a step-by-step procedure. On the surface, this is a straightforward procedure with few complications. The QPL diagram shows the steps clearly, but also highlights the information which must be recorded and communication with organizations outside of the goods inwards department.

This procedure deals with receipt of goods which were ordered through the purchasing procedures of Example 2, but which are handled by a different department of the company. The next chapter will illustrate how the two procedures, and the departments which 'own' them, can be structured into a consistent set of documents.

Goods inward procedure

(a) The goods inwards department is responsible for initiating and completing goods/services received notes (GSRN) for all goods received via goods inwards operations. The named acceptance authority, as identified by the off-site receipt concession form, is responsible for raising the relevant GSRN(s) for applicable off-site delivery consignments.

(b) All GSRNs are to be raised on Form PS-103, which is available from most stationery stores in the company.

(c) The GSRN is raised with reference to the supplier's advice note received with the goods and the relevant purchase order.

(d) Any damage noted, or discrepancies against either the supplier's advice note or the purchase order must be clearly identified on the GSRN.

(e) All individual packages received are to be clearly marked with the relevant GSRN number.

(f) If goods received may be sub-standard, they are to be held in quarantine at this stage.

(g) For valid delivery consignments received by goods inwards, goods are passed to the designated internal recipient defined by the purchase order (known as the 'consignee') by the end of the next working day from receipt. The consignee signs the GSRN to confirm receipt of such goods, and retains three copies.

(h) In the event that the consignee or other responsible authority is not available to receive the goods, then the goods are held by goods inwards in an area marked up as 'awaiting collection'. Such goods are checked on a regular basis.

(i) On acceptance of the goods, the GSRN is authorized by head of purchasing. Copies are distributed as defined in the code of practice of the requisitioner's department.

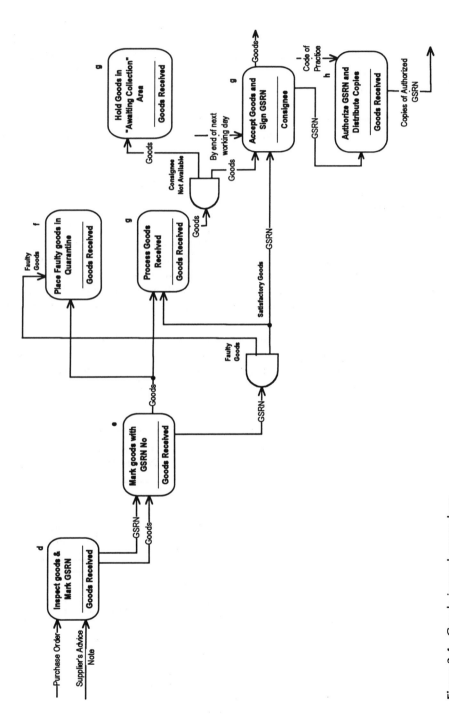

Figure 3.4 Goods inward procedure

3.9   WRITING GRAPHICAL PROCEDURES

There is a trend away from words alone as a means of giving instructions. Flow charts have been used to illustrate processes for decades, and they are being used with increasing frequency as more organizations see the importance of process-orientations. QPL is 'richer' than flow charting, particularly as it represents information as well as processes, but QPL itself is not suitable for a general audience, as it takes some training before one is able to read or write the notation. Fortunately, it is straightforward to convert directly from QPL to flow charting and other graphical notations, which can be read by a general audience. This section provides some examples.

Organization charts

Example 1 in the previous section has already provided an example of a 'written' organization chart. The text provides an implicit description of the organization of Eurolingua UK functions. To help make the structure of this organization clearer, we may want to supplement the text with an organization chart. This can be derived directly from the QPL diagram, by reflecting the top-down structure of processes, the application of authorities for functional roles, and the appointment of owners for processes. The organization chart which results is shown in Figure 3.5. Note that the QPL diagrams for Example 1 contain all the information in this chart. Its use is highlighting the managerial hierarchy, which, while implicit in the QPL, are not as clear.

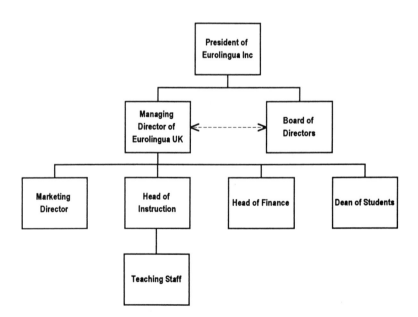

Figure 3.5   Organization chart resulting from Example 1

Flow charts

Because most people are familiar with flow charts, they are useful for supplementing or replacing textual information. As with organization charts, it is straightforward to convert from QPL diagrams to flow charts, as the essential elements of processes and decision points are both represented clearly in QPL.

The rules for conversion from QPL to flow charts are quite simple:

- process boxes in QPL are converted directly to one or more steps in the flow chart
- the flow of information, as shown by the information lines in the QPL chart, is converted directly to the flow lines in the flow chart
- control and case constructs in QPL are converted directly into decision points in the flow chart.

Figure 3.6 is a flow chart converted from the high-level QPL chart of Example 2 (Figure 3.3).

Procedures can usefully combine flow charts and text as well, to produce a set of instructions which are easy to understand and follow. Figure 3.7 shows an example, expanding on the first part of this purchasing example. The flow chart, on the left side of the page, provides a summary and overview of the major steps in the procedure. The text, on the right side, provides explanation and additional detail, where required.

3.10 SUMMARY OF CHAPTER 3

Much of this chapter has dealt with processes for analysing information and converting it into written procedures. This makes it possible to draw a QPL description of these processes, as shown in Figure 3.8. Such a diagram also serves as a summary of the instructional parts of this chapter.

Table 3.7 is a list of all the steps suggested in this chapter for writing procedures.

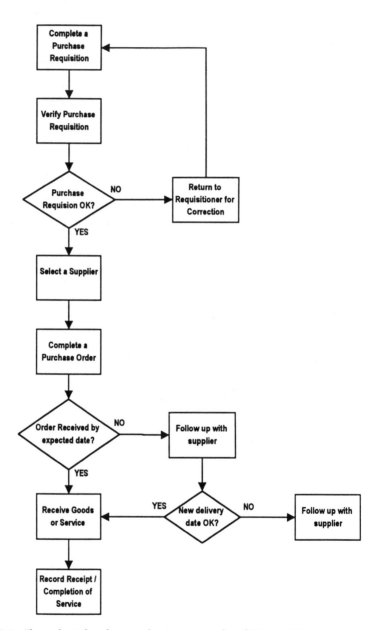

Figure 3.6   Flow chart for the purchasing example of Figure 3.3

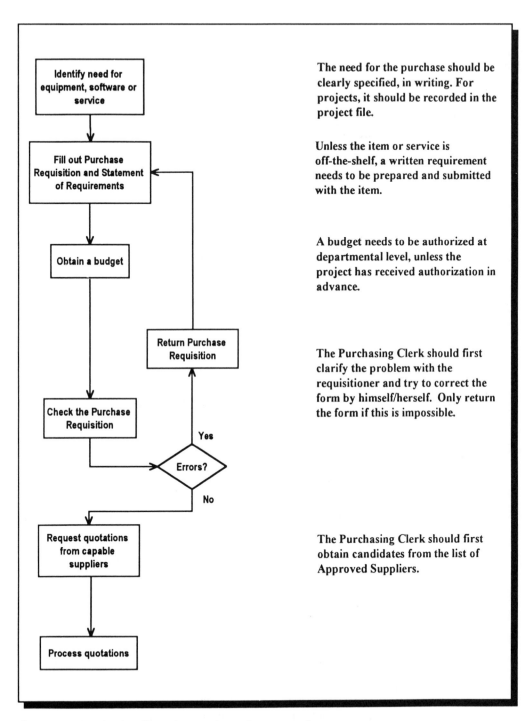

Figure 3.7 Combining flow chart and text in a procedure

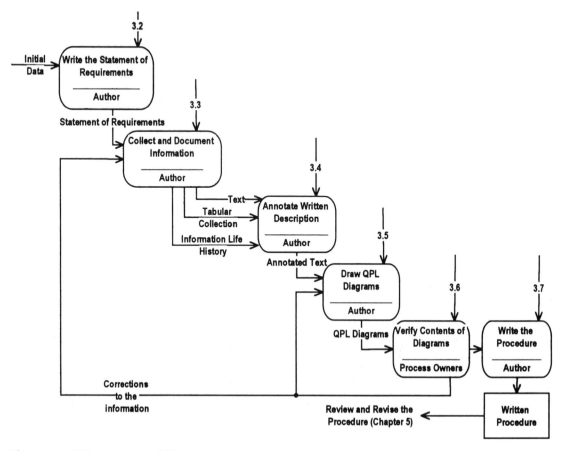

Figure 3.8 QPL summary of Chapter 3

Table 3.7 List of suggested steps for writing procedures

1.   Provide a description of the document to be produced—the statement of
     requirements.
2.   Collect and document all activities and information.
3.   Annotate the written description with the elements of QPL.
4.   Draw QPL diagrams.
4.1 Analyse the information by working top-down.
4.2 Identify the five QPL elements.
4.3 Draw QPL diagrams which represent the information collected.
4.4 Identify weaknesses or missing elements.
5.   Verify the contents of the QPL diagrams.
6.   Write the procedure, using the QPL diagrams.
6.1 Restructure the QPL diagrams into a form suitable for the audience.
6.2 Structure the steps into a nested hierarchy.
6.3 Write the procedure.
6.4 Verify that the procedure reflects the QPL diagram accurately.
6.5 Check the readability and usability of the procedure.
7.   Review and revise the procedure.

4

Structuring and coordinating processes

OVERVIEW

We now move from relatively simple processes discussed in the previous chapter, to those which capture the full complexity of whole organizations. Such processes involve many viewpoints of the organization—functional, departmental, informational, as well as process-oriented. There are three common ways to structure concepts: hierarchies, common characteristics (classes) and sequences. Each has a representation in QPL and can be used to structure organizations, their processes and the information which passes around them.

As in the previous chapter, the viewpoint is practical, and it is important to illustrate these concepts with real examples. The principles of structure are illustrated in writing standards and procedures for a range of organization types. Some pragmatic rules of thumb are introduced to help in the real problems which arise when capturing an organization and its processes in written documents.

Process structuring is a complex area, and a large body of technical research and literature is available to support it. While this chapter provides all the information which most readers will require, a summary of more extensive structuring principles is contained in Appendix 3. This provides an overview of the object-oriented principles underlying this chapter, as well as some additional material for advanced structuring techniques.

4.1 STRUCTURING

> All the world's a stage,
> And all the men and women merely players:
> They have their exits and their entrances;
> And one man in his time plays many parts.
>
> *Shakespeare, As You Like It*

We all play our part in many systems, and no one is totally their own boss. The politician needs to get re-elected, and the head of a company is responsible to the shareholders. Customers at a supermarket check-out counter are dependent on the clerk to check-out their purchases. The clerk is dependent on the cash register or bar code reader to total the purchases, and upon the manager when a price isn't clear. The bar code reader is dependent on the computer software which programs it, and the programmer is dependent on the correct specification for the program. And so the cycle continues.

With such inherent internal dependence and significant communications required, organizations need to structure their activities and their records. Without a structure to direct communications and establish clear responsibilities, only chaos can result.

The previous chapter established how to provide written instructions as individual standards and procedures. The problem of structure was not significant, since the tasks and processes involved were well-bounded, with a limited scope. Now the focus changes to writing and controlling such instructions when tight bounds cannot be drawn, or when the documentation has to match an existing, complex structure. This chapter provides techniques which will provide this structure. These techniques retain the basic QPL notation presented in the previous two chapters, but extend it to provide more power to cope with complexity.

Equipped with the ability to extend process descriptions to the whole of an organization, QPL can be used to capture and express the structure of an organization. This will form the basis for the complete set of documents—standards, procedures and work instructions—which cover the whole of the organization and tell its members about their responsibilities and about their communication with others, both within and without it.

This chapter contains an overview of the QPL structuring principles. A more complete and technical description is contained in Appendix 3.

To organize or not to organize . . .

Consider three words which have the same origin as the word *organize*: organization, organism, organic. These words share two concepts which are at the heart of organization—structure and processes. When we *organize*, we are following a process which produces an *organization*, a structure where the parts are clearly defined and related to each other. An *organism* is a coherent set of parts, depending on each other and their processes for mutual benefit. An *organic* structure is living and dynamic, with processes which coordinate the separate parts and which ensure that the whole is greater than the sum of its parts. All these words rest on the need for structure.

To form something into a coherent system, we first need to provide a structure which will group things into sensible units. These units could be arranged by functions, such as purchasing, sales or manufacturing. Or they could be arranged to minimize communication overheads, such as workgroups or geographic regions. However the units are arranged, they will reflect the goals, values and processes of the organization. For a commercial company, these will reflect the need to make a profit and to satisfy statutory regulations. For a public service, these will be more geared to empowerment, both of the people served and those who provide the service.

Along with structure, an organization must also take into account the processes into which its activities are grouped. These are the equivalents of structuring units, but here the focus is on actions, tasks and other activities. Organizations are not static, but are evolving, dynamic organisms, with the parts constantly exchanging information and acting on it. A major part of this chapter is devoted to the potential for structuring processes, in much the same way that objects or information are structured. Interestingly, this attention to processes provides a much improved structure for the organization as well.

The key to structure

As noted above, structuring involves combining units into coherent groups. The basis of this coherence lies in the three ways in which objects in the world are organized:

(1) By breaking objects into their component parts. For example, a country may be structured into states or provinces, which in turn may be broken down into counties and/or cities.

(2) By determining what groups of objects have in common. For example, apples and oranges have the common characteristic that they are both fruits; Red Delicious and Coxes are both types (or varieties) of apples, as they share certain characteristics with all other types of apples.

(3) By recognizing that objects appear in a certain order. For example, activities may be carried out in a given sequence, objects may be placed in specific positions and there may be a cause–effect relationship between certain events.

Compare these with the following excerpt from 'Classification Theory' in *Encyclopedia Britannica*:

> In apprehending the real world, men [people] constantly employ three methods of regulation, which pervade all of their thinking:
> (1) the differentiation of experience into particular objects and their attributes— e.g. when they distinguish between a tree and its size or spatial relations to other objects
> (2) the distinction between whole objects and their component parts—e.g. when they contrast a tree with its component branches, and
> (3) the formation of and the distinction between different classes of objects—e.g. when they form the class of all trees and the class of all stones and distinguish between them.

These are almost identical to QPL structuring principles, except that QPL extends this definition to add order to the differentiation emphasized in (1).

The next three sections expand on each of the three ways in which objects are organized, using the QPL notation to structure processes and information items. The three structuring principles provide insight into organizational structure. Then we will discuss some common structures, as well as a process-oriented approach to organization. The final two sections show how to produce effective instructional documents, where QPL is used to represent the structure of the organization and its processes.

There are several practical examples which build on those provided in the last chapter. Some rules of thumb for structuring documents and document sets are also provided.

4.2   THE THREE FORMS OF STRUCTURE

Whenever we are confronted with a problem or situation requiring better structure, we can make use of the fact that there are only three ways of organizing processes (or almost anything else):

- *hierarchy*—breaking the whole into its parts
- *classification*—determining what things have in common
- *sequence*—determining the order of things in time or space.

Each of these is discussed in turn.

Hierarchy

Hierarchy is the division of a whole (process) into its parts, so that the parts are mutually exclusive and, collectively, equate to the whole. This is an extremely common way of structuring, used everywhere. The list includes geographical areas, organizational structures, the collection of rooms into buildings, families and hundreds of other common structures encountered in everyday life.

Processes are often described in terms of hierarchy. For example, a common definition of a process defines it as a collection of activities, which in turn are collections of tasks. In this view, an insurance clerk may undertake the *process* of processing an insurance application. This can be broken down into the *activities* of checking the application, requesting a health check, providing a price, etc. One of these activities, such as requesting a health check, may involve various *tasks* such as determining which type of check is required (which varies by age group, gender, family history, etc.), determining availability of suitable clinics, telephoning the applicant with potential dates, etc.

Classification and inheritance

While hierarchical structuring is useful for many types of structuring, there are some areas where it is not sufficient. For example, we may want to study what different departments in a company have in common—where they use similar information, where they have cultural similarities, where their skills profiles are similar—to assist in restructuring the organization. In this case, the hierarchical structure of the company is not relevant, but shared characteristics are. This is the basis of classification, the structuring of processes or information by their common characteristics.

Classification is nothing new, of course—it extends at least as far as Aristotle, and achieved prominence in the work of the great classifiers in biology, such as Linnaeus. What classification strives to do is identify common characteristics in things: all birds have the common characteristics of feathers, reproducing through eggs, and wings (although not the ability to fly); houses have the common characteristics of being buildings which are capable of providing human habitation (adapted from *The Concise*

Oxford English Dictionary, 1990). These characteristics distinguish birds and houses from all other things (and each other). Mammals do not have feathers, even though they may reproduce through eggs. Flying insects do not have feathers. Tents are not buildings, even though they also provide human habitation.

The mechanism of using common characteristics to structure objects is called 'inheritance' (formally, we define inheritance as 'properties or characteristics which one or more processes may receive from a common process definition'). We say that an object, or group of objects, inherits all the characteristics from its parent class. For example, ducks inherit the characteristics of laying eggs and having feathers from their parent class, birds. Since both bungalows and palaces are houses, they have the common characteristics of being buildings and providing human habitation. We say that they inherit those characteristics from their parent class, houses.

Structuring processes by their common characteristics and inheritance is an extremely powerful method for understanding organizations and how they work. It provides us with a useful tool for reducing the complexity of procedures and work instructions, since aspects common to more than one process need only be described once. Chapter 6 makes use of classification as a basis for achieving compliance with a standard or other process definition.

Chapter 3 provides an example of process classification. The purchasing procedure of Example 2 describes how to do purchasing, and thus describes the essential characteristics of the class of purchasing processes:

- they arise from a need for goods or services
- they are the responsibility of the purchasing department
- their authority is derived from the set of purchasing procedures
- they result in the acquisition of goods or services and in the update of purchasing records.

All processes which have the above characteristics may be classified as purchasing processes.

Sequence

The final type of structure is also the easiest to grasp. Whenever we need to structure objects or processes by placing them in an order, we use sequence. This may include an order in time, such as the days of the week or the seasons. Or it may be an order by location, as the stops on a journey. Causal orders—if A occurs, then B occurs—are also sequences, as B always comes after A in time.

All process descriptions involve the sequence, as any two process steps need to be linked in a particular order, either in time or place. While the sequence is usually simple, with a succession of steps, it can also involve a causal sequence. For example, in Figure 3.3 a different sequence of processes follows 'Follow up with supplier/cancel', depending on the outcome. If the order is cancelled, then a new supplier will be selected. If it is not cancelled, then a new delivery date will be agreed.

4.3   HOW STRUCTURE IS REPRESENTED IN QPL

QPL notations for structure

Chapter 3 illustrated the structure of each procedure with a QPL diagram. However, there were limits to the complexity which could be described, because it lacked the more powerful structuring principles discussed in this chapter. This section extends the QPL notation to the three structuring principles just discussed.

Fortunately, little modification to the notation is required. When a process can be broken into sub-processes—the hierarchy relationship—it is represented with a thick shading. Thus, whenever a process box is so highlighted, we know that it can be broken down hierarchically into lower-level processes. Similarly, if any of the lower-level processes has thick shading, then we also know that it is composed hierarchically of lower-level processes. Figure 3.2 (the Eurolingua UK organization) contains several examples of such a process hierarchy.

Sequences are represented in QPL by the ordinary flow of information and control. Process boxes produce information items, which act as input to other process boxes. Not surprisingly, almost all QPL diagrams contain a sequence.

Classification and inheritance are represented by the use of authority: if a process A acts as the authority for another process B, we know that the latter is a member of the same class as A, and inherits its characteristics. QPL represents such inheritance with a dashed line from process A to process B, as shown here. Figure 4.1 shows similar inheritance, where a written policy is the authority. (A dashed line is used in QPL only to represent non-explicit authorities. In these examples, the authorities are non-explicit because there is no step-by-step, written description of the process which inherits characteristics. When the instructions for a process are explicit, a solid authority line is used.)

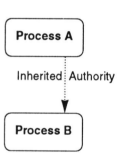

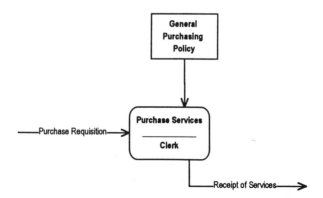

Figure 4.1   QPL representation of inheritance

Cardinality

Suppose a process can produce several items of the same class—for example, the process of issuing a request for quotation produces several copies of the request for quotation. Alternatively, a single information item may be used by several processes of the same class—say when a driver is shopping around for car insurance and provides the same information to several insurance companies over the telephone. In similar cases, it is useful to represent the number of possible occurrences of the process and the information item. This description is called the cardinality of the relationship.

In QPL, the possible cardinality values are:

- either zero or one occurrences of either a process or information item
- exactly one occurrence
- zero or more occurrences
- one or more occurrences.

In most cases of process representations, there is exactly one instance of a process and one of the information item. In this case, there is no need to represent cardinality explicitly on the QPL diagram. Where, however, there are other cardinalities, then it is shown on the diagram. The QPL notation for cardinality, and a more complete description of this concept, are given in Appendix 3.

Processes and classes

Many examples in this book contain process descriptions, such as purchasing procedures and manufacturing instructions. It is worth noting that there is a difference between a process description and a process itself. The former are abstract descriptions, and apply only to classes of things. When the process is activated, it operates on real and specific members of that class.

This is another powerful reason for introducing the concept of classification. It provides a means to reconcile structural differences between processes and the information they input and produce. Even if an organization's functions break down into a clean hierarchy of processes, they usually need to deal with information which is structured differently. For example, purchasing procedures break down this process into a hierarchy of functions, such as issuing the call for tender, evaluating tenders and completing the purchase order. But these operate on information which is not organized in the same hierarchy: calls for tenders, tenders, purchase orders. If we attempt to produce a common hierarchical structure, an inevitable conflict will result. By structuring the process in terms of inheritance and its characteristics, both viewpoints can remain compatible.

4.4   AN EXAMPLE

The three principles of structuring are illustrated by extending the high-level chart in Figure 3.3 (see Figure 4.2). Suppose we need to ensure that our purchasing procedures are compatible with the relevant parts of ISO 9001. This is indicated explicitly by

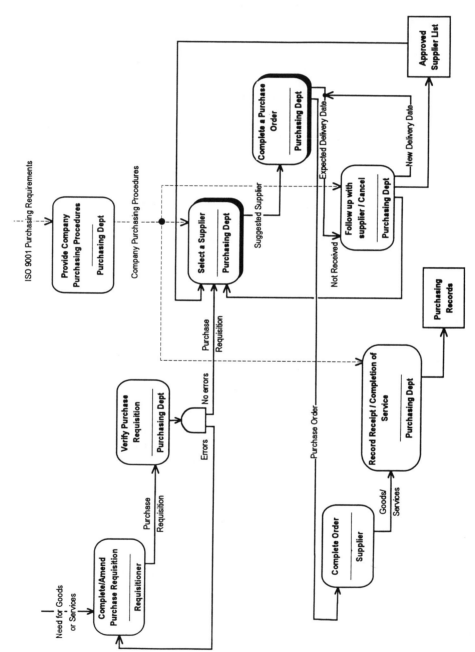

Figure 4.2 Modified purchasing procedure, showing the three structuring principles

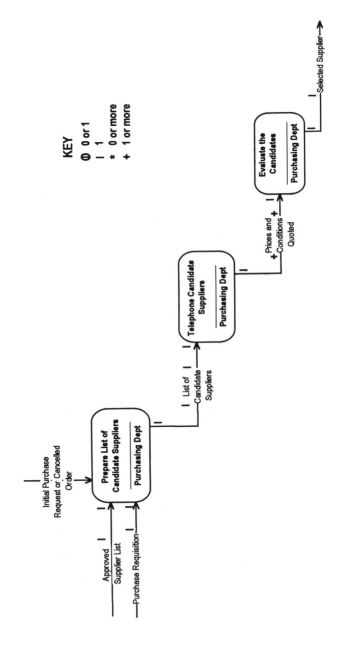

KEY
Ø 0 or 1
I   1
*   0 or more
+   1 or more

Figure 4.2 (continued)
Detail of 'Select a supplier'

showing first that the company purchasing procedures inherit all relevant characteristics of ISO 9001. Then we show that the relevant high-level processes inherit the characteristics of the company procedures. The dashed inheritance lines on the revised chart illustrate this use of classification for structuring. Two of the process boxes are shaded, indicating that they can be broken down into a hierarchy of processes, for more detailed descriptions. The sequence of process flow is apparent on the figure, starting with the completion of a purchase requisition, to the receipt of the goods or completion of service.

4.5   STRUCTURE IN ORGANIZATIONS

Organizations are structured in many different ways. Some of these, particularly the hierarchical and functional, are old styles which have been around for hundreds of years. Others, such as matrix and workgroup, are relatively new forms which owe much of their popularity to the spread of Japanese working practices and total quality approaches.

Underlying these various structures are the processes and information which represent the actual activities of the organization. Example 1 in the previous chapter shows how to generate a richer form of representation than the usual organization chart. QPL provides a representation which shows not only the hierarchical components (normally the process owners or roles in the organization, along with the authorities) but also the processes which represent the activities of the organization, and the information which the processes produce and store.

It is possible to do a QPL representation of any structure, even when its processes and information are not obvious at first. One can start by taking any information available and converting it into QPL primitives: process, information items, authorities, process owners/responsibilities and conditions. For example, we can convert an organization chart, like that in Figure 3.5 by calling each function a *process owner*, in QPL terminology. The next questions to ask are:

- Can an owner/function be broken down into others?
- What processes does each owner/function carry out?
- What information does each owner/function use and what does it produce?
- What authorities—standards, procedures, terms of reference, etc.—does the owner/function use to carry out its operations?

Answering these questions will provide us with the other information needed to complete all elements of the QPL diagram for this organization. Similarly, we can start with any other way of representing an organization and, by asking similar questions repeatedly, develop the QPL representation of its processes and information. Chapter 3 contains further details on annotating documents to create such a QPL representation.

We sometimes observe some surprising results after converting to a QPL representation of an organization; for example, that the underlying processes bear little relationship to the functional organization. So a strictly hierarchical functional organization may have processes and information which are structured more like a workgroup structure. An apparent matrix organization may have processes which are more like those in a task-oriented structure.

Such discoveries can provide valuable insights when dealing with organizations. When viewed from a QPL perspective, apparent differences in organizational structures often reduce to differences of style and form, rather than substance and content. In Chapter 6, which deals with issues of compliance and regulation, this ability to see the true process structure, stripped of the varnish of historical and cosmetic differences, will prove invaluable.

If an organization maps on to QPL more or less directly, the following QPL structures will tend to be used:

Organizational structure	QPL structure
Hierarchical	Straightforward hierarchical decomposition of processes
Matrix	Two large process groups, representing production processes and personnel processes, with limited and clear lines of communication between them (representing information about staffing requirements, forward load, staff capabilities, etc.). Within each of the two groups, there are hierarchical and sequential processes, representing project/task management for the production side and staff management for the personnel side.
Workgroup	A structure with well-defined authorities and training processes, and where roles/responsibilities are assigned to a process, rather than fixed. This represents the key characteristics of a workgroup organization: flexible jobs within the workgroup and attention to process flow between different groups. (For a discussion of Japanese workgroup concepts, see Pascale and Athos, 1986: 125–9.)
Task oriented	This is already a process-oriented approach, and we would expect a nearly direct mapping onto the QPL diagram.
Objectives (goal) oriented	As this management approach is oriented around objectives, the latter are the key to the representation in QPL. Objectives are a form of requirements, which is a set of information items. The processes to be modelled in QPL must result in these information items as their final outputs. They can also provide feedback to the objectives-setting process.
Functional	There is no general QPL representation of such an organizational structure. However, if the functions are drawn cleanly and there is minimal overlap between them, then each function will correspond to a major high-level process, with possibly some overlap between processes. Either the functional department, or its head/leader, may take responsibility for the process, and the authority derives from the departmental manual or procedures.
	The use of inherited authority is usually a good surrogate in QPL for processes which transcend several functional areas.

These QPL representations are idealized and represent organizational structures which have been well tuned to its needs and operations. In such a situation, turning the QPL into a set of procedures and work instructions will be very straightforward indeed. However, in practice, things are rarely this simple, and compromises need to be made. The QPL may need to be adjusted to suit the organization better, or it may be advisable to duplicate information when the documents are written. The final section of this chapter provides some practical guidance on these and other topics.

It is essential that organizations consider their processes and objectives when determining the best form of structure. A process-oriented structure results in fewer internal conflicts than other orientations, such as functional. This is almost self-evident when one thinks of processes—if a department or workgroup is responsible for the whole of a process, then there is much less chance of a conflict over rival claims to ownership. For example, if the purchasing process is shared by three different functions—the purchasing, accounts and goods inwards departments—there is a potential for conflict and competing ownership claims whenever the process crosses from one functional boundary to the next. If there is a problem in, say, the completion of a form by one department but used by another, then needless acrimony and delays can easily result. A structure which is more process-based can resolve this problem. In this example, we can train people within a workgroup to handle all three functions. As computers are used increasingly to streamline processes and simplify tasks, this concept of multiple roles becomes increasingly feasible and attractive. (For a stimulating discussion of these and other alternative forms of work organization, see Handy, 1989.)

In general, a structure oriented around processes has the following advantages:

- clearer lines of authority and ownership
- use of more coherent record-keeping, coordinated with real processes
- fewer lines of communication required, with less risk of misunderstood information
- less formality required to achieve the same level of quality
- less risk of a broken process, resulting in unnecessary delays or lost paperwork.

Even when dealing with a less-than-ideal organization, however, QPL is still extremely useful. The remainder of this chapter provides practical guidance for structuring instructional documents in any type of organization.

4.6 PROVIDING STRUCTURE IN INSTRUCTIONAL DOCUMENTS

Having introduced structuring methods and reviewed the ways in which organizations can be structured, you are now ready to go a step further than the previous chapter: how to structure a set of instructional documents for the whole organization. You will probably feel that this is less of a problem now than would have been expected, since a host of resources are now available for structuring the documents. Indeed, all that is needed now is to apply these resources to the problem in hand.

First, let's have a short recap on the two structuring principles of this chapter.

(1)   There are only three methods of organization:

    (a)   hierarchies—breaking the whole into its parts
    (b)   classification—determining what things have in common
    (c)   sequence or causality—determining the order of things, in time and space.

    Each method of organization can be represented in QPL.

(2)   Classes and inheritance provide the means to describe processes and information in terms of their common characteristics. If several processes have common characteristics, we need only describe them once, as a general class. We can then speak of the individual processes as inheriting characteristics from the general process.

There are three levels of instructional documents:

●   Standards and directives, which provide a regulatory framework or codes of practice. Alternatively, they may also provide policy and describe the structure of the organization and its communication channels. They specify what a product or service should 'look like' and the 'why' of its operations.

●   Procedures, which provide the processes, rules and information needed to implement the standards and directives, and which apply to the whole organization. They specify the 'who', 'what', 'when' and 'where' of its operations.

●   Work instructions, which provide the details needed to carry out procedures accurately (the 'how'). They may also provide additional detail for the specific function, department or individual process.

With minor variations, the three levels can be used for the instructions of all organizations. They are used to illustrate the remainder of this chapter.

Each level of document is supported by the above structuring principles:

●   Standards and directives are supported by hierarchy, since they are limited only to the general description of policy, structure and communication needed to describe the whole. They do not need to describe details of how they are to be implemented, which can be provided by the lower levels of the hierarchy.

●   Procedures are supported by inheritance, since they inherit the key attributes of standards and directives, yet provide a framework which work instructions can inherit.

●   Work instructions are supported by inheritance and sequence. They inherit the general features of processes common to the whole organization. Description of process details is facilitated by the sequence, which permits specific decisions, information flows and relationships to be notated precisely and concisely.

The structuring principles, combined with the three levels of instructional documents, provide a series of steps for producing these documents:

(1)   Start with known facts about the organization's structure, then expand into process and information descriptions using QPL.

(2)   If the resulting process/QPL description clashes with the organization's structure, modify the QPL diagrams to provide a compatible structure.

(3) Check that the relationships between processes make full use of the structuring principles of hierarchy, classification and sequence. Abstract the aspects of processes which are general, and define them as 'generic' processes. Define the specific processes which will inherit characteristics from the generic processes. Iterate back to step (2), if necessary.

(4) Determine where the information on the QPL diagrams fits into the three types of document: standard/directive, general procedure or work instruction.

(5) Write the three levels of documents, verifying them regularly against the QPL diagrams.

(6) After the documents are completed, validate them with the actual users to determine if they match expectations and are both readable and usable.

Table 4.1 shows the application of these steps for a typical company.

4.7 RULES OF THUMB FOR STRUCTURING DOCUMENTS

This chapter has provided a challenge, by introducing a large number of new concepts to assist in structuring instructional documentation. However, as a practical book, the emphasis is on useful information and guidelines, in the form of real documents. You need not know the 'theory' behind them, but you should be very aware of their readability and usefulness. The following guidelines provide some practical tips for structuring documents. (For some creative suggestions for structuring, see Booch, 1991.)

Table 4.1 Application of the structuring principles for a typical company

Step	Parts/roles involved	Relevant documents
1	Chief executive and major departments	Organization chart Initial QPL representation
2	Chief executive and major departments	QPL representation
3	All	Detailed QPL representation
4	All	Full set of document outlines or contents lists
5	Document authors	Full set of standards/directives, procedures and work instructions
6	Document authors and document users in all departments	Full set of standards/directives, procedures and work instructions

Structuring by use

As instructional documents exist only to be used, that is the first principle in structuring them. This obviously applies to the processes themselves, but it also applies to the other basics of QPL, such as information, authorities and roles. The three structuring principles provide the key—as noted in the previous section. Hierarchical elements can be structured according to the hierarchical structure of the organization. Thus, for a three-level hierarchy of directives, procedures and work instructions, we structure authorities into the same hierarchy (Figure 4.3). The framework of laws, regulations and industry-wide standards provide the authorities for the highest level, the organization's own directives and other policy documents are the authority for the procedures which implement them, and those procedures are among the authorities for the third hierarchical level of work instructions. Chapter 6 expands this use of inherited authority to all aspects of compliance.

Redundancy

At one extreme, there are procedures which never repeat information and are hard to read; at the other extreme, some procedures seem to repeat everything several times, and are boring (and often hard to read as well!). In writing instructional documents, we need to strike a balance. Ideally, each idea should be stated only once, yet the reader should not need constantly to cross-reference documents or tie together concepts which are in different parts of the documents.

Using the structuring principles of this chapter, it is possible to produce QPL diagrams with no redundancy. In particular, when processes and information items inherit characteristics, those characteristics need be documented only once. By definition, no redundancy results.

In practice, real documents need to be readable as well, and this involves deliberate redundancy. For example, they should repeat inherited instructions if the reader might otherwise ignore them and miss important detail. They should also repeat such instructions if the reader needs to understand the full context of inherited instructions, but there is a possibility of misinterpreting the inheritance.

With experience, document authors learn to interpret the QPL as they write, inserting redundancy where required. However, in the early stages of using the notation, it is advisable to expand the diagrams when planning the actual writing of the document—at step 1 (see Chapter 3), where the QPL diagrams are restructured into a form suitable for the audience. It is sensible to read the diagrams as they will appear to the audience (visualizing the text and figures, of course). Where there are areas where it will be difficult to read the document, or where misunderstandings could occur, the QPL can be amended or notated. For example, where inherited authorities could cause confusion, a note on the diagram will remind the author to avoid this by restating the inherited authority. Another deliberate redundancy is to provide details of all levels of a hierarchical process, rather than to describe each level separately.

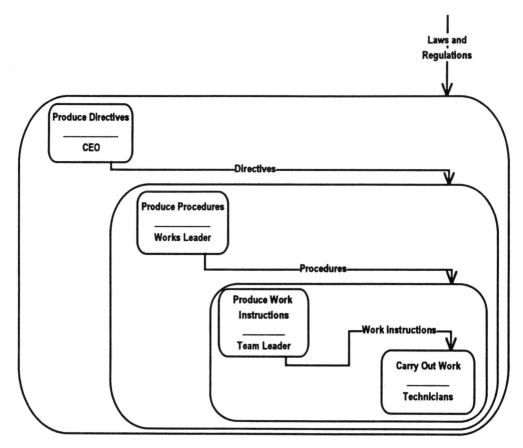

Figure 4.3 Example of a process hierarchy

Multiple inheritance

While classification is a powerful tool for providing common or generic instructions, we sometimes encounter the confusing situation where a process inherits characteristics from more than one process, which may be incompatible. This is called multiple inheritance.

Multiple inheritance occurs when a process inherits characteristics from more than one 'parent' process. Typically, it is used to minimize redundancy, in documents, with a set of generic procedures, coupled with a specification of which apply (i.e. are authorities for) to a specific work instruction. For example, when writing the quality plan for a one-off job, the author needs to refer only to the generic procedures which apply to this job, rather than the laborious and error-prone task of writing a complete set of work instructions from scratch.

While this method of writing procedures is extremely efficient and can minimize the risk of violating procedures, a number of precautions need to be taken:

● We must check carefully that the generic procedures are totally *consistent* and can never produce internal contradictions when inherited by a specific work instruction.

● The generic procedures must be *complete*—we must check that they cover the full range of possible tasks which the work instructions will cover.

● Staff specifying which procedures to use on a job need to be *well trained* about all the generic procedures, their range of applicability and how to apply them to specific situations. As noted earlier, the use of inheritance and other QPL constructs produces little or no redundancy in the resulting documents, but at the risk of poor comprehension by users. Training minimizes this risk.

We will return to the subject of multiple inheritance in later chapters. Chapter 5 provides techniques for checking consistency and completeness. Chapter 6 illustrates how to use multiple inheritance when complying with several regulations or directives.

Compromises

As noted above, instructional documents are practical, and in writing them the author needs to compromise between the optimal structure which QPL can produce and the actual needs of the document users. Some of the areas where compromises are required are outlined below.

User needs and training

The first and most important area of compromise involves the users of the documents we are writing. What will they use them for? How well trained are they likely to be? Do they carry out only routine tasks, or do they require specific guidance for a wide range of jobs? The structure and style of the document set should be heavily influenced by these and other considerations concerning the user.

Organizational structure

As noted in Chapter 3, the structure of the organization should strongly influence the shape of the documents. While the emphasis of this book is strongly on a process-oriented view of business organization and operations, the reality is that they often are organized differently. The documents produced should reflect the actual organization, and the underlying QPL can be modified to this end. Note, however, that it is possible to produce a process-oriented description even for a functional organization: by producing a set of generic process descriptions to define all relevant processes, and then by providing the specific guidance interpreting these processes, for each of the functions or departments.

History and culture

If we are writing instructional documents for an existing organization, its history and culture will have a major influence on the acceptance of those documents. They must be respected. For example, the organization may have a strong tradition of personal and informal communication, not well-suited for formal quality systems, but extremely efficient for its own needs. The instructional documents can reflect this culture by documenting the flows of information in the form of channels (i.e. non-persistent information). It will, of course, be necessary to determine which of this large amount of information needs to be recorded, and to initiate appropriate procedures for suitable information stores and archives. But this must be kept to a minimum to avoid conflict with the organizational culture.

At the opposite end of the organizational spectrum, we may encounter a culture which requires everything to be specified and documented. A QPL analysis may demonstrate that this is quite unnecessary to satisfy quality requirements or to comply with external regulations. If so, the organization may be persuaded to alter its practices over time. But at the beginning, it is better to document and reflect its actual working practices. Later, they can be assisted to evolve to a less prescriptive and detailed form.

4.8   SUMMARY OF STRUCTURING PRINCIPLES

In QPL there are three ways of providing structure to procedures and instructions:

- *hierarchy*—breaking the whole into its parts
- *classification*—determining what things have in common
- *sequence*—determining the order of things in time or space.

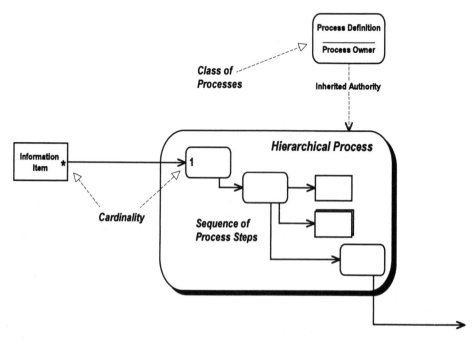

Figure 4.4   QPL structuring notation

Classes and inheritance are used to describe process and information in terms of their common characteristics. Individual processes inherit characteristics from more general, or parent, classes of processes; this provides a means of representing processes very compactly.

Cardinality provides a means for describing the relationships between processes and information items, in terms of the number of possible occurrences of each.

Figure 4.4 is a summary of the QPL structuring notation.

5

Process analysis

OVERVIEW

The QPL approach to process design is based on a combination of creating process descriptions and analysing them for faults and weaknesses. Process analysis consists of the application of several checks to a process description to determine where it is incomplete, inconsistent or not achieving its objectives. This chapter covers static analysis, which deals with the aspects of processes directly represented on a QPL diagram. Dynamic analysis covers the changes to processes and is covered in Chapter 7.

There are three kinds of check in static process analysis: logical, failure mode and technical. Logical checks analyse the structure of the process and the flow of information. They reveal faults in the process description and also ensure that it can be expressed clearly in a written procedure or guidance document. Logical checks are broken down further into four types of checks. Incompleteness checks reveal gaps in the process description and missing processes or information links. Inconsistency checks reveal ambiguous use of information or unclear instructions. Hierarchical incompatibility checks reveal inconsistencies between a process description and those of its sub-processes. Inheritance incompatibility checks reveal differences between what processes are supposed to do and what they actually do.

Failure mode checks emphasize the risk of faults occurring in a process and concentrate on what might go wrong. Technical checks require additional experience by the reviewer and are used to determine the correctness or adequacy of a process. Usually they are based on expert judgement.

This chapter is arranged in the form of reference material, and tables are provided to facilitate error checks. The chapter concludes with a complete case study which checks and corrects a procedure.

5.1 WHAT IS PROCESS ANALYSIS?

> *Dumby:* Experience is the name every one gives to their mistakes.
> *Cecil Graham:* One shouldn't commit any.
> *Dumby:* Life would be very dull without them.
>
> *Oscar Wilde, Lady Windermere's Fan*

No one is perfect and we all make mistakes. On a simple level, that is why we need to analyse processes—to ensure that they are accurate and that they produce useful results. Using QPL, analysis is part of a highly creative process. In designing processes, analysis is used not only to catch errors, but also to indicate activities which are ineffective at achieving their objectives. It assists us in designing processes which optimize production, while ensuring that the results are desired and consistent.

Following the approach of Chapter 3, QPL enables us to document existing processes. The same approach can be used to develop and document new processes. Process analysis is then used to review the process descriptions and determine errors or weaknesses. These results are used, in turn, to revise and improve the process. This iterative approach—development and description, analysis, further development and description, etc.—is the basic approach to process design using QPL.

There are two kinds of analysis—static and dynamic. Static analysis deals with the unchanging aspects of process, things which are directly represented in a QPL diagram. They include the relationships between process steps, information items, controls, authorities and process owners. Dynamic analysis deals with aspects of change, such as the rate of processing information or materials, and adaptability of processes under changing conditions. This chapter deals with static analysis, while Chapter 7 discusses dynamic analysis along with the wider issues of change management.

The techniques of process analysis can also be used for compliance auditing, where the process is checked against an external set of criteria or other authority. Common examples are compliance checks against ISO 9000, the internationally recognized set of quality standards, and against the Food and Drug Administration's (FDA) Code of Good Manufacturing Practice (FDA, 1989). Compliance reviews, audits and checks are covered in Chapter 6, which treats all aspects of compliance.

Three kinds of checks are used in static analysis:

- *Logical*, where the structure of the process and the flow of information are checked for internal consistency, with no omissions or loose ends. This also ensures that the process description is consistent and well formed with respect to QPL conventions and can be expressed clearly in a written procedure or guidance document.
- *Failure mode*, where the process may pass the above checks, but could still be applied incorrectly, resulting in incorrect results or other problems. The name failure mode is used, as it corresponds with failure mode and effects analysis (FMEA), which is a method commonly used to analyse processes and determine situations where they could break down or give incorrect or inconsistent results.
- *Technical*, where the above checks are not sufficient to detect errors in the process description. Additional information, not available internally or through rules of well-formed QPL, is used to determine the correctness or adequacy of a process. A common example is when an expert or authority in a discipline provides a judgement based on expertise or experience.

Unlike most of the other chapters, this one is organized as a reference to facilitate QPL analysis. The principles have already been laid down in Chapters 2, 3 and 4, which explained the form of the QPL notation and how it is used to structure descriptions of complex processes. They also provided the basis for well-formed process descriptions—where a process is described in a way which leaves no gaps or inconsistencies. This chapter formalizes the earlier chapters by providing the rules for well-formed QPL. The rules correspond to simple common sense and apply to all process descriptions, even when a QPL diagram has not been produced. The problems which arise from violating the rules are also easy to visualize, and the text which explains the rules provide simple examples of violations in ordinary use.

At the end of the chapter, a complete case study is provided, based on a straightforward and very common purchasing process. The text of the procedure is provided, along with its QPL equivalent. The analysis checks provide the basis for analysis of this procedure and determine how to revise it. This revision will prevent the potentially damaging consequences resulting from rule violations, and improve the effectiveness of the purchasing process.

This is a reference chapter and rather dense with detail, and it is not designed for reading from beginning to end. It would be difficult to retain the information without some practical work to anchor the principles in reality. Therefore, it is advisable to skim through it first, just to obtain an overview. This can be done by reading Tables 5.1–5.5, along with a few explanations of the rules to clarify their application. Then read the case study at the end, as it provides a working illustration of how the rules are applied. As required, look at the rules themselves to see how they are applied to the procedure.

Later, you can return to this chapter, as required, to carry out practical analysis of procedures, directives, codes of practice and working instructions—any document which gives directions for carrying out actions.

5.2 LOGICAL ANALYSIS

Classes of errors

Whenever there is a situation where a process description does not fit the natural logic which accompanies QPL, this is called a logical error. There are 22 logical errors in total, which can be divided into four groups:

- *Incompleteness*, where there are gaps in the process description, such as a missing process or information item (ten types of error)
- *Inconsistency*, where the usage of information items varies in different parts of the process, resulting in ambiguous use of the information, or unclear instructions (eight types of error)
- *Hierarchical incompatibility*, where a process is not compatible with the sub-processes which constitute it (two types of error)
- *Inheritance incompatibility*, where there is a conflict between a process used as an authority and a process which inherits it (two types of error).

The rest of this section lists the errors possible within each group.

Error tables

Table 5.1 shows the ten types of incompleteness error, along with a short description of each. This is followed by similar tables for the three other types of logical error—

Table 5.1 The ten types of incompleteness error

Type of error	Description
Information errors	
(a) Unused information	A process generates an information item which is never used by a process step or sent to a destination. (A destination is a consumer of information external to the process.)
(b) Uncreated information	An information item is used by a process step but is never generated or provided by a source. (A source is a provider of information external to the process.)
(c) Unused source	A source exists on the diagram but does not produce any information items.
(d) Unused destination	A destination exists on the diagram but does not receive any information items.
Process errors	
(e) Unconnected process	A process is not connected to any sources, destinations or other processes.
(f) Hostile process	A process has no inputs or control.
(g) Infertile process	A process produces no outputs.
(h) Broken path	There is no possible path of information between a related source and a destination.
(i) Missing authority	No authority is shown for a process.
(j) Missing ownership	No process owner (role) is shown for a process.

inconsistency (Table 5.2), hierarchical incompatibility (Table 5.3) and inheritance incompatibility (Table 5.4).

Incompleteness errors

As this category of error is quite large, it has been divided into two types, depending on whether the error relates mainly to information or to processes. Figure 5.1 provides a QPL 'picture' illustrating each type of incompleteness error. Two new terms are introduced in the descriptions, to cover the origins and destinations of information outside of a process. A source is a provider of information external to the process. A destination is a consumer of information external to the process. An example of a source is a person requesting an insurance policy, where the person supplies a completed form, but the details of filling in the form are not relevant to the process. A typical example of a

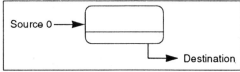

Table 5.2 The eight types of inconsistency error

	Type of error	Description
(a)	Misprocessed information	An information item is processed inconsistently with its type (channel, information store or archive).
(b)	Misused information	An information item is used inconsistently with its class.
(c)	Inconsistent information	A process uses an information item in a way which is incompatible with its content.
(d)	Absent input	A process requires information which none of its inputs can provide.
(e)	Absent output	A process provides information which none of its outputs can take.
(f)	Incompatible information	An information item is split and, after one or more of the threads is transformed by a subsequent process step, rejoined. This will make them incompatible.
(g)	Authority mismatch	A process is inconsistent with, or has a different scope from, its authority.
(h)	Interface error	The input or output for a process does not link with the equivalent input or output for an adjoining process.

Table 5.3 Types of hierarchical incompatibility error

	Type of error	Description
(a)	Hierarchical mismatch	There is a mismatch between the input or output of a process and one of its sub-processes.
(b)	Hierarchical incompleteness	When a process is broken down into its component sub-processes, the parts do not match the full process.

Table 5.4 Types of inheritance incompatibility error

	Error of type	Description
(a)	Inheritance mismatch	A child process is incompatible with the parent process, when it handles information items which are members of a class handled by the parent.
(b)	Cardinality mismatch	The cardinality of a child process is incompatible with that of a parent process.

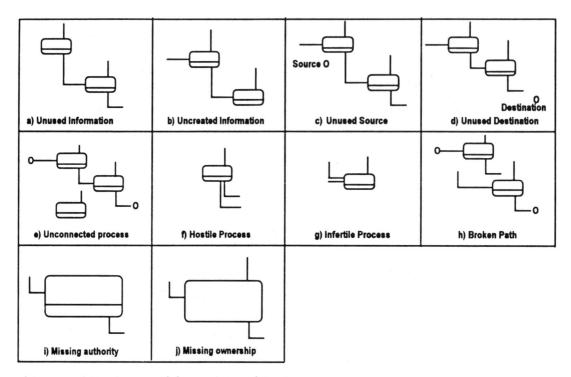

Figure 5.1   QPL 'pictures' of the ten incompleteness errors

destination is the final customer, who receives information, goods or a service; again, the details of what the customer does with them is not relevant to the process. In QPL diagrams, a source or destination is represented by a small circle or just by writing its name.

Information errors

(a) Unused information

Description: A process generates an information item which is never used by a process step or sent to a destination.

This error is quite common; in fact, it is the most common error in most office environments. Typically, they generate and file information, 'just in case'. It is always much easier to create information than to destroy it when it is not required.

Examples:

● Records of correspondence are kept in archives, but there is no standard process for retrieving information systematically.
● All incoming correspondence is automatically copied and filed. The copy is unnecessary, since the original copy is always filed after it is initially processed.

Likely causes: Such an error results from two main causes: inertia and excess caution. In the first case, as office procedures evolve they tend to retain obsolete information, which may have been useful in the past but is no longer required or likely to be accessed. In the second instance, information is retained even though it is known that it is highly unlikely ever to be needed.

Sometimes this error results simply from bad design of business processes: the designer assumes that information will be used later in the process, but does not check that it actually will happen. This results in large quantities of unwanted records and other documents.

Damage which can result: At the very least, such errors create excessive paperwork; the excess makes it more difficult to locate the documents which will be required later. More dangerously, such an error may be a symptom of a misunderstanding between two parts of the organization. The owner (role) of one process may assume incorrectly that a second process will make use of the output from the first. Alternatively, the two owners may be referring to the same information by different names (see '(b) Uncreated information' below).

This error is most damaging when information is added continually to an archive but never removed or destroyed. The archive continues to grow unnecessarily, and it may get harder and harder to locate required information.

Correcting the error: Determine if there is a genuine use for the information item; if so, use it as input to other processes or to the destination. If the information is not required, modify the process to eliminate it entirely. In some cases, it will be necessary to arrange a meeting to determine the actual use of or common name for such information.

(b) Uncreated information

Description: An information item is used by a process step but is never generated or provided by a source.

In this error, we make the assumption that another process produces the information item, but we do not actually identify it. This may result from a genuine error, or from a simple oversight in forgetting to name the process which produces the information.

Examples:

- A designer in a large manufacturing organization requires a design brief before producing the required drawings and specifications for a new product. However, the organization does not have a standard process for creating such a brief, nor even a standard format for it. As a result, the designer often will not receive such a brief and has to create one by asking for the required information. This is wasteful of time and can also produce inaccurate results, since the designer may not be aware of all customer requirements.
- This error is also common for material inputs to processes. If an organization depends on large stocks of materials rather than controlling the processes of

producing or ordering such stocks (say in a just-in-time system), then the production process will halt whenever stocks are exhausted.

Likely causes: Most often, this error results from incorrectly scoping the process: the information item is created outside the process. This can be corrected by widening the scope or by specifying an external source for the information item.

The error sometimes results from poor communication among process owners. As with unused information, a process owner assumes that another process generates information, but further investigation finds that this process does not exist.

Damage which can result: As with unused information, uncreated information errors may be a symptom of a misunderstanding between two parts of the organization. The owner of one process may assume incorrectly that a second process will produce the required input. Alternatively, the two owners may be referring to the same information by different names.

If undetected, this error will result in one of two undesirable consequences:

- processes will be suspended because required information is never produced, or
- the organization will initiate emergency (ad hoc) processes to create the information, with no time to organize them properly or ensure that the information is correct.

If this happens, at the very least the results will be inefficient, and at worst the whole process can be seriously disrupted, with possible faults in the results of the process.

Correcting the error: Determine if the process genuinely needs the information item; if so, determine where it originates and describe the process which creates it. If the information is not required, delete the information item from the process. If the problem results from poor communication between process owners, arrange a meeting to determine how the information item is created and transmitted.

(c) Unused source

Description: A source—which is always external to a process—is provided in a process description, but it does not produce any information items.

Since the only reason for including a source is to identify providers of information items which are external to the process description, this is an obvious oversight.

Example: During interviews in developing the process model, we are told that some information is provided by a source external to the organization. Therefore, the source is included in the process description. However, when we contact that source, we are told that no relevant information is provided.

Likely causes: Incomplete interviews, or misunderstanding of roles by people involved in a process. Poor scoping of the process, which assumes that information is created outside its scope, when it should be provided by an internal process.

Damage which can result: Information which is required to complete the process description is omitted, resulting in an incomplete description. As with the uncreated information error, processes may need to be suspended, or the organization may need to initiate emergency and ad hoc processes to obtain the information, with no time to check the quality of the information.

Correcting the error: See '(b) Uncreated information'.

(d) Unused destination

Description: A destination—which is always external to a process—is provided in a process description, but it does not receive any information items.

Since the only reason for including a destination is to identify users of information items which are external to the process description, this is an obvious oversight.

Example: During interviews in developing the process model, we are told that some information is used by a destination external to the organization. However, when we contact that destination, we are told that no relevant information is actually required or used.

Likely causes: Incomplete interviews, or misunderstanding of roles by people involved in a process. Poor scoping of the process, which assumes that information is used outside its scope, when it should be provided to an internal process.

Damage which can result: Information which is required to complete the process description is omitted, resulting in an incomplete description. As with the unused information error, superfluous or redundant information may be provided. We may also fail to provide genuinely needed information to an organization external to the process, i.e. a genuine destination for an information item.

Correcting the error: See '(a) Unused information'.

Process errors

(e) Unconnected process

Description: A process is not connected to any sources, destinations or other processes.

This error is unusual, as it implies that a process step exists in total isolation from other process steps. It also occurs under certain types of extreme information errors: if the process' inputs are all uncreated information and its outputs are all unused information.

While it is unlikely that such a process is designed deliberately, it may occur when 'busywork' is considered necessary, i.e. when work is created for its own sake and not to provide useful products. It is also a strong symptom that internal communications are very poor in the organization.

Examples:

● During a period of slack work, an employee is given a job which is not really of any use, but his supervisor feels that he would be bored otherwise. To avoid interference with the 'real' work of the factory, however, this work is kept totally separate from its operations. As a result, the employee feels a sense of isolation, with accompanied stress levels. This negates the whole point of the assignment, which was to improve the morale of the employee.

● In a research laboratory, staff work in small, independent units, with no defined information paths. They are encouraged to publish results when they are ready, but there are no direct channels of communication between staff. As a result, much valuable information is not exchanged, and new opportunities are lost.

● In the sales department of a company, salespeople work individually, with no defined information paths. They are required only to report on prospects in their monthly reports, and these reports are seen only by the sales manager, who is only interested in the total volume of sales in the month, and likely sales in the future. As a result, valuable information is not shared between the sales staff, and sales prospects are lost.

Likely causes: In most cases, an unconnected process results from a mistake during our analysis: we identify a likely process and then either miss its connections or identify them incorrectly, so that they cannot be connected to other processes.

As noted above, unconnected processes can also be created deliberately, to make work. They may also exist if the value of shared information is not widely appreciated in the organization, and processes are seen in isolation from the information they deal with.

Damage which can result: If the process was designed deliberately to be unconnected, employees will soon discover that their work is not valued. Disenchantment and boredom may result. Valuable opportunities, visible when information is shared, may be missed.

If the unconnected process results from an error when the process is analysed, the damage is the same as with unused or uncreated information.

Correcting the error: If the error is deliberate, the QPL analyst should discuss this with the source of information and advise of the possible negative consequences. If it is decided to retain the process step after this, then three actions are possible:

● The process step can be connected to other process steps.
● It can be treated as an external process—i.e. isolated from other, fully connected process steps.
● It can be removed from the analysis altogether by treating it as outside the scope of the process.

If the error is not deliberate, the same actions as with unused or uncreated information should be taken.

(f) Hostile process

Description: A process has no inputs or control. This process gets its name because of its 'unwillingness' to receive any inputs or to 'permit' any controls.

In principle, such a process can never be run, because the inputs which it needs to be activated are never supplied to it.

A routine process—one which is activated at regular intervals, or at a particular time each day—may appear incorrectly to be a hostile process. Because it does have a control, which activates the process at the prescribed time, there is no error.

Example: The company handbook states that a department is responsible for dealing with customer enquiries, but it does not provide any information about how the process is initiated, i.e. how enquiries are directed to the department.

Likely causes: This error usually arises from a simple oversight. Either the inputs and control for a process are left vague, or it is assumed that the process owner is aware of them and doesn't need them to be specified.

Damage which can result: As with many other errors, the usual damage from this error arises from misunderstandings. At some point, the process owner makes different assumptions about the inputs than others, resulting in incorrect synchronization with other processes. This may have knock-on effects, throwing the whole system out of balance.

Correcting the error: Additional process specification is required, to clarify the exact inputs to the process and the conditions under which it is activated. It is also necessary to determine which sources or other processes produce the inputs and controls, so that the correct linkages are established.

(g) Infertile process

Description: A process produces no outputs. This process gets its name because of its 'inability' to produce anything useful.

Example: The emergency room (casualty department) at the local hospital is provided with a list of cases and situations which it will handle, along with a set of procedures for determining that the prospective patient is eligible for treatment. However, no procedures have been produced for admission and treatment. As a result, eligible patients may wait far longer than is necessary, and sometimes serious mistakes in treatment occur.

In this situation, the inputs and conditions for the process are quite clear. But the essential outputs from the process—informing medical staff that urgent treatment is needed, and providing essential details about the patient's condition—are ignored. It is not surprising that patients are sometimes forgotten or incorrectly treated!

Likely causes: Often, infertile processes are the result of obsolete practices, where the process once produced useful outputs, but is no longer required. In other cases, the error results from oversights, ambiguities or unwarranted assumptions.

Damage which can result: As with hostile processes, the usual damage from this error arises from misunderstandings. At some point, the process owner makes different assumptions about outputs than others, resulting in incorrect synchronization with other processes. This may have knock-on effects, throwing the whole system out of balance.

Correcting the error: Additional process specification is required, to clarify the exact outputs from the process. It is also necessary to determine which destinations or other processes make use of the outputs, so that the correct linkages are established.

(h) Broken path

Description: There is no possible path of information between a related source and a destination. This error is manifest when it is certain that there is a causal connection between a source and a destination, yet there is no continuous path of information and processes linking them.

Examples: This error is common in mature organizations where everyone knows that certain inputs result in desired results at the end, yet no one can describe how this comes about.

In other cases, two processes may possess the property of 'action at a distance', where there is no direct link between them, yet one influences another. A common example of this is where two process owners have reached an understanding about common situations and resolve them without formal communication. This could be in the form of a casual telephone call, a word over lunch or simply a set of unwritten rules which both parties obey.

Likely causes: As we see from the above examples, the broken path error usually exists by a failure to identify the actual communication links between processes.

Occasionally, however, the error is genuine and can mean that it is only by convention that people assume that a source and a destination are connected. In reality, there is no connection between them and it is through connections with other sources and destinations that they *appear* to be linked.

Damage which can result: As seen from the examples above, we may make assumptions about the causal relationships between sources and destinations which come about by chance rather than design. These relationships may be valid during normal conditions, but under unusual or extreme conditions, the lack of connections will be obvious and may cause a system breakdown.

Correcting the error: Examine the information flows from the source and to the destination and determine if any links between them have been overlooked. If they remain unconnected after this examination, check that there is a genuine connection between source and destination. If there is, then redesign the process to incorporate the necessary link.

(i) Missing authority

Description: No authority is shown for a process.

Examples:

- A non-trivial process exists and is carried out routinely, but it has never been described in a document.
- Various staff carry out an operation. Some of them have been properly trained to do so, but others have not.

Likely causes: Insufficient attention to documentation of a process or to qualifying the staff who will be responsible for the process.

Damage which can result: Without an authority acting as a basis for the activities of a process, it is usually difficult or impossible to propose sensible measures for improving it. It is also difficult to determine the quality of staff required to execute the process, or alternatively the training which they need to execute it competently.

If something goes wrong in carrying out the process, it will be very difficult to determine what went wrong, since there is no baseline document or set of qualifications to review.

Correcting the error: Document a description of the process, or state the criteria for qualifying a suitable person or machine for the process.

(j) Missing ownership

Description: No process owner (role) is shown for a process.

Examples:

- A process is described, but no terms of reference or job description are provided for the person responsible for it.
- Various staff members may carry out a process, but it is not clear how they are selected or how one is chosen for a particular 'shift'.

Likely causes: Insufficient attention to the responsibility for carrying out a process or to keeping records of those who have carried it out.

Damage which can result: If the owner of a process is not specified, then over time it will become increasingly unclear who is responsible and even what their responsibilities are. This will result in poorer standards for executing the process. There will also be problems in keeping records of who was responsible at a particular time, which will decrease accountability and hinder process improvement.

Correcting the error: Provide a clear job description, terms of reference, or list of criteria for assuming ownership of the process.

Inconsistency errors

(a) Misprocessed information

Description: An information item is processed inconsistently with its type (channel, information store or archive).

Examples: A purchasing department keeps records of only the latest purchase from each supplier, so that it can review the quality of that purchase. However, the parent organization also wants it to provide historical information on supplier performance, which it cannot do without previous records.

In this situation, the parent company is requesting the department to retain purchasing records as an archive, but the department itself is treating them only as an information store.

Reversing this example, the purchasing department unnecessarily may keep all previous records, when it is required to retain only the latest transaction with each supplier.

Likely causes: Insufficient attention to the persistence characteristics of information (see Chapter 2). Attempt to treat an information item in more than one way, depending on the context. Overcaution in retaining previous versions, when only the latest will suffice, or imprudence in not keeping records of past versions when traceability is required.

Damage which can result: Useful information may be thrown away. Information may be treated inconsistently, resulting in processing errors and misunderstandings.

Correcting the error: Ensure that the correct persistence characteristics are ascribed to the information item (see Chapter 2), and that all processes treat it in accordance with those characteristics.

(b) Misused information

Description: An information item is used inconsistently with its class. This differs from an misprocessed information error, which deals with the persistence of information rather than its class.

Examples:

- By mistake, a date is used as an authority for a process.
- A control is not in the form of 'IF condition ...' or 'WHEN ...', etc.

Likely causes: This form of error is usually caused by a simple mistake rather than a misunderstanding or incorrect usage.

Damage which can result: Damage is rare, as this sort of error is obvious and is easy to detect.

Correcting the error: Obvious.

(c) Inconsistent information

Description: A process uses an information item in a way which is incompatible with its content.

Examples:

- The 'process invoices' process requires information which is not present on the invoice form, the only input to this process.
- The 'receive order' process requires a packing note to process the order. However, the shipper does not attach such a note to orders.

Likely causes: Usually caused by a simple lack of attention. Often results from uncontrolled changes, either to a process or to information which it processes, so that they do not remain compatible after the change.

Damage which can result: The process will operate incorrectly. If the process does manage to execute, the output probably will be corrupted.

Correcting the error: Correct the inconsistency between process and content of the information item. If possible, institute proper change control to avoid future occurrences of the problem.

(d) Absent input

Description: A process requires information which none of its inputs can provide. As a result, it can never be activated.

Examples:

- A new machine in a factory requires an operator to be specially trained, yet such training is not catered for. As a result, the machine remains idle.
- Trains or planes fail to depart on time because an essential human resource or necessary parts are not specified in the process and, hence, ignored.

Likely causes: Sometimes this problem arises because of incomplete analysis of the process and its requirements for activation. Often, if we keep digging, we will discover inputs which are hidden from the view even of participants in the process.

It can also arise because of a belief of 'fortuitous' processes—that it is not required to specify all inputs, as 'something will turn up' (the Macawber Syndrome). This is a dangerous belief, as sooner or later, it is bound *not* to turn up (Murphy's Law!).

Damage which can result: The damage from this error results from the unpredictability of the process. Clearly, the process must be getting the input it requires, or it could never be executed. However, the analysis has failed to uncover the source of the input, and it will be uncontrolled and unpredictable until it is found. At the least, the results will be a highly variable and unpredictable output, and at the worst, the result could be catastrophe if the process is not activated at a critical moment.

Correcting the error: Complete the analysis to reveal all inputs to the process. Alternatively, if the 'presumed' input is not actually required, alter the process description.

(e) Absent output

Description: A process provides information or material which none of its outputs can take.

Examples:

- As a by-product of a manufacturing process, excess heat is produced, but no mechanism is provided to transfer the heat, resulting in excessive temperatures.
- Routine operation of a clerical process results in useful feedback information which could be used to improve the process, but no mechanism is provided for channelling this information.

Likely causes: Insufficient analysis or assumptions about what outputs are required, without inspecting the process in detail.

Damage which can result: As noted in the examples, processes often produce valuable by-products which will be lost if an explicit output mechanism is not provided. Alternatively, there could be a hidden output on which other processes or destinations are dependent. If so, then the chain of processes will be unpredictable and could become unstable.

Correcting the error: Complete the analysis to reveal all outputs from the process. Alternatively, if the 'presumed' output is not actually required, alter the process description.

(f) Incompatible information

Description: An information item is split and, after one or more of the threads is transformed by a subsequent process step, rejoined. This will make them incompatible.

Examples:

- Procedures management within an organization is faulty, allowing different versions of its codes of practice to be in use at the same time.
- Two 'duplicate' processes are supposed to produce the same products; however, one of them is faulty. Since the products are then mixed in the same bins with no identification, it is impossible to trace the cause of the fault.

Likely causes: Assumptions that processes will always execute correctly often lie behind this error. Processes do sometimes go wrong, and by performing checks on their products, we are able to catch them before they cause problems. However, if the output from another process is merged with the product, the problem will be much harder to correct. See '(b) Process validation omissions' in the next section.

Sometimes, this error masks a redundancy error, one of the failure mode errors described in the next section. This occurs when two processes operate in parallel yet produce the same output. See '(h) Process redundancy' in the next section.

Damage which can result: This error usually results in information which is incompatible, and can lead to a chain of incorrect data promulgated down the process chain. It can also lead to processes getting out of synchronization.

At the very least, such errors lead to inefficient processes which are wasteful of valuable resources and, possibly, processing time.

Correcting the error: In many cases, the desired result can be obtained by introducing cardinality, so that identical processes operating in parallel are replaced by a single process with cardinality greater than one. This produces the desired results without introducing the problems of inconsistent products.

If the problem results from redundancy, then the processes need to be redesigned to ensure that only the minimum number of required processes are included.

(g) Authority mismatch

Description: A process or aspect of a process is inconsistent with, or has a different scope from, its authority. This is a particular case of the inconsistent information error described in (c) above.

Also see inheritance mismatch (one of the inheritance incompatibilities errors) for a related type of error. The process balance criterion, described in Chapter 7, provides a detailed discussion of this error and its cure.

Examples:

- The wrong procedure is listed as the authority for a process: e.g. where an international standard is used, rather than appropriate law, as the authority (see ISO 9001, 4.4.4, for an example) (ISO 9001, 1994).
- A medical doctor exceeds the limits of his competence in making a diagnosis, leaving himself open to a lawsuit.

- The instructions for a process cannot be carried out competently by anyone within an organization, and no training is provided to achieve the required level of competence. As a result, it is impossible to carry out the process as specified in the instructions.

Likely causes: Insufficient understanding of regulatory and other requirements to which the process is subject. Gradual slippage over time, where the process is modified in practice, without a corresponding change in the description of the process. Insufficient training of staff to match the requirements of an organization's rules and procedures.

Damage which can result: The stated authority for a process becomes less and less relevant, making it harder to trace the reasons why actions were carried out. The process will also have a tendency to drift, introducing errors and variable product quality. If the problem is lack of training, then staff morale will suffer and the quality of results will be inadequate.

Correcting the error: Investigate the areas where the authority and the process differ and then correct them.

(h) Interface error

Description: The input or output for a process does not link with the equivalent input or output for an adjoining process. From the viewpoint of the first process, an output is sent to a second process, but from the second viewpoint, the output is not received.

Examples:

- The owner of the goods inwards process believes that copies of purchase orders are sent to it directly from the purchasing department. In reality, these documents are filed and sent from the accounts payable department. When there is a delay in receiving a purchase order, goods inwards tend to try to resolve it with the wrong department, purchasing, rather than with accounts payable. This results in delays in receiving orders and possibly even rejecting them unnecessarily.
- The sales department sends orders to the manufacturing department, on a magnetic tape which they call 'Net customer requests'. The manufacturing department refers to the same tape as 'Sales orders'. Since the sales department has another file also called 'Sales orders', a confusion results when describing the whole process.

Likely causes: This is a common problem—staff often are unaware of the connections between their process and others. If the analyst, while documenting the processes, does not do compatibility checks, this error will be promulgated into the process description.

Damage which can result: As seen in the examples, it is difficult to resolve problems involving the interface between processes. In more extreme cases, information may even be lost because it is incorrectly identified and not recognized as information shared between processes.

Correcting the error: This error is easy to spot, particularly when the process is mapped with QPL. Normally, it is necessary to arrange a conference with the relevant process owners to resolve consistent naming and transfer of the affected information item.

Hierarchical incompatibility errors

(a) Hierarchical mismatch

Description: There is a mismatch between the input or output of a process and one of its sub-processes.

In network terms, we can divide the communication links within the process into internal and external links. Internal links connect two sub-processes. External links connect a sub-process to an entirely distinct process. The external links of the sub-processes should add up to those of the full process, but with this error they do not.

Examples: The purchasing manager (owner of the purchasing process), specifies that input to the purchasing process will come from requisitioners and external suppliers, and output will be purchase orders to the suppliers and memos to the requisitioners. However, the purchasing clerk, owner of one of the sub-processes, believes that there is an additional external link to the accounts department, who receive a copy of the purchase order after the order is placed.

Likely causes: This error tends to result from one of two causes:

- misunderstandings between the owner of the full process and owners of the sub-processes
- incomplete analysis of the full range of external inputs and outputs.

Damage which can result: See '(b) Uncreated information' under incompleteness errors.

Correcting the error: Complete the analysis more thoroughly, or resolve conflicts or misunderstandings between the owners of the full process and the sub-processes.

(b) Hierarchical incompleteness

Description: When a process is broken down into its component sub-processes, the parts do not match the full process (i.e. the sum of the parts does not add up to the whole). The collected descriptions of individual sub-processes, and their inputs and outputs, does not match that of the full process.

Example: The full purchasing process is supposed to process purchase orders, order materials from suppliers and maintain records of acceptable suppliers for future reference. However, when its sub-processes are described, we discover that none of them is responsible for maintaining the records of acceptable suppliers.

Likely causes: This error tends to result from one of two causes:

- misunderstandings between the owner of the full process and owners of the sub-processes
- incorrectly scoping the full process, so that it is unclear what the sub-processes need to do to complete the full process.

Damage which can result: See '(b) Uncreated information' under incompleteness errors.

Correcting the error: Complete the analysis more thoroughly, or resolve conflicts or misunderstandings between the owners of the full process and the sub-processes.

Inheritance incompatibility errors

(a) Inheritance mismatch

Description: A child process is incompatible with the parent process, when it handles information items which are members of a class handled by the parent.

This is an error encountered frequently when attempting to comply with a large number of rules or procedures and is dealt with at greater length in Chapter 6. It arises when child processes, which inherit the properties of all authorities to which they are subject, contradict those authorities. This can occur in many ways:

- the inputs and/or outputs of the child processes contradict those of the authority
- the child processes do not put into effect all processes required by the authority
- the child processes do not have roles which match those stated in the authority etc.

Examples:

- The quality control unit in a pharmaceuticals laboratory does not have access to laboratory facilities (contradicts FDA Good Manufacturing Practice: '211.22 (b) Adequate laboratory facilities for the testing and approval (or rejection) of components ... and drug products shall be available to the quality control unit.') (FDA, 1989)
- An organization does not check the qualifications or provide training for staff involved in verification activities (contradicts ISO 9001, '4.1.2.2 The supplier shall identify resource requirements and provide adequate resources including the assignment of trained personnel for verification activities' (ISO 9001, 1994).
- Company procedures specify that 'timesheets are to be returned to the departmental administrators by noon on Monday', yet there are several departments that do not have administrators because they are too small. In this case, who will receive the timesheets?

Likely causes:

- Misunderstanding of the authority.
- Misunderstanding the information items or roles required by an authority, leading to incorrect inheritance within the process.

- Poor definitions of processes or information items in the document used as the authority.

Damage which can result: The process can be in violation of the relevant laws or regulatory requirements, leading to financial or other penalties. In extreme cases, where safety or security is an issue, it could lead to dangerous situations and uncontrolled results.

Correcting the error: Ensure that the authority is fully understood and reflected in the process description. Check the scope of all information items and roles in the authority.

In the case where the authority itself is ambiguous in its application, qualify the authority by passing it through an intermediate document. In practice, organizations do this by writing down explicit interpretations of external standards or regulations; these interpretations are the authorities for their processes, not the external standards themselves. This is the approach taken in the ISO 9000 series of quality standards, which require the organization to write quality manuals, plans and procedures addressing the requirements of the international standard. In practice, the organization's processes are based on, and audited against, these documents, not directly against the standard.

(b) Cardinality mismatch

Description: The cardinality of a child process is incompatible with that of a parent process.

The child process must never be more restrictive than the authority, although it can provide for additional possibilities. If, for example, the authority states that at least three information items of a given class will be provided as input to a process, then a child which required at least four inputs of the class would be acceptable. However, it would not be acceptable if only a single input item was permissible for the child process.

It is not possible to provide a table of possible mismatches, since the interpretation of 'more restrictive' varies with the interpretation of the authority. In the above example, three is obviously the minimum cardinality for the input. However, if the authority stated that a maximum of two inputs were acceptable, then a child process which allowed for three or more inputs would not be acceptable. In this case, the maximum cardinality of input items is two.

Example: A government department is obliged to request competitive tenders for all procurements in excess of $10 000. However, the procedures manual for the spares division says that a single tender is acceptable if:

- the supplier has supplied the same goods or services before
- in the past, prices and the quality of supply were both acceptable.

Obviously, the single tender may be rejected if it is not acceptable, in which case a competitive tender will be issued.

As represented in QPL, the process descriptions in the authority and in the process are identical, as are the information items. However, the cardinalities are incompatible. For the authority, a one-to-many relationship applies between the 'request tenders' process and two information items, the request for tender, and the tender. In the process itself, a one-to-one relationship is used when the above conditions are met.

Likely causes: This error usually arises from a failure to make the cardinalities explicit in either the authority or the description. It may, of course, also arise from a simple error in matching the cardinalities.

Damage which can result: Significant yet unexpected misinterpretation of requirements or regulations.

Correcting the error: Carefully check the cardinalities in the authority and make them explicit where necessary. Also determine where any restrictions in the authority occur. Then check for conflicts between the child processes and the authorities. Where they do occur, remove the conflicts by changing the authority or the child process.

5.3   FAILURE MODE ANALYSIS

In the logical errors described above, each error describes a situation where there is a genuine mistake: the outcome will either be undesired or will be logically inconsistent. There is, however, a further class of errors, which are not clear-cut mistakes or faults, but which could still result in damage to the results and present a threat to quality. These represent 'probabilistic' errors, where the fault will not always appear, but may occur with a given set of circumstances. They are called 'failure mode errors' after the method known as FMEA, or failure mode and effects analysis. This method is designed to analyse processes and the ways in which they fail to produce desired results (Garvin, 1988: 16, 136).

Logical errors are always mistakes and always need to be corrected, as incorrect results will invariably occur. Failure mode errors are not necessarily mistakes, but they do introduce a risk into the processes which we are describing. For example, the process may describe transmission of a message by mail: if the message gets lost, is there a means of catching the fault before any damage is done? This is a case of a failure mode error, but we may choose to ignore it, if the risk is low or if the consequences of failure are not significant.

Types of error

(See Table 5.5 opposite.)

Table 5.5 The ten types of failure mode error

	Type of error	Description
(a)	Information validation omission	There are no checks to catch incorrect or incomplete information items.
(b)	Process validation omission	There is no mechanism for catching or correcting an incorrectly applied process.
(c)	Reception omission	There is no mechanism for checking that an information item is received by a process after being sent by another process.
(d)	Transmission omission	There is no mechanism for checking that an information item required by a process has been sent by another process.
(e)	Information feedback omission	Information on the effect of a process is not returned to it as an input.
(f)	Process improvement omission	Information on the effect of a process is not returned to it as an authority.
(g)	Non-activated process	A process can never be activated (e.g. one of its inputs will never exist).
(h)	Process redundancy	An unnecessary process step is included (i.e. the results of the overall process would be identical without the step).
(i)	Information redundancy	Some of the information content of an information item is never used by any process.
(j)	Process exception	A process is not designed to handle a possible situation within its scope.

Description of each error type

(a) Information validation omission

> *Description*: There are no checks to catch incorrect or incomplete information items.

> *Example*: 'Process purchase orders' occasionally results in incorrect orders being sent to the supplier. Since there are no checks on the orders before they are sent out, such a mistake could result in an incorrect shipment of goods, and either payment for undesired items or bad relationships with the supplier.

> *Likely causes*:

> ● Assumption that processes are always executed correctly.
> ● Failure to model all aspects of a process, resulting in unpredictable or uncontrolled consequences.

Damage which can result: No control on the inevitable variability of outputs. Damage could range from mild customer irritation to a risk to safety and security.

Correcting the error: List all likely variations of output from the process. Incorporate checks and correction mechanisms, either in the process or externally (i.e. to 'filter' each output before it is used as input to another process). Anticipation of possible errors and making processes 'fail-safe' is at the heart of the Japanese technique known as the Poka-Yoke—literally 'mistake proofing'—system (Dyer, 1990).

(b) Process validation omission

Description: There is no mechanism for catching or correcting an incorrectly applied process.

This differs slightly from the previous error: although the information output is checked and corrected if necessary, the process itself is not.

Example: In the previous example, incorrect purchase orders were sometimes sent to suppliers. Now the problem has been corrected, by instituting a check by a second purchasing clerk. However, the head of purchasing is still unhappy, because five percent of purchase orders are found to have errors. Thus, although these incorrect orders are never sent to suppliers, the process itself is still faulty.

This example is the conventional concept of 'quality inspection', which puts the emphasis on finding errors after they occur rather than on prevention. Many commentators have noted the weaknesses of this approach, which fortunately is increasingly rare due to competition with the high-quality products of Japan and other countries, which have extremely low defect rates. For a vivid example of these differences see Womack, Jones and Roos (1990).

Likely causes:

● Insufficient training of staff.
● Ambiguous or excessively complicated process steps, which are difficult to observe.

Damage which can result: The knock-on effects of this error can lead to many other problems or weaknesses in the system, including poor staff morale, inefficient production or excessive rejection rates.

Correcting the error: These errors cannot be detected by inspection of the outputs of the process, as the inspection mechanism focuses on the products of the process, not on the process itself. Instead, it is necessary to introduce feedback mechanisms, such as:

● external process audits, or
● internal quality circles or quality improvement teams, which monitor processes from within and suggest improvements.

(c) Reception omission

Description: There is no mechanism for checking that an information item is received by a process after being sent by another process.

Example: A critical order is required urgently. A purchase order is sent to the supplier, with a short deadline. When the order does not arrive at the due time, the supplier is telephoned. Their representative replies that the order was never received and was probably sent to the wrong address. A delay of two weeks results.

Likely causes: This error arises from the assumption that communication between processes always occurs correctly, and that messages are never lost or misinterpreted. *The interfaces between two processes are the most error-prone parts of the whole operation.*

Damage which can result: Significant delays, as in the example.

In the extreme case, this error can result in work which is never completed. In real life, customers move to competitors. A company may never even know that there is a problem, if customers vote with their feet and are not asked why they were dissatisfied.

Correcting the error: Introduce a confirmation process whenever there is a significant risk of important information not being received by another process.

(d) Transmission omission

Description: There is no mechanism for checking that an information item required by a process has been sent by another process.

Example: For the example given at (c), the error has been corrected, and the purchaser now confirms that the supplier receives each purchase order. When a critical order is due, it assumes that there is no cause for worry, since the order was received. However, after three days, the situation has become one of panic, and the supplier finally is contacted. It acknowledges that it did receive the order, but apologizes that it cannot be processed until an essential part from yet another supplier is received.

By this time, it is too late to find an alternative supplier, and the purchaser has no choice but to wait.

Likely causes: See '(c) Reception omission'.

Damage which can result: The most common damage is the delay in starting a process, which will result either in delays in completing the process or in rushing through the work, resulting in errors and excessive stress to staff. If even an ad hoc mechanism is not available for contacting the sender of the information, then the process will never execute, and a catastrophic situation could result.

Correcting the error: As with the previous error, introduce a confirmation process wherever there is a significant risk of information not being sent by another process when it is required. This can be done by requesting regular progress reports from the other process to obtain early warning of a problem, or by contacting the process owner when the input is due.

(e) Information feedback omission

Description: Information on the effect of a process is not returned to it as an input. This error is closely related to the information validation omission described above under '(a) Information validation omission'. It is illustrated in Figure 5.2.

Examples: Customers complain that the Sunrise Yellow paint purchased from Deluxe Paint Company is less yellow than previously and will not match the same paint from an earlier batch. Upon investigation, the company determines that a change in pigment suppliers means that more of the pigment is required to produce the same shade as before.

Likely causes: Failure to carry out internal control checks and to keep trend records.

Damage which can result: As seen in the above example, the quality of products will suffer and customers may be lost. If the error can be corrected, it will be more expensive than if the checks had been built in.

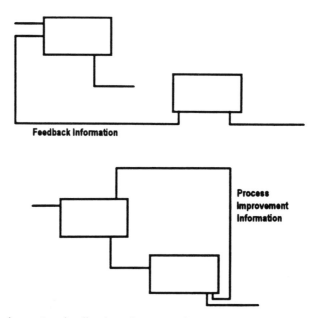

Feedback Information

Process Improvement Information

Figure 5.2 Information feedback and process improvement omissions

Correcting the error: Wherever possible, design processes with such feedback loops built in. This correction should be tied in with corrections of the information validation omission described in (a), to make use of the information detected there.

(f) Process improvement omission

Description: Information on the effect of a process is not returned to it as an authority. Unlike the previous error, the feedback changes the way in which the process is carried out, rather than providing information which will be used by the unchanged process.

This error is closely related to the process validation omission described above under '(b) Process validation omission'. It is illustrated in Figure 5.2.

Example: A company produces electronic components. Records show that the number of rejected components varies widely—some days there are almost no faulty parts, yet on others, the fraction of rejects is very high.

This indicates that the process of producing the components needs to be improved. However, there is no mechanism for such improvement by updating the process description. (The processes implicit in the Malcolm Baldrige Award criteria provide many examples of feedback loops for process improvement. See Appendix 2 for a QPL chart of this process.)

Likely causes:

● Overly complex processes, which are difficult to understand and to change when required.
● Unwillingness to create a 'learning culture', where processes are continually reviewed and improved.

Damage which can result: The organization will be slow to change. If mechanisms for process authority feedback are not in place, the processes will be altered infrequently and at greater expense than a culture where processes are under continuous review and improvement.

Correcting the error: Wherever possible, design processes with authority feedback loops built in. This correction should be tied in with corrections of the process validation omission described in (b), to provide a use for the information detected there.

(g) Non-activated process

Description: A process can never be activated (e.g. one of its inputs will never exist). Although in theory the process will operate correctly if activated, one or more of the required inputs will never actually be available.

This error is closely related to that of the hostile process (incompleteness errors, (f)). Hostile processes have no inputs. Non-activated processes do have inputs, but at least one of them will never contain real information. Formally, we say that this input has no instances, even though its class exists.

Example: An organization is concerned to cater for all possibilities and zealously provides procedures for all conditions, even though some of them never occur in practice. For example, the Eurolingua language school (described in Chapter 3, Example 1) has a rule that all teachers require a formal qualification certifying that they can teach English as a foreign language (TEFL). Despite this, they include in their procedures a process which caters for teachers without qualifications. This process is never activated, as all teachers are qualified!

Likely causes:

● Excessive desire for reassurance.
● Inadequate analysis of the scope of inputs, to determine the range of processing required.

Damage which can result: Procedure manuals will tend to become unwieldy, due to superfluous information. The presence of non-activated processes can also indicate faulty analysis of tasks and result in incorrect or inefficient designs.

Correcting the error: As with hostile processes, additional process definition is required, to clarify the exact inputs to the process and the conditions under which it is activated. Processes which supply input may need to be investigated to determine the range of possible values of this information.

(h) Process redundancy

Description: An unnecessary process step is included—the results of the overall process would be identical without the step.
    This error is related to that of incompatible information—(f) inconsistency errors—and to that of unconnected processes—(e) incompleteness errors.

Examples:

● None of the authorities for a process require traceability to be included, yet the process makes provision for this additional and time-consuming activity. The additional process steps for traceability are redundant, since they are unnecessary in this instance.
● The work specifications for telephone installers include a lengthy description of how customers are to be billed, even though billing is not part of the installation process. These descriptions are redundant as installation work specifications, since they do not contribute to the results of the process.

Likely causes: This error often results from the evolution of procedures, which retain process steps no longer relevant or required. It also results from unnecessary repetition of process steps and from processes which exceed the scope of their authorities.

Damage which can result: This error results in overly complicated and long procedures. Indirectly, it can produce errors, since their frequency is directly related to the complexity of the procedure.

Correcting the error: For each process step in a process, check that it actually contributes to the final result (the 'value chain'). Also check that the process step does not repeat the work of another step in the process.

(i) Information redundancy

Description: Some of the content of an information item is never used by any process. Alternatively, information is repeated, unnecessarily, in more than one information item.

Examples:

- An application form asks for details of hobbies and interests, but this information is never used in deciding whether to employ the applicant.
- Identical details about an order are included on two forms, the purchase order and the order confirmation, even though the process obtains all required information from the purchase order only. The order confirmation, therefore, contains redundant information.

Likely causes: Like redundant processes, redundant information often arises historically: the information was genuinely required in the past, but modifications to processes have made it obsolete. Even information stores and archives can become redundant if the processes they were designed for are changed significantly.

Damage which can result: In addition to the waste and inefficiency inherent in redundant information, this error can lead to mistakes if duplicated information is not kept up to date. Unused information also makes it more difficult to identify redundant processes (which often have the sole function of processing information which no longer has any use!).

Correcting the error: For each process, identify all information which is used, created or transformed by it. Remove parts of information items which are not processed.

Cross-check information items to determine any duplicated information. If there is, remove it if possible. Alternatively, ensure that processes are in place to update all duplicates simultaneously and consistently.

(j) Process exception

Description: A process is not designed to handle a possible situation within its scope. Certain types of feasible inputs, or certain feasible situations, will result in unforeseen consequences.

Example: A manufacturing company's accounts receivable procedures provides for invoicing customers—conventional paper invoices are used. When one of its customers asks that invoices be abolished and replaced by direct electronic funds transfer, the company is unable to accommodate them until it radically changes the procedure.

Likely causes:

- Failure to note all possibilities within the scope of a process.
- Lack of attention to detail.
- Omitting to do failure mode and effects analysis.

Damage which can result: Results of the process are unpredictable if such a situation should occur. The results could result in injuries to people, loss of property or damage to customer goodwill.

Correcting the error: Failure mode and effects analysis is particularly powerful in avoiding this error.

5.4   TECHNICAL ANALYSIS

The errors described above as logical or failure mode cover the full range of errors which can be detected by systematic analysis. Once a process has been broken down into its component parts and revealed the underlying structure, we can apply these checks to discover the underlying faults and weaknesses in the system. This leads to significant improvements in efficiency and quality, based only on the QPL diagrams describing the process.

However, these systematic error checks are not sufficient to catch all errors, because many errors are embedded in the technical content of a document. These require review by a technical specialist, who will make use of knowledge and experience to determine if the information is correct and well-considered. Procedures for the disposal of toxic waste, or for the installation of an electricity supply may have logical errors, of course, but only a specialist can provide the additional assurance that the procedure is adequate for its purpose.

In reality, the distinction between the above reviews and the technical review is not great, because technical errors always reduce to a single type of logical error: inheritance mismatch. This error states that a process conflicts in some way with the knowledge which is considered an authority for the process; this is exactly what a technical specialist does when reviewing the content of a document. Therefore, the use of QPL and its structuring techniques can still be of significant value to the specialist, since it provides a notation for sub-dividing the steps embedded in the document, for structuring them, and finally for relating them to the knowledge and experience embedded in authorities. This provides the expert with a systematic procedure for ensuring that all relevant knowledge has been taken into account, and that the document does not have any significant omissions. Chapter 6, which deals with compliance issues, provides further information about techniques for linking expertise to a process.

5.5 A WORKED EXAMPLE

A procedure for a purchasing process

How does process review work in practice? The best way to find out is to experience the techniques in the previous sections, on a real procedure. Such a procedure, based on a real set of purchasing procedures, is shown below, with its accompanying flow chart (Figure 5.3).

ABC Corporation purchasing procedures, Issue 1.2, June 1, 1993

Introduction and scope

Step (i)	This procedure describes the purchasing procedures to be followed by all employees of the ABC Corporation.
Step (ii)	The following roles are involved in this procedure: <ul><li>the requisitioner, who requests an item of equipment, software or service,</li><li>the budget holder, who will provide the funds for the purchase from his or her allocated budget</li><li>the purchasing department, which is responsible for selecting suppliers and issuing purchase orders</li><li>the goods inward department, which receives and checks the purchase when it is received</li><li>the quality assurance department, which is responsible for the overall effectiveness of this and other procedures in the corporation.</li></ul>
Step (iii)	This procedure includes all steps of the purchasing process. However, it does not cover maintenance of the approved suppliers record, which is specified in procedure P002.
Step (iv)	Note that there is a general corporation rule that at least two suppliers must be considered for all purchases, to preserve competition in supply.

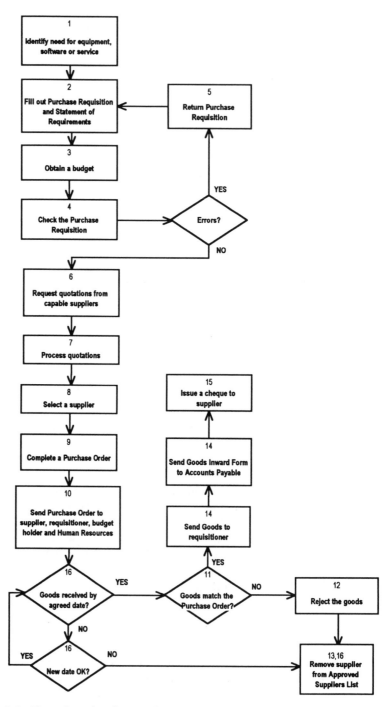

Figure 5.3 Flow chart for the purchasing procedure

Body of procedure

Step 1	An employee identifies a need for equipment, software or service.
Step 2	The employee fills out a purchase requisition (PR) and writes a statement of requirements.
Step 3	The employee obtains a budget from a budget holder and obtains his or her authorization. The PR is sent to the purchasing department (PD).
Step 4	The PD checks the PR.
Step 5	If errors are found, the PR is returned to the requisitioner (go to step 2).
Step 6	If there are no errors, the PD requests quotations from capable suppliers on the approved suppliers record.
Step 7	Suppliers send in quotations by the deadline set by the PD.
Step 8	On the deadline for quotations, the PD opens the envelopes. Quotations over the spending limit are rejected. The remaining quotations are graded by established criteria in the PD Handbook. The supplier with the highest grade is selected.
Step 9	The PD completes a purchase order (PO) and includes a date when the goods are to be received. The PO is sent to the selected supplier.
Step 10	The PD sends copies of the PO to the requisitioner, budget holder and to human resources.
Step 11	The goods are received. If they match the PO, they are accepted.
Step 12	If the goods do not match the PO, they are rejected.
Step 13	If the goods are rejected, the supplier's quality rating is downgraded, or the supplier is removed from the approved suppliers list (ASL). The approved suppliers record is also updated (this document, which is only to be seen by the purchasing manager, contains all previous records of additions to and removals from the ASL, also giving reasons for this).
Step 14	If the goods are accepted, they are sent to the requisitioner, and a copy of the goods inward form is sent to the accounts payable department.
Step 15	Accounts payable issue a cheque to the supplier.
Step 16	If the goods or services have not been received or completed by the date agreed with the supplier, then the PD checks with the supplier. If a new date is feasible, then it is recorded, and this action is repeated on that date. If a new date is not feasible, and the supplier cannot provide a reasonable explanation, then the supplier is removed from the ASL. A new supplier is selected, starting with step 8.

Analysing the process

Now we can analyse this procedure, using the reviewing rules presented in this chapter. The QPL diagram for this procedure is shown in Figure 5.4.

The following codes for QPL reviewing checks are used in Table 5.6 to identify the five classes of errors:

1 Completeness
2 Consistency
3 Hierarchy

4 Inheritance
5 Failure mode.

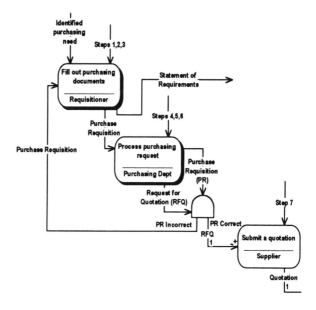

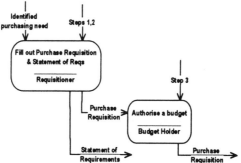

Figure 5.4 QPL diagram for the purchasing procedure

Process Purchasing Request

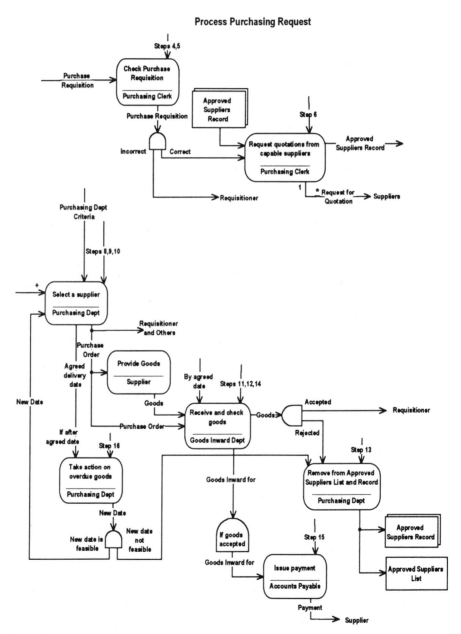

Figure 5.4 *(continued)*

Table 5.6 Analysis of introduction and scope

Step No	Procedure step	Error(s)
(i)	This procedure describes the purchasing procedures to be followed by all employees of the ABC Corporation.	
(ii)	The following roles are involved in this procedure: • the requisitioner, who requests an item of equipment, software or service • the budget holder, who will provide the funds for the purchase from his or her allocated budget • the purchasing department, which is responsible for selecting suppliers and issuing purchase orders • the goods inward department, which receives and checks the purchase when it is received • the quality assurance department, which is responsible for the overall effectiveness of this and other procedures in the corporation.	**1c Unused source/1d Unused destination** This source and destination is never used.
(iii)	This procedure includes all steps of the purchasing process. However, it does not cover maintenance of the approved suppliers record, which is specified in procedure P002.	**2g Authority mismatch** Sub-process contradicts the scope of the whole process (see step 13).
(iv)	Note that there is a general Corporation rule that at least two suppliers must be considered for all purchases, to preserve competition in supply.	**4b Cardinality mismatch** This will be contradicted by step 13, which has no way of checking that the number of suppliers has dropped below a limit. Thus, the cardinality of the authority is one (process) to 2 + ('two or more'), while the process itself has cardinality one to 0 + .

Table 5.7 Analysis of body of procedure

Step No	Procedure step	Error(s)
1	An employee identifies a need for equipment, software or service.	
2	The employee fills out a purchase requisition (PR) and writes a statement of requirements.	**5a Information validation omission** No check that the requirement is correct.

continued

Table 5.7 (*continued*)

3	The employee obtains a budget from a budget holder and obtains his or her authorization. The PR is sent to the purchasing department (PD).	
4	The PD checks the PR.	**5f Process improvement omission** Feedback on this process is never obtained (e.g. there could be significant delays if faulty PRs are posted back to the requisitioner, when a phone call could have cleared them up).
5	If errors are found, the PR is returned to the requisitioner (return to step 2).	
6	If there are no errors, the PD requests quotations from capable suppliers on the approved suppliers record.	**2a Misprocessed information** By mistake, the AS record is used in this procedure, instead of the AS list, thus violating rules of confidentiality. *This error is detected because an archive is input to a process that requires only an information store.* **5e Information feedback omission** Records of recent (good quality) suppliers aren't being fed back to this step, which could facilitate the process (and cut down the numbers asked to bid).
7	Suppliers send in quotations by the deadline set by the PD.	
8	On the deadline for quotations, the PD opens the envelopes. Quotations over the spending limit are rejected. The remaining quotations are graded by established criteria in the PD Handbook. The supplier with the highest grade is selected.	**1b Uncreated information** This spending limit has never been mentioned before. **1a Unused information** An information item (the statement of requirements) is never used.
9	The PD completes a purchase order (PO) and includes a date when the goods are to be received. The PO is sent to the selected supplier.	**5c Reception omission** There is no check that the supplier received the PO. **5d Transmission omission** Date is not agreed with the supplier in advance, nor confirmed afterwards.
10	The PD sends copies of the PO to the requisitioner, budget holder and to human resources.	**2h Interface error** The PD never asks the requisitioner if the goods are needed earlier than the specified date. **5h Process redundancy** Since the human resources department doesn't do anything with the information, why are they sent a copy?

continued

Table 5.7 (*continued*)

11	The goods are received. If they match the PO, they are accepted.	**1a Unused information** An information item (the statement of requirements) is never used (see step 8). **2b Misused information** Information on the PO is used incorrectly (the description of the goods or service is used as if it were the statement of requirements). If necessary, we need to provide an additional checking step against the requirement, and postpone payment until then.
12	If the goods do not match the PO, they are rejected.	**1h Broken path** Doesn't state explicitly what to do with the faulty goods. Also, there is a break in the chain—the supplier must either receive its payment or the (returned) goods.
13	If the goods are rejected, the supplier's quality rating is downgraded, or the supplier is removed from the approved suppliers list (ASL). The approved suppliers record is also updated (this document, which is only to be seen by the purchasing manager, contains all previous records of additions to and removals from the ASL, also giving reasons for this).	**1j Missing ownership** Fails to identify a process owner for this step (could be purchasing or could be the quality assurance department, which was named as a role but given no jobs to do, in step ii). **2e Absent output** Does not specify where downgrading is recorded. **5b Process validation omission** Despite the importance of this process step to the company (and the possibility of lawsuits by rejected suppliers), this step has no checks built in.
14	If the goods are accepted, they are sent to the requisitioner, and a copy of the goods inward form is sent to the accounts payable department.	
15	Accounts payable issue a cheque to the supplier.	**2b Misused information/2d Absent input** Accounts payable is not told what the value of the cheque should be, since it is not on the goods inward form and they do not receive a copy of the PO or the supplier's invoice.
16	If the goods or services have not been received or completed by the date agreed with the supplier, then the PD checks with the supplier. If a new date is feasible, then it is recorded, and this action is repeated on that date. If a new date is not feasible, and the supplier cannot provide a reasonable explanation, then the supplier is removed from the ASL. A new supplier is selected, starting with step 8.	**2h Interface error** The output from this process (the ASL) does not agree with the input to step 6 (the ASR). **2d Absent input** The requisitioner is not asked whether the new date is feasible.

The revised procedure

Based on the above comments, the procedure can be improved in many ways. The following example shows the final result. The QPL diagrams for the revised procedure are shown in Figure 5.5.

ABC Corporation purchasing procedures, Issue 1.3, December 1, 1993

Introduction and scope

Step (i)	This procedure describes the purchasing procedures to be followed by all employees of the ABC Corporation.
Step (ii)	The following roles are involved in this procedure: ● the requisitioner, who requests an item of equipment, software or service ● the budget holder, who will provide the funds for the purchase from his or her allocated budget ● the purchasing department, which is responsible for selecting suppliers and issuing purchase orders ● the goods inward department, which receives and checks the purchase when it is received ● the quality assurance department, which is responsible for maintaining the approved suppliers list.
Step (iii)	This procedure includes all steps of the purchasing process. However, it does not cover maintenance of the approved suppliers record, which is specified in procedure P002.
Step (iv)	Note that there is a general corporation rule that at least two suppliers must be considered for all purchases, to preserve competition in supply.
Step (v)	In certain key steps in this procedure (2 and 13) the document produced by the step must be checked by someone other than the author of the document, to ensure that unacceptable errors are not made. The person doing the check must be qualified to carry out the step.

Body of procedure

Step 1	An employee identifies a need for equipment, software or service.
Step 2	The employee then fills out a purchase requisition (PR) and writes a statement of requirements. A second person on the employee's team must check and approve the statement of requirements before it is issued.
Step 3	The employee obtains a budget from a budget holder and obtains his or her authorization. The PR is sent to the purchasing department (PD).

Step 4	The PD checks the PR.
Step 5	If errors are found, the PR is returned to the requisitioner (go to step 2). (See Notes below.)
Step 6	If there are no errors, the PD requests quotations from capable suppliers on the approved suppliers list. (See Notes below.)
Step 7	Suppliers send in quotations by the deadline set by the PD.
Step 8	On the deadline for quotations, the PD opens the envelopes. Quotations over the spending limit (specified on the purchase requisition) are rejected. All quotations which do not comply with the statement of requirements (step 2) are rejected.
	The remaining quotations are graded by established criteria in the PD Handbook. The supplier with the highest grade is selected.
Step 9	The PD agrees a date with the supplier and checks with the requisitioner to ensure that this is acceptable. It then completes a purchase order (PO). The PO is sent to the selected supplier. (See Notes below.)
Step 10	The PD sends copies of the PO to the requisitioner and the budget holder.
Step 11	The goods are received. If they match the PO and the statement of requirements, they are accepted.
	The recent suppliers list is updated. This list has records of successful orders for the previous six months and is used to select capable suppliers quickly (step 6).
Step 12	If the goods do not match the PO, they are rejected and returned to the supplier with a letter of explanation. The PO is amended to indicate that the goods were rejected and is sent to the quality assurance group in step 13, for amendment of the approved suppliers list.
Step 13	If the goods are rejected, the quality assurance group downgrade the supplier's quality rating on the approved suppliers list, or remove the supplier from the list (following the supplier approval procedures). A copy of the amended PO, with evidence that the order was rejected, is also retained.
	This step must be confirmed by the quality assurance manager before a supplier is removed from the approved suppliers list.
Step 14	If the goods are accepted, they are sent to the requisitioner, and copies of the goods inward form and the PO are sent to the accounts payable department.

Step 15   Accounts payable issue a cheque to the supplier.

Step 16   If the goods or services have not been received or completed by the date agreed with the supplier, then the PD checks with the supplier to obtain a new date. The requisitioner is then asked if this date is acceptable.

If a new date is acceptable, then it is recorded, and this step (16) is repeated on that date. If a new date is not feasible, and the supplier cannot provide a reasonable explanation, then the supplier is to be removed from the approved suppliers list (step 13). A new supplier is selected, starting with step 8.

Notes

Step 5   At regular intervals, not exceeding three months, the results of this step are to be examined. If more than five percent of purchase requisitions are returned to requisitioners, then the purchasing manager must hold a review of this step.

Step 6   To facilitate selection of good suppliers, the recent suppliers list may be used for this step. This list is described in step 11.

Step 9   The supplier should be contacted after two days to ensure that the PO was received.

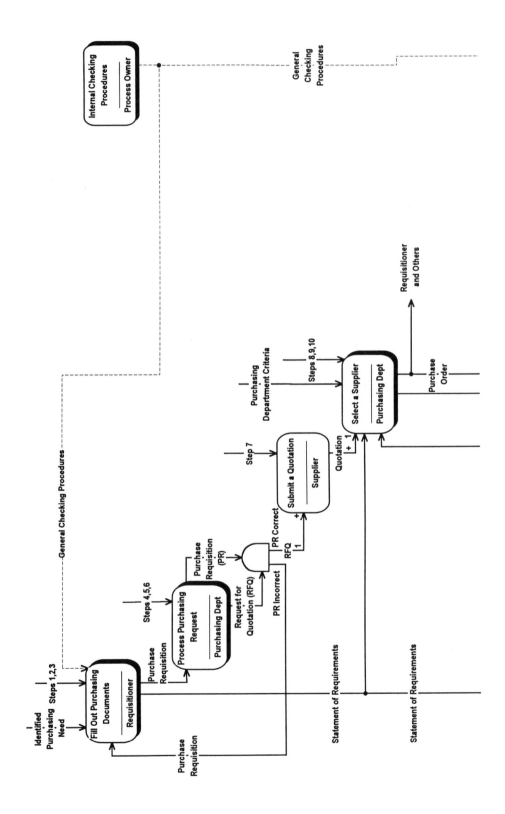

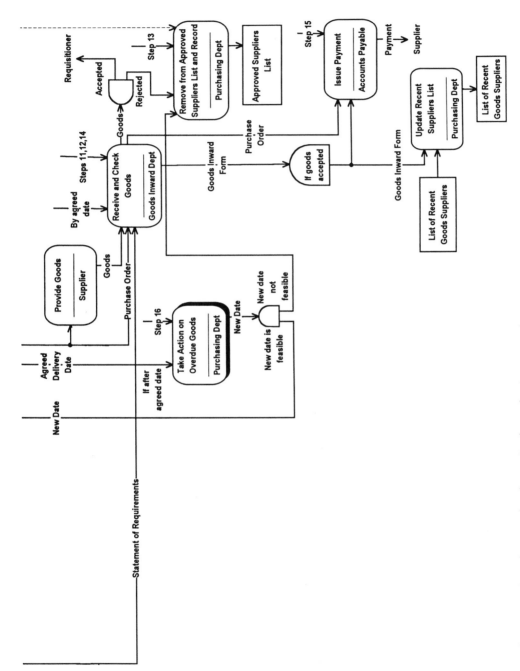

Figure 5.5 QPL diagram for the revised purchasing procedure

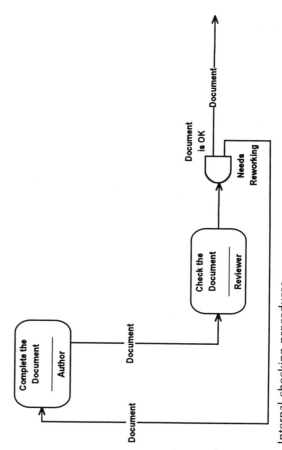

Internal checking procedures
Figure 5.5 (continued)

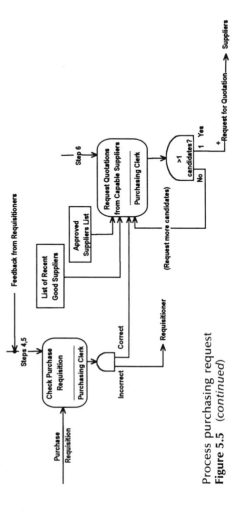

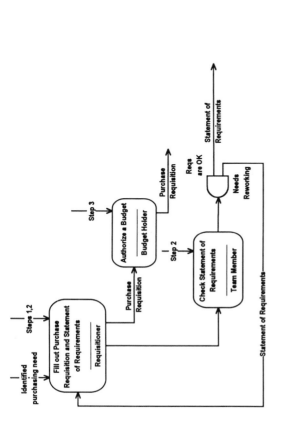

Process purchasing request
Figure 5.5 *(continued)*

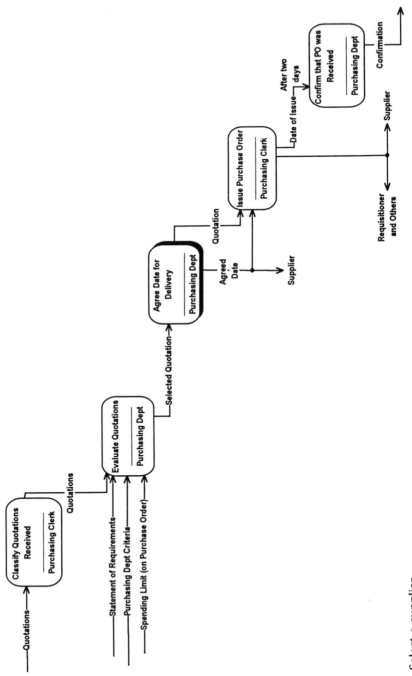

Select a supplier
Figure 5.5 *(continued)*

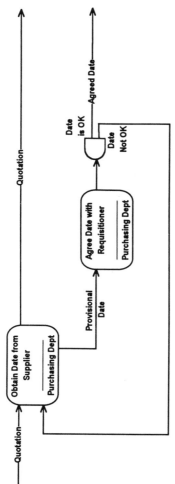

Agree date for delivery

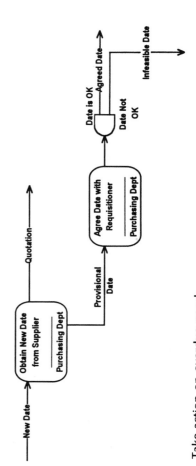

Take action on overdue goods
Figure 5.5 (continued)

6

Compliance and creativity

From all her words and actions, mix'd with love
And sweet compliance, which declared unfeign'd
Union of mind, or in us both one soul.

Milton, Paradise Lost, Book 8

OVERVIEW

All organizations need to comply with standards, regulations and other rules. At the highest level, companies produce goods which must comply with national and international regulations, such as those of the Food and Drug Administration (FDA) in the USA, or those of the European Commission in the European Union.

But compliance does not involve only the rules imposed from outside the organization: it also applies within it. It sets its own standards and ways of working which are expected to be followed throughout the organization. For larger organizations, it is not practical to impose a single set of regulations applicable to all activities and staff. So it provides broad and comprehensive rules, and it is left to individual parts or departments to establish their detailed rules. However, these detailed rules need to be compliant with those of the whole organization.

In this fashion, a chain of compliance is established, which extends from the treaties and laws of countries, through the policies and procedures of companies, and finally down to departments and workgroups within companies. Each part needs to establish rules and procedures which suit its own needs, but it also needs to ensure that the wider requirements are satisfied.

This chapter shows how to use QPL to support compliance-oriented activities. It explains how to connect organizational processes to the standards and regulations which they must comply with—by means of authority and inheritance. Using QPL to convert these documents into process descriptions, we can provide a framework for modelling organizational processes and judging where they need to comply with higher-level regulations or standards.

Checking compliance is an extension of process analysis, introduced in Chapter 5. The standard analysis checks are used to indicate where parts of the process fail to comply with the authorities which regulate its behaviour. This is illustrated in this chapter with an example of a compliance audit using QPL.

When it is extended to the design of processes under constraints, compliance becomes a highly creative process. A design cycle which incorporates compliance checks is used. This approach produces processes which are suited to the individual needs of the organization but also comply with the wider requirements of standards and regulations.

GUIDE TO CHAPTER 6

The first section provides an introduction to compliance—what it is, how to achieve it, and how to maintain it. The remainder of the chapter explores the various aspects of compliance and provides examples of how to achieve compliance in modelling processes. The sections following look at:

- The nature of compliance in terms of the QPL notation and concepts by introducing the two QPL criteria for compliance. You will also see how to express compliance in QPL and how to connect parts of the template process into the relevant parts of the operational process.
- How to check for compliance using auditing techniques. It also provides an example of an audit, using QPL and the ISO 9001 process template in Appendix 2.
- Problems associated with compliance (including problems of conflicts of interest and conflicting authorities), with guidance on their pragmatic solutions.
- A summary of the chapter, with an overview of the use of QPL for the design of compliant process and for compliance auditing.

Appendix 2 provides frameworks for complying with three common quality criteria, ISO 9001, the Malcolm Baldrige Award and the European Quality Award. They provide high-level QPL descriptions of each process and discuss issues related to their interpretation, when designing organizational processes.

GLOSSARY FOR CHAPTER 6

This chapter introduces a number of new terms. The principal ones are defined below.

Compliance   The development and checking of a process to ensure that it does not contradict a standard or set of regulations.

Compliance audit   A specific type of review which identifies areas where an organization's processes fail to meet the requirements of a given regulation or other requirement.

Compliance violation   An inconsistency or contradiction between an organization's processes and those to which it must comply, as revealed by a compliance audit or other check.

Configurable   A feature of QPL which enables templates to be connected into operational processes for compliance checking. We say that the template's processes are configured when they are all connected to the processes of an organization.

Conformance   The development and checking of products and other concrete objects produced by a process, to ensure that they do not violate a standard or other definition of the product.

External compliance   Compliance with a law, regulation or other requirement external to the organization.

> **Internal compliance**   Compliance with a policy, procedure or other requirement internal to the organization.
>
> **Operational process**   A process, as documented by a procedure, work instruction or other document, which can be checked for compliance against a template.
>
> **Template**   The process model of the regulation, standard or other document which must be complied with.

6.1 INTRODUCTION TO COMPLIANCE

What is compliance?

In the life of every organization, a time arises when it must be asked if its processes achieve the goals for which they were designed. These goals might include any of the following:

- Perhaps they need to comply with various regulatory requirements in the pharmaceutical, financial services, oil or mining industries.
- In the European Union, organizations need to comply with more than 250 laws, which provide for a Single Market for trade and normalize practices throughout the Union. (As of 1 January 1993, the start of the European Single Market, there were 282 such laws (*The Times* (London), 1 January 1993: 1).)
- Contracts specify the basis for relationships between two or more organizations and often require activities which are tailored to meet their requirements.
- An organization may just want to comply with certain standards and criteria to demonstrate that it is a quality organization: ISO 9000, the Malcolm Baldrige Award and the European Quality Award are examples.

The above examples involve external regulations, standards and criteria. Less formally, organizations also need to meet requirements at many levels, even though those involved may be unaware of it. Whenever individuals carry out a procedure or work instruction, they comply with the directions given in that document. Such compliance also ensures that the parts of an organization communicate effectively and that they operate with a common level of understanding about their objectives and values.

In each of these situations, the processes which constitute systems need to be designed not only to meet the organization's own requirements but also the requirements of these external regulations and standards. This is the heart of compliance: the development and checking of processes to meet a set of requirements.

The compliance audit

Compliance with a regulation is checked by means of the compliance audit. This is a particular type of review which identifies areas where an organization's processes fail to meet the requirements of the given regulation. In QPL, such an audit is carried out by assigning the given regulation as an authority for the process being evaluated. Then the implications of the authority are examined, mainly to note if the sub-processes are consistent with the authority. Compliance violations occur when the reviewing errors listed in Chapter 5 are found.

Traditionally, compliance and its auditing has relied on a combination of training, experience and common sense. These demand a great deal of interpretation by the auditor, along with an understanding of the organization and its technical work. In most cases, a sample of the procedures or actual working practices are used for comparison with this norm. Often, the auditor relies on intuition or a hunch when exploring a line of reasoning or possible area of non-compliance. Together, these non-systematic aspects of auditing can lead to wide variations in auditing results: two auditors with similar training and experience can produce widely different results, based on their differing views, interests and backgrounds.

QPL provides a systematic method of compliance auditing which is an alternative to the traditional experience-based method. It does not deprive the auditor of his or her valuable experience and the creative use of detective work and hunches during an audit. But it provides an assurance of consistent auditing at a common basic level, and a systematic means of documenting the results of the audit. Since QPL is process-oriented, it provides repeated checks on cause and effect relationships, and guides the auditor in pursuing lines of enquiry.

While compliance work tends to put most emphasis on checking for violations during audits, it is also part of process design and requires a high degree of creativity. The regulations to be complied with provide a constraint on an enterprise's activities and their structure, but those activities must be designed to suit its own needs, not those of the regulation. The goal of good process design is to provide processes which match the enterprise's needs most effectively. Compliance auditing assists this creative activity by directing it along the channels permitted by the authority.

Compliance and conformance

These terms are usually confused and used interchangeably. However, they refer to at least two very different aspects of quality: one process-oriented and the other product-oriented. To avoid confusion, this book will use them only as follows.

Compliance: The development and checking of a process to ensure that it does not contradict a standard or set of regulations or other requirement.

Conformance: The development and checking of products and other concrete objects produced by a process, to ensure that they do not violate a standard or other definition of the product.

For example, a company making children's toys needs to *comply* with various EC regulations and might also comply with ISO 9002, but the toys themselves *conform* to standards for such products. A pharmaceuticals company must *comply* with the FDA regulations for manufacturing drugs (a process), but the drugs *conform* to specified formulations and packaging regulations, which deal with products.

The remainder of this chapter deals only with the process-oriented view, namely with compliance. Conformance is a separate issue, which is left to the individual technical disciplines dealt with in a standard.

Steps for achieving compliance

When an enterprise wishes to establish that it is compliant with a standard or regulation, it goes through a sequence of steps which tend to follow a common pattern. Figure 6.1 shows the steps in this sequence.

Step 1: Set policy

To start the process of compliance, the enterprise needs to set its policy. It needs to decide which regulations and standards are appropriate for its activities and the kind of approaches to compliance it wishes to follow. It may choose a traditional approach, where specialists such as quality controllers are responsible for enforcing its mandatory practices and procedures. It may delegate this responsibility to line managers and others involved in the production and/or delivery of goods or services. Or, in line with recent trends, it may choose the path of total quality and encourage *all* staff to take

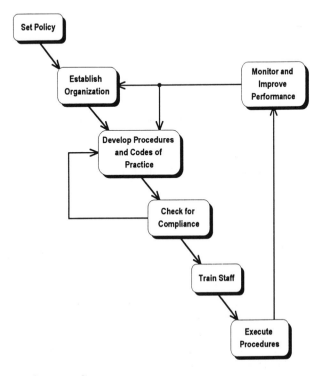

Figure 6.1 Steps for compliance

an active role in the processes. With proper training, such a policy encourages all members to learn the rules and procedures and to take a keen interest not only in their practice, but also in their weaknesses and possible improvements.

Step 2: Establish organization

Following identification of its policies, goals and values, the enterprise then needs to establish an operational framework. This will depend on the nature of its work, as well as the feasibility of different approaches to internal communications. Traditionally, organizations are based in functional departments, with similar or related skills in each department. However, this approach is giving way to more broadly based, less hierarchical structures, making use of the opportunities offered by modern tele-communications to replace bureaucratic levels of management.

The organization also needs to review responsibilities for compliance. For conventional compliance monitoring, this would be a quality assurance department or its equivalent, which ensures that procedures are developed, promulgated and observed. More distributed compliance systems need more emphasis on training and communications channels, for widespread ownership of procedures and a common understanding of how they are put into practice. A common acknowledgement of everyone's responsibility for ensuring compliance is always required.

A single person is usually required to take responsibility for the overall compliance process and for links with the external bodies which will carry out the eventual compliance audit or assessment.

Step 3: Develop procedures and codes of practice

The development of the operational documents for an organization is a significant activity which will affect all aspects of its work. When compliance is also a consideration, then the organization also needs to take into account the regulations and other rules which will constrain its operations. A considerable amount of effort in later steps can be saved if they are taken into account at this early stage.

Step 4: Check for compliance

After the procedures and codes of practice have been developed, they need to be checked for compliance with the regulations and policy determined in step 1. This involves a review of the former, to see which parts need to be checked for compliance. The regulations and policy are then interpreted to determine if there is a conflict between their requirements and the proposed procedures and codes of practice.

Any compliance violations are noted and sent back to step 3, where the procedures documents are revised. The dynamic flow between these two steps sets up a cycle of development and checking, where working documentation is evolved—documents produced in a single attempt are more likely to fail. The result is a set of procedures and codes of practice which meet both the needs of the organization and the policies and regulations to which it is subject.

Step 5: Train staff

After the procedures and codes of practice have passed a final compliance check in step 4, the organization can now devote its energies to implementing them. This starts with the training of staff. In addition, the procedure documents need to be promoted internally, to educate staff how their work will be affected.

Step 6: Execute procedures

After staff are properly prepared, the procedures are ready for operation. Since they have already been checked for compliance, this should not be a problem at this stage. However, it is essential to establish an ongoing monitoring programme, to determine local problems in the implementation of procedures and to provide feedback on the effectiveness of training programmes.

Step 7: Monitor and improve performance

Modern organizations are always improving their processes, obtaining the necessary data needed to monitor their effectiveness. This leads to a quality improvement loop, from the previous step of executing procedures to the steps which can modify the organization and its procedures. Thus, based on the results of this step, the next step will be either step 2 or step 3.

An example of a quality loop—the Rooney Loop—is described in Appendix 4.

A systematic approach to compliance

Following the seven steps given above, any organization can create a system which meets its needs and complies with the relevant policies and regulations. Most organizations follow steps more or less the same as these. However, there is a wide range of variation in how well they go about this. Some go down an excessively formal route, resulting in red tape and bureaucracy. Staff know what to do, but they are deprived of initiative: they are disempowered. Other organizations produce a workable system, but which has many loose ends and inefficient processes built in. Others are haphazard in their approach and go through many attempts before they achieve a compliant set of procedures.

QPL provides a systematic and logical framework for management and quality systems, and this also applies to systems for compliance. It does this with the *process template*, which is the set of standards or regulations which must be complied with. However, it is also a model of a strategic process, a guide for improving the organization and its processes. As shown earlier in this book, QPL provides a common language for describing processes at all levels, the detailed as well as the strategic, and it provides a foundation for linking process design with process compliance.

The remainder of this chapter explores the use of QPL in this context and provides examples of how it is done in practice.

6.2 COMPLIANCE IN A QPL FRAMEWORK

QPL's process-oriented view of an organization provides a framework for compliance. This is achieved with a configurable process model of the standard or regulation to be complied with, which is called the template process. The organization wishing to achieve compliance does not have to tailor its systems directly to the processes of the standard or regulation, but rather configures that document to its own operational processes. This section will demonstrate how to configure these template processes, through the use of authorities and inherited properties.

Levels of detail and class membership

In QPL, compliance is based on two simple ideas: levels of detail and class membership. Before going into the way these work for processes, they can be illustrated with a simple example. Rather than our usual QPL network, let's take a more common type of network, the transport network.

Suppose you want to visit a friend in another city and need to plan the route. You look at your road atlas, which shows major roads between cities and within them. This tells you the main route to your friend's house, but how do you get to the house once you reach the city? This requires a more detailed street plan.

But once you read the street plan, you notice an odd thing: the two maps you are using do not agree. None of the roads on the atlas's map seems to appear on the street plan, so you have no way of knowing where to go in the city once you reach it. Clearly the two maps do not agree. We say that the more detailed map does not *comply* with the other map, because the details of its features do not correspond to those of the other map.

At first, compliance appears to be only a matter of detail: the second map complies with the first if its details are consistent with it. However, compliance is more than that. The classes of information between the two maps must also be compatible. For example, the roads in the two maps could be in identical locations, but with different types of vehicles permitted. Suppose that the first map indicated that a road was a high-speed road, from which bicycles and pedestrians were banned. However, the second map indicated that it was an ordinary road, which anyone could use. While the location of the roads is identical on the two maps, the classes of vehicle are different. The more detailed map does not comply with the other map, because it indicates a different class membership for the same road.

This example illustrates the two ways in which a network can fail to comply with another, basic network. First, by having more detailed information which contradicts that of the basis. Secondly, by indicating a different class membership than in the basic network. The same approach to non-compliance is taken with a QPL network, where the links are information items rather than roads or footpaths, and where the 'nodes' are processes rather than physical locations on a map.

Hierarchy and class membership

Hierarchy in QPL

The previous chapters contain many examples where a process step is expanded into a network of sub-processes. Each sub-process can be further expanded into additional hierarchies of processes. This helps us to chart, analyse and understand the complexities of organizations, by concentrating only on a particular level of detail at one time.

As with the maps of the previous example, the more detailed process descriptions in the hierarchy must agree with the higher-level process descriptions if they are to remain compliant. Chapter 5 provides two checks for this kind of compliance, under the category 'Hierarchical incompatibility'. Hierarchical mismatch errors focus on information items—the links in the network. Hierarchical incompleteness errors focus on process and sub-processes, and mean that the sum of the parts is not equal to the whole.

Class membership and the elements of QPL

What is the QPL equivalent of class membership? On a map, it is obvious that certain streets are restricted in what can travel on them: a car may not travel on a footpath, and heavy goods vehicles are not allowed on some roads.

What is the equivalent for a QPL network? For the most part, class membership is concerned with the information items which are input to and output from processes. In checking an operational process for compliance with a template, we enquire whether its information items are members of the class of the template process. If they are not, then there is a compliance violation. For example, if a standard requires that a process handles all vehicles, but the procedure specifies that it is applicable only to automobiles, then the procedure is not compliant.

Class membership also applies to elements other than information items. The owner for a process must be a member of the class of process owners permitted in the template. In the case of control, any conditions in the process must be at least as restrictive as those in the template.

The conditions for class membership compliance are expressed through the two inheritance incompatibility errors discussed in the previous chapter.

Expressing compliance in QPL

QPL expresses compliance through the authority construct. As defined in Chapter 2, an authority provides a description of a process, or basis for decisions within a process. However, an authority need not be a complete description of a process, and it is this situation where we say that the process complies with the authority. Whenever a process description is shown as an authority for a process on a QPL diagram, then the process must comply with that authority. Figure 6.2 shows a simple example of this way of indicating compliance. The dashed line indicates that process B needs to comply with process A, but that A is not an explicit and detailed description of B. A dashed line is used in QPL only to represent non-explicit authorities. In this example, the authority is non-explicit because there is no step-by-step description of the process which inherits characteristics. When the instructions for a process are explicit, an information item is shown as the authority, and a solid information line is used to connect it to the process.

Connecting a template to an operational process

The QPL approach to compliance starts with identifying the standards, regulations and other requirements to be complied with. We then build a process model—the *template* of these requirements. Then the template is connected into the QPL description of the organization's processes (the 'operational processes').

In QPL, this connection is established first by identifying the template as an authority to the overall operational process. Then we examine how the parts of the operational process are affected by the template: in other words, we determine the connections between sub-processes in the template and sub-processes in the operational process.

For complex templates, establishing connections can be quite complicated. Therefore, it is simplified by dealing with only a limited number at a time. This can be done by dividing the template into its main sub-processes, and checking the connections of each of them in turn. Figure 6.3 shows an example from the ISO 9001 process description of Appendix 2. In this case, the sub-process dealing with inspection and testing is shown.

By this stage, the process to be complied with (the template) has been sub-divided into more manageable sub-processes. Next, these will be connected with the appropriate parts of the process being checked for compliance.

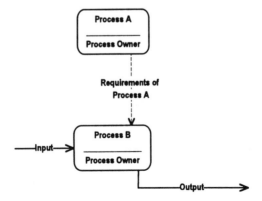

Figure 6.2 Indicating compliance in QPL

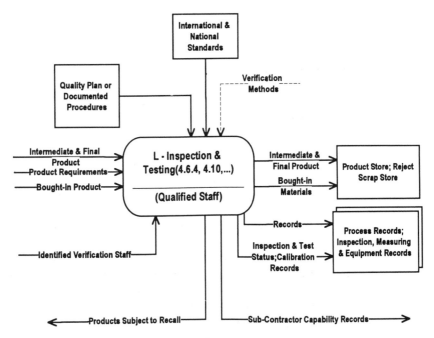

Figure 6.3 ISO 9001 subset for inspection and testing

An example

The purchasing example of Chapter 5 provides an illustration of how to connect a process template into an operational process. The sub-set of ISO 9001 dealing with inspection and testing (L), shown in Figure 6.3, will be connected to the revised purchasing process (Figure 5.5). The only sub-process to which this authority applies is that for 'Receive and check goods'. Therefore, the sub-set of the template is connected only with this process step, as shown in Figure 6.4 (which is a fragment of the full process). If we were to connect all relevant ISO 9001 sub-processes to this operational process, then we would also connect J—Purchased product conformance.

Adding part of ISO 9001 as an authority for this purchasing step has implications for process design, as the process may need changes to achieve compliance. This is explained in the next section.

6.3   AUDITING: THE MEASUREMENT OF COMPLIANCE

After the process template is connected to the operational process, we are ready to examine the latter for compliance. The formal mechanism for this is the compliance audit, the subject of this section. QPL provides a framework for the audit, through its graphical representation of processes and compliance and with the process analysis checks listed in Chapter 5.

In compliance auditing, we check that an operational process meets all the requirements of the template process. As noted earlier, this reduces to two checks:

- that the operational process contains no direct contradictions of the template process
- that class membership of the operational process is compatible with that of the template process.

In practice, these checks are applied with the same analysis techniques discussed in Chapter 5. The error types are identical for compliance auditing. However, since they are applied after connecting in the template process, errors revealed will tend to be compliance violations. Correcting the errors leads to a process which is compliant with the template.

The auditing approach of this chapter applies to formal compliance checks of process definitions—usually in the form of procedures, work instructions and codes of practice. However, compliance audits often include a check on how these documents are actually applied in the organization (see BS 7229, 1989: Paragraphs 3.1 and 4.1). This is a check to see that people in the organization actually do what the documents say they do. This type of audit can also be handled in QPL, by treating the system at a very low level and noting the actual processes of people being audited. In addition to the written authorities of procedures etc., we also need to note unwritten authorities which affect people's actions. For example, a workgroup may have a long-standing habit of taking a break at a particular point in the day, and such a regular practice will act as an authority for their work. In this situation, the auditor must also check that the breaks do not conflict with other rules of the organization, as well as with the standards or regulations being audited against.

SOME OTHER VIEWS OF COMPLIANCE AUDITING

Below are extracts showing two writers' definitions of compliance auditing.

The assessment of a quality system against a particular standard or set of requirements by internal audit and review is known as a first party assessment or approval scheme. If an external customer makes the assessment of a supplier against either its own or a national or international standard, a second party scheme is in operation. The external assessment by an independent organization, not involved in any contract between customer and supplier, but acceptable to them both, is known as an independent third party assessment scheme. The latter usually involves some form of certification or registration by the assessment body. ...

Many organizations have found that the effort of designing and implementing a written quality management system, good enough to stand up to external independent third party assessment, has been extremely rewarding in:

- involving staff and improving morale;
- better process control;

- reduced wastage;
- reduced customer service costs.

(Oakland, 1989: 168–9)

The task of the auditor [for an ISO 9001 audit] is to:

- confirm that the documented QMS [quality management system] has the capability to be effectively used in the management of the organization and the products of the organization
- confirm by way of sample auditing the use of the documented QMS in the management of current work
- confirm that the practices employed meet the methods and principles contained in ISO 9001 taking into account the ISO guides.

(TickIT, 1992)

Using QPL for compliance auditing

It is useful to think of compliance auditing as a set of steps from initial process description through correction of any violations which are uncovered by the audit. Initially, we prepare a QPL description of the operational process which is to be compliant with a higher-level process template. Next, we express compliance through the authority construct, connecting the template's sub-processes into their correct positions in the operational process. Then compliance is inspected with the analysis checks of Chapter 5. This provides a list of compliance violations. Finally, the list is used to assist in redesigning the processes.

These steps are described in more detail below.

Step 1: Design the process

The first step is to design and document the organization's processes, as described in Chapters 3 and 4. At this stage avoid too much attention to the standards which need to be complied with. Focusing on external standards rather than internal requirements distorts the organization's procedures and diverts them from addressing its own needs and culture. However, it is wise to keep a knowledge of compliance requirements in the background, so that no direct contradictions will be embodied in the processes.

Step 2: Connect the template's sub-processes to those described in the organization's procedures

This is described in Section 6.2.

Step 3: Review the combined process

Now the criteria of Chapter 5 are applied in a reviewing process. Since the template sub-processes are connected as authorities, the error types will determine exactly which compliance violations have occurred. Corresponding to the compliance requirements of hierarchy and class membership, most violations will be one of the four types listed under hierarchical incompatibility and inheritance incompatibility (Tables 5.3 and 5.4.) However, other errors can arise when templates are connected to a process. For example, a process owner specified in a template may be missing in the process (missing ownership in Table 5.1), or a procedure may not cover the full scope of the template (authority mismatch in Table 5.2).

The most common types of compliance violations are listed in Table 6.1. They are shown with their error type names, from Tables 5.1 to 5.4. The table also provides a suggestion for correcting the violation. Where the term 'process' is shown in the table, it refers to the operational process or its description in a procedure or other document.

While any of the other types of error can also result in a compliance audit, they tend to indicate problems with the process itself rather than in compliance with the template. It is advisable to correct these errors first, and then to recheck the combined process to reveal compliance violations.

Step 4: Redesign the process to avoid compliance violations

Step 3 provides a list of the compliance violations in the process. It is also a list of constraints for redesign of the process. For example, an inconsistent process (the

Table 6.1 Common compliance violations

Description	Error types	Correction
General violations		
Incomplete process—the scope of the standard or regulation is not dealt with completely.	Authority mismatch Hierarchical incompleteness Broken path	Add additional sub-processes or otherwise increase the scope of the operational process.
Inconsistent process—sub-processes in the operational process use information in different ways (i.e. the operational process is inconsistent in its interpretation of the template).	Inheritance mismatch	Reinterpret the template to achieve consistency, or redefine the sub-processes to achieve consistency in applying the template.
Non-comprehensive process—there are certain feasible conditions or types of information which cannot be handled by the process.	Inheritance mismatch	Widen the scope of the operational process.

Table 6.1 (*continued*)

Description	Error types	Correction
Process violations		
The details of the process contradict those of the template.	Authority mismatch Inheritance mismatch	Redefine the operational process to ensure agreement with the template.
Information violations		
Information items in the template are incorrectly represented by the process (e.g. the template states that a form should contain a particular item, but the operational process omits this item).	Inheritance mismatch	Correct the operational process.
An information item in the template is of the wrong type (e.g. an archive in the template is represented in the operational process as an information store).	Inheritance mismatch Misprocessed information	Correct the representation of the information item and modify sub-processes, if necessary.
Authority violations		
An authority in the process is missing, unclear or inexplicit.	Authority mismatch	Add an explicit authority where required.
The authority for the process contradicts that of the template.	Authority mismatch	Re-examine the connections from the template to the sub-processes. Then modify the authority in the process to provide compatibility with the template.
An authority for the process has a lower scope than that of the template (an authority for a sub-process does not have sufficient scope to cover the requirements of the template).	Authority mismatch	Widen the scope of the authority within the operational process.
Ownership violations		
Definition of an owner in the process conflicts with that of the template.	Inheritance mismatch (Possibly) missing ownership	Redefine the process owner in the operational process, or make the owner more explicit.
Control violations		
The conditions for executing the process or one of its sub-processes conflict with those in the template.	Inheritance mismatch	Redefine the condition in the operational process, or make it more explicit.

operational process is inconsistent in its interpretation of the template) suggests that we need to look at the authorities for the conflicting sub-processes. Then the sub-processes need to be redesigned to provide a common way of working. A violation resulting in a non-comprehensive process—where the template requires the process to handle conditions it was not designed for—demands an obvious redesign, with a wider range of conditions.

When the process has been redesigned to handle the compliance violations, it needs to be rechecked; new errors, either internal to the process or new compliance violations, may have been introduced. We also must be careful not to introduce new complications, red tape or inefficiencies in our attempt to design compliant processes. That is where the creativity of process design is to be found. Adequate process design provides processes which are compliant with the demands of internal policy and external standards. Creative design does the same, but also creates processes which are efficient, effective and empowering to those who put them into effect.

An example

As an example of compliance auditing, we will continue the example of the previous section, which connected the inspection and testing (I&T) subset of the ISO 9001

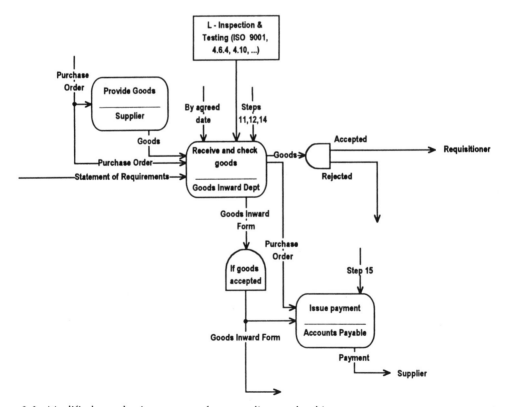

Figure 6.4 Modified purchasing process for compliance checking

standard to the purchasing example of the previous chapter. Figure 6.3 is the I&T subset of ISO 9001, while Figure 6.4 shows its connection to the purchasing process. It is now straightforward to do a compliance audit on the purchasing procedure, based on the template and its connection to the process. The results are shown in Table 6.2, which lists each violation, the description of the error from Table 6.1 and the correction required.

It is also worth noting that much of the procedure does agree with the ISO 9001 template. These include:

- Inputs agree with the template—both the 'Bought-in product' and 'Product requirements' are included (as 'Goods' and 'Statement of requirements'). The third input in the template—'Intermediate and final product' does not apply to purchasing.
- 'List of recent suppliers' fulfils the same function as 'Supplier capability records' in the template, and so compliance is achieved.

Table 6.2 Purchasing process: inspection and testing compliance violations

Compliance violation	Type of violation	Correction required
No authority comparable to 'Quality plan or documented work instructions' is shown.	Missing authority	Write up steps 11, 12 and 14 as work instructions and ensure that staff are trained in their use.
There is no evidence that purchasing staff are qualified to carry out inspection and testing.	Missing ownership	Document how purchasing staff are to be qualified or trained to carry out this role, or use technical specialists for inspection or testing.
The procedure does not provide for the possible involvement of an ultimate purchaser in the inspection process.*	Missing ownership	Document how such involvement is to be achieved.
The procedure does not provide a store for rejected bought-in items (it only assumes that they will be returned immediately, which is overly simplistic).	Unprocessed information —information item is of the wrong type (channel rather than an information store).	Provide for storage of suspect or rejected goods inward, until they can be returned to the supplier or used elsewhere.
The procedure does not specify that the annotated purchase orders are to be archived after inspection, as required by the template ('Inspection, measuring and equipment records').	Inheritance mismatch (template information is incorrectly represented by the procedure).	Provide explicit instructions in the work instructions on how to file and store purchase orders.

* 'Where specified in the contract, the supplier's customer or the customer's representative shall be afforded the right to verify at the subcontractor's premises and the supplier's premises that subcontracted product conforms to specified requirements' (ISO 9001, 1994: Paragraph 4.6.4.2).

● The amended purchase order does provide a record of I&T status, thus partially fulfilling the template's requirement that this information be retained. (However, the procedure does not indicate that it be stored as an archive, as required by the template.)

6.4 PROBLEMS WITH COMPLIANCE

From the discussion to this point, it may appear that compliance is straightforward, if not trivial. It seems to follow automatically, once we have established the processes of an organization and of the templates which are relevant. Unfortunately, compliance often is not as simple as this. A substantial amount of interpretation is often required, or there may be ambiguities which need to be resolved. This section is a brief discussion of some of the problems which arise, along with guidance for resolving them in the QPL framework.

Conflicts of interest in compliance

In certain cases of unwritten authorities, a conflict of interest may appear. This is common in legal cases, where specialists in the same technical field are called upon to provide expert opinion by opposing sides in a lawsuit or trial. At first glance, this appears to contradict the concept of a single process template, since equivalent authorities will attempt to justify different processes.

The legal process itself provides the resolution to this apparent contradiction. The opposing legal counsel will attempt to find the weaknesses in the opposite technical opinion, thus weakening their case. The result of this process will be an opinion, by the judge or jury, which is a single authority. In forming their judgement, they will consider the arguments of both sides and from them derive a consolidated opinion of the correct authority which applies to the case.

What to do with supersets?

An interesting problem in compliance occurs when a procedure deals with a process of wider scope than a template. For example, a purchasing procedure for a company deals with far more than just the requirements of ISO 9001, including financial recording, staff management and communication between purchasing and other departments. If the procedure is of wider scope than the template, can it still be compliant?

With the QPL approach, it is clear how to handle this situation. When the sub-processes in the template are connected to the operational process, it will be clear which parts of the latter are not affected by the template: they will not have authorities based on the template. Clearly, those sub-processes in the procedure are outside the scope of the template and thus are outside the scope of compliance checking.

Multiple compliance

In a complicated world, companies increasingly need to comply with more than one regulation, law or standard. In QPL terminology, their operational processes are subject to more than a single template. This provides a difficult environment for these companies, where they are tempted to pay more attention to the needs of compliance than to those of their customers, employees or shareholders.

For example, European companies are subject to almost 300 regulations produced by the European Commission. In addition, they have to comply with national laws, international standards relevant to their products and contracts with their customers.

The approach of this chapter should make it easier to achieve multiple compliance, as it allows us to note the authorities for only one sub-process at a time. The same compliance checks can be applied, and redesign of the processes will lead to compliance with the multiple authorities.

This raises the question of whether it is possible to check whether two regulations or other templates are non-contradictory. This is a central issue in multiple compliance, since it is obviously impossible to comply with two regulations which require contradictory processes. Unfortunately, this cannot be proven except in limited (and usually trivial) circumstances. In the general case, two templates can be demonstrated only to be contradictory by use of a counterexample, i.e. by connecting them to an operational process and demonstrating that they require contradictory processing by a sub-process to which they both apply.

Authority exceptions

There are certain circumstances where an authority can be overridden at a lower level. For example, a line manager can delegate to more junior members of staff, or a company manual can provide lists of spending authority for different grades of staff. The question arises how to check compliance in this situation.

Such exceptions can be broken down into two possibilities:

- the template process states explicitly where exceptions can occur and how to delegate authority
- the template process makes no allowance for exceptions.

The first case is obviously well defined and should cause no problems when checking for compliance to such a rule.

The second case, however, is harder to check. At first, it would seem obvious that if no exceptions are allowed for, then any exception constitutes a compliance violation. However, a grey area arises when a situation falls outside the scope of an authority. For example, a manager may be tasked with certain authority for a range of circumstances. What happens outside that range? This situation is common in battlefield situations, where the unforeseen is commonplace and not included in procedures, yet those in charge must make decisions.

Fortunately, this situation is straightforward, from the point of view of compliance. From the perspective of those carrying out a procedure, they are responsible for complying with it only within the limits of its applicability. Outside those limits, the question of compliance does not apply, unless there is a higher authority to which both the procedure and those responsible for its execution are accountable.

When this situation occurs, we must also ask, of course, whether the procedure needs to be revised to incorporate the conditions which it does not currently handle. This may be a compliance violation—such as an incomplete process or non-comprehensive process—if there is a higher authority. Where there is no higher authority, then a failure mode error may apply: that of process exception.

6.5   SUMMARY OF THE QPL APPROACH TO COMPLIANCE

The key points of the QPL approach to compliance are:

- *Compliance* is the development and checking of a process to ensure that it does not contradict a standard or set of regulations.
- A *template* is the process model of the regulation, standard or other document which must be complied with.
- Compliance is established on a QPL diagram by *connecting* one process to another process, as an authority.
- A template is connected to an operational process by connecting each of its sub-processes to the applicable sub-processes of the latter. As before, they are connected as authorities.
- *Compliance auditing* checks that an operational process meets all the requirements of the template process. This reduces to two checks:
  - that the operational process contains no direct contradictions of the template process (hierarchical compatibility)
  - that class membership of the operational process is compatible with that of the template process (inheritance compatibility).
- The compliance audit is carried out using QPL's standard analysis checks, after the template has been connected to the operational process.
- Process design is the creative act of creating workable processes which comply with external and internal requirements for an organization.

Designing processes for change

OVERVIEW

The modern world is changing rapidly and demanding a rapid pace of change from all organizations. This results from a combination of factors: a more open and competitive world economy, improved training of workers, better technology and a greater emphasis on quality and customer satisfaction. The old functionally oriented and hierarchical organization is being replaced by the process-oriented organization, emphasizing the whole value chain from inputs to customer delivery.

To cope with change we need to address the dynamics of organizations. Earlier chapters have dealt with process statics—the aspects which do not change. This chapter deals with dynamics—changes to inputs and outputs, cycle time for a process, incorporating internal changes into a process and dealing with external changes which affect a process and an organization.

QPL provides a framework for designing dynamic processes, supplemented by powerful techniques that focus the designer's attention on the objectives and help to avoid inefficient and ineffective processes. Four guidelines are particularly useful:

- *Process balance*, ensuring that all elements of a process are in balance, so that a change to any of them can be met by a balancing change in another element.
- *Flow process analysis*, analysing processes for inefficiencies, particularly in wasted effort or inefficient materials transfer and storage.
- *Simplicity*, where QPL provides a simple measurement which guides the process designer toward an optimal combination of process steps and the instructions for those steps.
- *Adaptability*, providing for the key enablers of empowerment and process feedback.

Process analysis, introduced in Chapter 5, also applies to dynamic processes, and a checklist is provided to supplement the lists in previous chapters for static aspects.

The QPL approach can also be applied in business process re-engineering (BPR) and change management. There are QPL-based techniques for re-engineering, including the use of process simplification, hierarchies and inheritance. QPL templates—introduced in Chapter 6—provide an approach to benchmarking and process improvement. Finally, QPL offers an approach to change in organizations, providing a model of the transition from an existing to a new process.

There is an intrinsic impermanence in industry, and indeed the management task is to recreate the company in a new form every year. Industry is a bit like the human body. The cells are continuously dying and unless new cells are created, sooner or later the whole thing will collapse and disappear. These three potent forces—people, technology and competition—mean that industry cannot afford to become institutionalized. We have to be more adaptable, and quicker on our feet than many of the other great national institutions which create the external conditions under which we operate. I would imagine that industry confronts and copes with more forms of change than any other branch of our life.

John Harvey-Jones, 1989: 18

7.1 PROCESSES AND PROCEDURES IN A CHANGING WORLD

For a business in today's environment, there is no possibility of standing still to reflect on one's success. The competition is always innovating, either to produce new and better products or to reduce their costs. Competition is on a global level, and it is never certain exactly who will be the major players in the future. Political, regulatory and economic environments and the conditions of trade are changing rapidly, as are the markets for goods and services. Business customers are changing too: they want long-term and cooperative relationships with suppliers.

This list of external changes is matched by the changes within organizations. The pace of changing technology is as rapid as it has ever been. Middle management is being replaced by a combination of computer and communications-based technology and a more responsible and empowered workforce. The workforce is better educated than ever and demands collaboration, not commands, in carrying out the organization's objectives.

The traditional approach to process change places the emphasis on the internal and the functional. Managers are seen as controlling processes rather than facilitating or owning them. There is little or no measurement of current processes, and thus no way to determine if the changes have achieved their objectives or even if they are an improvement.

The new, process-oriented organization, however, puts the emphasis on customers and the value-added processes which serve them. Measurement is built into all processes, providing a clear view of the current situation, the proposed changes and the results of change.

The QPL approach supports this sort of evolving and vital organization. Previous chapters have dealt with the constant, unchanging aspects of processes. This chapter concentrates on the dynamics of processes—that is, how processes change information and objects, and how they themselves are changed. It deals with three aspects of change:

- how processes handle changing information
- how the environment of and technology used by processes can change
- how to change processes over time.

In dealing with organizational change, process designers have a choice of paths to follow. They can act as a break on the change by digging in their heels and insisting that the existing systems are perfectly adequate. Alternatively, they can facilitate change and work sympathetically with senior management, with those implementing changes and with those affected by the changes. The goal of any quality system is the continual improvement of processes, through critical analysis, deep understanding and creative thought. Later, the chapter provides guidelines for designing adaptable processes, harnessing feedback, and planning for improvements.

7.2 STATICS AND DYNAMICS

> You could not step twice into the same river; for other waters are ever flowing on to you. All is flux, nothing stays still.
>
> *Heraclitus, c. 500 BC*

A static system is an illusion

Organizations often appear to be static and unchanging, but in reality they are continually transforming themselves, like Heraclitus' river. This becomes obvious when an enterprise is undergoing rapid change, to cope with changes in its environment. But it is also true even when the enterprise is not actively reorganizing. Input and output consist of streams of discrete and changing information items, such as application forms or membership cards. Authorities need to change regularly to cope with new conditions, and the people filling roles are also changed periodically.

If it is not always obvious that change is part of reality, this is merely due to being too far away from the process. When we get closer, the change is easier to see. Chapter 6 illustrates the principle of compliance with a map of streets and other transport links. This resembles the view from an airplane at high altitude, where it is difficult even to distinguish the traffic on roads. Even if we can identify heavy goods vehicles or cars, we cannot see pedestrians at that altitude, without the aid of a telescope or binoculars. However, as the plane descends, we gradually become aware of smaller objects moving along the roads and paths, first a horse, then a cyclist, finally pedestrians and pets.

Once we are in the airport terminal we stop thinking about transport networks altogether, and just notice the bustle of people moving in all directions. Yet the airport is just as much a network of traffic links as the roads noticed a few minutes before. People, airport buses, carts and luggage trucks are in a constant state of motion, with a clear reason for moving from one location to another (to catch a plane, to get home, to get a bite to eat, etc.). All networks are dynamic systems, facilitating the flow of objects or information.

A QPL diagram is also a dynamic system, with its process boxes dealing with a stream of changing information or material objects. For example, look at the fragment of the purchasing process in Figure 6.4. 'Receive and check goods' accepts goods and a purchase order as input, and passes them on to other processes. None of these remains constant. The process box may regulate the receipt and checking of several items in a shipment. The same process will be used for the hundreds or thousands of purchase orders which are processed each year.

In the previous chapters, systems have been treated as static, as it was unnecessary to add additional concepts for change. Also, it was easier to view a snapshot of the system, frozen at a point in time. But in the real world, systems deal with change. The methods developed to this point need to be extended to deal with the different types of change.

Types of change

What types of change are relevant to processes? There are four aspects:

● Changes in the quantities of input and output (as shown in the previous example).
● Changes in time, mainly the time needed by a process to complete a cycle (i.e. to transform a unit of input into a unit of output).
● Internal changes, such as the use of feedback loops for process improvement and other changes to the process—the need for continuous internal change is one of the foundations of total quality management. For example, one of Deming's fourteen key principles is: 'Improve constantly and forever the system of production and service, to improve quality and productivity, and thus constantly decrease costs' (quoted in Scherkenbach, 1986: 35).
● Imposed changes in the external environment, such as a change in the conditions of trading or the need to expand output.

Changes in input and output

A process transforms a stream of input into one of output. Thus, processes are always concerned with changes in information items. In addition, there is a natural and normal variation in those items; the attributes of individual items differ slightly. For example, the process of renting a car deals with differing types of models and different renters, although the process for the rental itself remains the same. On the output side, there is also a variation in the quality of what is produced, such as the cleanliness of the car. One of the main goals of quality management is to control and reduce this variation. W. Edwards Deming, one of the pioneers of modern quality management, defines quality as 'a predictable degree of uniformity and dependability, at low cost and suited to the market' (quoted in Oakland, 1989: 285). This accepts some degree of variation, as opposed to the more conventional, and perhaps unrealistic, definitions of 'in accordance with the specification', 'fitness for purpose' or 'right first time'.

Changes in time

As any manufacturer or supplier of services knows, delivery of goods on time is one of the essential components of quality. Customers will not stay with any supplier which is unreliable in its delivery times. Since production and delivery ultimately depend on the processes used by the supplier, we need to consider two key measures of time:

- lead time, the time between receipt of an order and the start of the process which fulfils it
- cycle time, the time which a process consumes or requires to convert an item or unit of input into output.

For example, if a company provides a service repairing washing machines, it needs to pay attention to the time spent responding to a call-out, and to the average time spent on each job. In this highly competitive industry, the company which can simplify its processes and reduce lead and cycle times will have a distinct advantage over its competitors on two counts, both for the reduction in employee costs and for the improved service to the customer.

Time has another role in process management: the coordination of process steps within a process. This most commonly occurs when there are several steps contributing to a single process step. These need to be synchronized, and the most common mechanism is that of time. 'Be sure to provide your delivery by 10 a.m. tomorrow' is a typical statement.

In QPL, time is treated as an implicit information item; that is, one which is available to all processes, and which does not require an explicit flow line to connect processes. This can be done because accurate clocks and watches enable people and machines to synchronize themselves and the processes which they manage. However, if we make this information item explicit, it can serve other uses. For example, Figure 7.1 shows a feedback loop which measures the elapsed time of a process and uses it as feedback for process improvement.

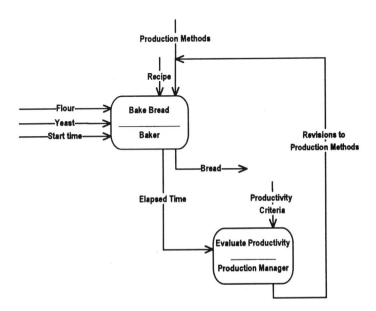

Figure 7.1 Explicit use of time in a QPL feedback loop

The next section provides other examples of implicit information which can sometimes be treated as explicit, such as distance travelled and resource usage.

Internal changes

Internal changes result from a drive for improvement in operations, and can range from gradual changes, such as work on small-scale processes by quality improvement teams, to the major changes resulting from BPR or the introduction of new technology.

For smaller-scale changes to processes, the techniques of flow process analysis (sometimes shortened to 'process analysis' in industrial engineering) can be extremely useful. One of the pioneers of this subject, Junichi Ishiwata (1991: 18), provides five considerations which direct the analysis:

(1) Study the flow of processes.
(2) Find where waste exists in the flow of processes.
(3) Consider whether the processes can be rearranged into a more efficient sequence.
(4) Consider whether the flow of processes is smooth enough and whether there are any problems in the equipment layout or the transport system.
(5) Consider whether everything being done at each process is really necessary and what would happen if superfluous tasks were removed.

Section 7.3 provides more material on flow process analysis and how QPL is used to support it.

Imposed changes

Unlike internal changes, which are about the internal operations of a process, imposed changes are those which occur in the environment of the process. They include any of the elements of QPL which can affect a process: its input and output, the authority which regulates the process, the role which is responsible for the process and the conditions for activating the process. Typical examples are:

- A competitor cuts the price of a similar product, resulting in a reduction in orders (change to an input—orders for the product).
- A warehouse is flooded, resulting in a sudden loss of storage capacity for the manufactured product (change to an output—the manufactured product—which can no longer be stored once produced).
- A new law regulating drugs manufacture means that an established process can no longer be used (change to an authority—the new law).
- An old skill, such as traditional furniture manufacture, gradually dies, resulting in a shortage of craftspeople able to make a particular type of table (change to the owner of the process of making this type of table).
- The average age of applicants for car insurance is decreasing, resulting in more high-risk applications—those under 25 years old and those with high-performance cars (change in the condition for a process—the proportion of high-risk applications increases).

While each of these cases results in a change in the external environment, outside the control of the process itself, a change to the process is often required. For example, if a drop in orders arises from price competition, it may be necessary to redesign the process to make it more efficient. A loss in storage capacity for an output may mean that the process is halted temporarily, or it may mean that the process needs at least a temporary connection to another process which can utilize the output immediately. If no qualified person can be found for a process, then we must either train someone to the required level of skill, redesign the process, or accept that the process must be abandoned. In each of these cases, the cause of the change is external to the process affected, but the change is directed primarily at the process itself.

How QPL handles dynamics

QPL provides a comprehensive framework for process design. Previous chapters covered aspects of static processes. The remainder of this chapter shows how to design for the dynamics of processes and for BPR. The following sections look at:

- Guidelines for good process design, providing a comprehensive set of guidelines for designing processes. These are general purpose and apply to all aspects of processes. They also assist the design of robust processes capable of withstanding change or, when required, facilitating change. They also provide techniques for obtaining feedback and using it for process improvement.
- A checklist for dynamic processes, which can be used to check that dynamic processes have a basic stability and comply with the rules of well-formed QPL. The checklist supplements the reviewing rules provided in Chapter 5.
- Applications to BPR and change management. QPL is suitable for modelling existing processes as well as processes to be implemented. The same language also models the authorities which those processes must comply with. Later we provide a framework for implementing process re-engineering, using a succession of process models and measured by their compliance with these authorities. It also covers other relevant issues, such as benchmarking and process improvement.

7.3 GOOD DESIGN PRACTICE

Good things only happen when planned; bad things happen on their own.
Crosby, 1979: 66

The whole of this book is about designing good processes. The early chapters concentrated on how to represent simple processes and the flow of information between them, and this was expanded to include guidelines for structuring processes. Later, it focused on analysis of process descriptions to ensure that they were well formed, and the last chapter covered the design of processes which need to be compliant. This section provides a few concise guidelines for the dynamic aspects of process design. The guidelines also provide a basis for processes which provide a platform for change and which are adaptable when required. They could also be called guidelines for viable design, for they deal with the conditions for processes which will withstand the many changes which organizations need to undergo.

Process balance

Following the end of the Cold War and the rise of a globally integrated economy, companies are finding that change cannot be avoided or even slowed. The pace is ever quicker, and yesterday's winners become today's has-beens. There are many companies now in the second rank which only a few years ago appeared to be unassailable.

To meet these challenges, an organization needs to be robust—capable not only of surviving changing circumstances but of exploiting them for success. In QPL terms, this means that the organization is capable of reacting to a change in *any* of the elements in its environment. For example, if demand drops, then an organization needs to take action, such as: reduce production, reduce costs and improve quality. If changes in authority are required, then it needs to be clear to all where that authority is applied, so that detailed procedures and staff training can be changed accordingly. With each of the other QPL elements, similar actions need to be applied during a period of change.

The design needed to optimize processes under change is summed up by the principle of process balance. This principle states that a process or group of processes is balanced when a change to one of its elements can be countered by a change in another element. Typically, the element which may change is external to the process and poses a threat to its viability. The element which changes to meet this threat is within the control of the process. Some examples of process balance are:

- The output from a process needs to match the input, so there is no accumulation of materials (or information) and no shortage. (Balancing effect: if there is a change in the rate of input, the rate of production can be changed to produce a corresponding change in the rate of output.)
- The authority for a process must be matched by the process owner/role; in essence, this just means that the person responsible for a process is capable of carrying it out correctly. (Balancing effect: if the authority is changed, then the process owner needs to undergo some additional training, or a new, properly qualified person needs to be appointed to the role.)
- Information (material) balance: the rate at which an information item is produced is matched by the rate at which it is consumed. This means that there is always a planned place for all outputs in a balanced process: an output is either used immediately by another process step, or it is placed in a planned storage place. (Balancing effect: a change in the production rate of one process is balanced by a equivalent change in the consumption rate of another process.)

A simple example will help to illustrate the balancing principles. Suppose you decided to invite some friends to a dinner which you will cook. The processes involved include cooking dishes for the meal, keeping the dishes warm before they are served, seating guests at the table, and so forth Process balance is applied in the following examples:

- Input–output balance—The cooking processes need to be at a sufficient rate to complete all dishes at the same time.
- Authority balance—The cooks must have the capability to prepare the dishes they have selected.
- Information balance—There is no point having all the dishes on the table at a precise time, if the hosts forget to tell people when to arrive. As a result, some of the meal will remain uneaten until the late guests do arrive, and it will probably be cold by then.

Techniques from the discipline of flow process analysis can also assist in developing process balance. This is covered in the next topic.

On a wider, cultural level, there is an equivalent of the rule of process balance: that of process viability. This rule states that, for long-term viability, an organization needs to be capable of responding to changes at least as quickly as the changes themselves. When applied to warfare, this means that a nation needs to be capable of responding to a threat in less time than the time it would be overwhelmed by that threat. In the case of competition, this principle means that a company needs to be able to change its internal practices, or produce different types of goods, at a faster rate than competition can bring out new and more competitive products. In the theory of information or cybernetics, this is called the Law of Requisite Variety (Bateson, 1972).

Industrial engineering and flow process analysis

Industrial engineering includes a long-established set of techniques, dating to the early part of the twentieth century, for studying industrial and clerical processes, analysing the results and making improvements. Besides flow process analysis, it includes motion study, time study and factory and office layout analysis.

Flow process analysis describes the operations in terms of key activities and data. The activities are operations, transportation, storage and inspection. The key data are time spent in an activity and distance which an item or form needs to travel. Flow process analysis relies on charting processes with techniques similar to the flow diagrams of QPL, along with careful measurements of the key variables. Figure 7.2 shows an example of a flow process chart, along with the symbols for flow process analysis. (For an excellent description of flow process charts see Ishiwata, 1991.)

Once the processes are charted, with measurements recorded, they can be analysed. Then the processes can be improved to decrease time spent and distance travelled, reduce the numbers of inspections and improve production layouts, among other changes.

A QPL chart can be modified to provide the information needed for flow process analysis, by adding the variables to be measured explicitly. Figure 7.1 shows an example of this, where time was added to a QPL diagram so that it could be used for process improvement.

Normally, QPL just treats movement of information or materials with the communication lines which link processes. However, if distance and layout are also to

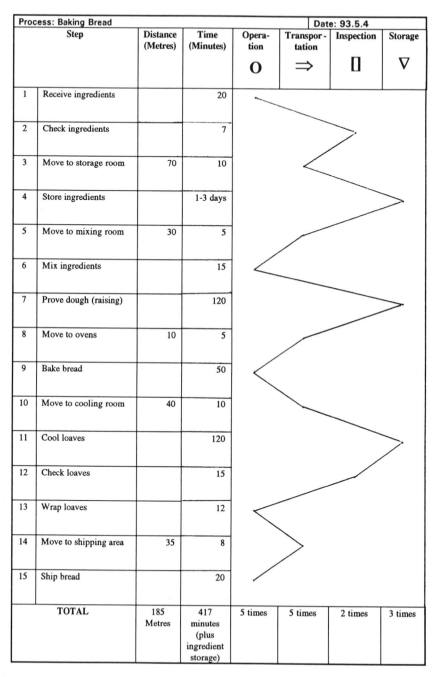

Process: Baking Bread		Distance (Metres)	Time (Minutes)	Opera-tion ○	Transpor-tation ⇒	Inspection []	Storage ▽
	Step						
1	Receive ingredients		20				
2	Check ingredients		7				
3	Move to storage room	70	10				
4	Store ingredients		1-3 days				
5	Move to mixing room	30	5				
6	Mix ingredients		15				
7	Prove dough (raising)		120				
8	Move to ovens	10	5				
9	Bake bread		50				
10	Move to cooling room	40	10				
11	Cool loaves		120				
12	Check loaves		15				
13	Wrap loaves		12				
14	Move to shipping area	35	8				
15	Ship bread		20				
	TOTAL	185 Metres	417 minutes (plus ingredient storage)	5 times	5 times	2 times	3 times

Date: 93.5.4

Figure 7.2 Example of a flow process chart

be considered in a flow process analysis, then transportation processes need to be explicit. To do so, we add a 'transportation' process to the process diagram. Figure 7.3 shows how this is done, using the bakery example of Figure 7.1.

Once the QPL diagrams have been 'instrumented' with these explicit information items, the measurements are used to determine where the process can be improved. For example, if a process step takes an especially long time to execute, making it difficult to coordinate other processes, then effort should be made in speeding it up. If the distance travelled by a component is longer than necessary, then the layout of the shop or office floor should be re-evaluated to make it more efficient.

Complexity and the complexity index

Why do people always complain about red tape? Is it the number of rules we need to follow, the number of forms required, or simply about the difficulty of following instructions? There isn't much that can be done about the number of regulations required for modern living, as we live in a complex world, which requires order to control the chaos. But there is always plenty of room for simplifying those necessary procedures and forms, and particularly for improving the clarity of instructions.

How do we measure whether a set of instructions are efficient: whether they provide all the information required to execute them, without providing unnecessary additional information? This is called the complexity index for instructions, and is calculated by a simple formula. First calculate the complexity of an instruction, which is defined as the total number of pairs of authorities and process steps. That is, the sum of the product of the number of steps times the number of authorities per step. As an equation, this is:

$$\text{Complexity} = \Sigma (\text{Process steps} \times \text{Number of authorities for each step})$$

The complexity gives a measure of the complexity of carrying out an instruction.

Because some instructions involve many steps, we also want a measure for the 'ideal' amount of authorities to provide for them. The best instructions provide exactly one authority per process step, so that the executor of the instructions knows exactly what to do at each step. Therefore the complexity index is defined to reflect this difference between the best and the actual. It is the average number of authorities per process step, or:

$$\text{Complexity index} = \frac{\text{Complexity}}{\text{Total number of process steps}}$$

The complexity and complexity index for an instruction include process hierarchies: for nested process steps, the steps within an aggregated process are counted individually, as well as the aggregated process. If one or more authorities are inherited through a single authority for a process, then that counts only as a single authority (since the executor of the process needs to look only at that single authority to understand what needs to be done).

An example will help to explain these definitions. Suppose a parcel delivery service uses three types of vehicles: cars, vans and motorcycles. Drivers may use all three

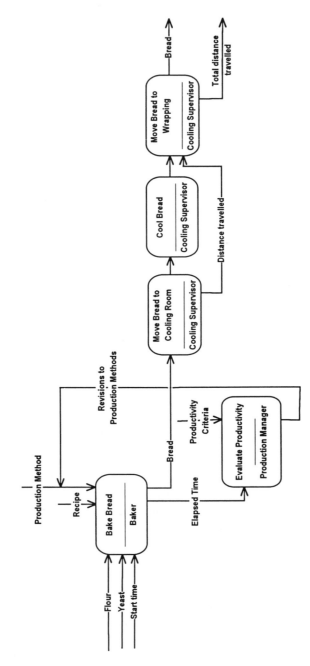

Figure 7.3 Explicit use of distance in a QPL diagram

types, depending on the number of parcels to be delivered and the urgency. Now suppose that the drivers' manual provides four general rules, which apply to all types of vehicles, plus specific rules for each type: cars—four rules, vans—five rules, motorcycles—two rules. For example, a general rule could state that all drivers are to drive to the destination and return by as direct a route as possible. A specific rule for motorcycles could state that a helmet is to be worn at all times, while one for cars could state that it is to be locked whenever unattended.

There are at least three ways of writing these rules as instructions:

(a)   For each type of vehicle, repeating the general rules for each type (structuring by type of vehicle).
(b)   Describing each rule in turn, with an indication of its applicability to each type of vehicle (structuring by rule).
(c)   Describing the general rules first, then providing the specific rules for each type of vehicle (hybrid structure).

Figure 7.4 illustrates these three ways of structuring the instructions, with each rule being represented as a process step. The complexity and complexity index for each of the three is shown in Table 7.1. These have been calculated on the basis of 15 rules, 4 general, plus 11 specific. When a hierarchy of rules is used, as in the structuring by rule and the hybrid structure, the complexity also includes one count for each higher-order process box. For example, the complexity for the hybrid structure is counted as 4 + 15, i.e. 4 higher-order boxes, plus 15 rules within boxes. The complexity index for all three is found by dividing the complexity by 15, since there are 15 steps or rules.

Some might object that it is not reasonable to include each of the three vehicle types in all fifteen rules, since some of the rules are specific to only one type of vehicle. However, this argument does not hold if you consider what it is like to plough through 15 rules to determine which are applicable to a specific type of vehicle. You have to check each rule, and for each determine whether or not it applies to the vehicle type of interest. Thus, a total of 60 checks will be needed, even though the majority of them will be pointless. This demonstrates why this way of structuring the instruction is so inefficient in use.

This example shows the large range of complexities possible even with simple rules. The complexity varies by a range of more than three, simply by arranging the rules in different orders. It shows clearly why the presentation of instructions is so important and can have such an influence on the quality of the result.

In structuring instructions, the complexity index can be a valuable guide for determining effectiveness. Ideally, you should aim for one authority per process step, so that the index is one. When the index is much greater than one, this is an indication that the instructions are too complex, while if the index is much less than one, then the instructions are probably underspecified (i.e. insufficient guidance is provided). As the above example shows, we can get relatively close to the ideal 1.0. But when a process is inherently complex, the necessary redundancy in instructions will lead to an index somewhat above this. The complexity index should never be below 1.0, as that would indicate that at least one process step has no authority or documented instructions.

Complexity and the complexity index can be used as a quick way of determining whether there is room for improvement in the way an organization has documented its procedures. Alternatively, they provide a guide for structuring new procedures. The

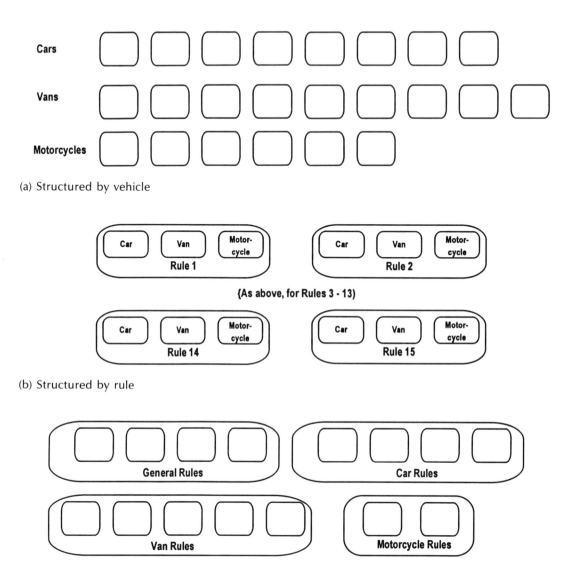

(a) Structured by vehicle

(b) Structured by rule

(c) Hybrid structure

Figure 7.4   Three ways of structuring instructions

Table 7.1   Complexities and complexity indexes

	Complexity	Complexity index
Structuring by type of vehicle	23	1.53
Structuring by rule	60	4.00
Hybrid structure	19	1.27

process designer can use the index in a way similar to the use of readability indices for writers and design a structure properly matched to the needs of the organization. There are several measures of readability.[*]

Adaptable cultures and authorities

In designing organizational processes, we need to provide a set of flexible procedures and rules, which can be modified readily to suit changing conditions. Perhaps the most powerful way of achieving this is through empowerment of the process owners. This means that the people directly involved in a process take responsibility for its results, and also that they have a major influence on how the process is designed. This can be done through a combination of participation in designing processes and building feedback loops into all processes. Some ideas for encouraging participation are discussed in the following chapter, while feedback loops are discussed below.

An excellent example of local control of processes is provided by the NUMMI (New United Motor Manufacturing Inc.) plant in Fremont, California, a joint venture of General Motors and Toyota. It provides some excellent examples of how employees on the shop floor can be involved in developing their own procedures, in the areas they know best. A case study in the *Harvard Business Review* (Adler, 1993) makes this clear:

> Indeed, standardization is not only a vehicle and a precondition for improvement but also a direct stimulus. Once workers have studied and refined their work procedures, problems with materials and equipment quickly rise to the surface. Moreover, since each worker is now an expert, each work station is now an inspection station—and a centre of innovation. . . . In systems designed for what experts call usability, the operator both learns from and 'teaches' the technology. Using learned analytical tools, their own experience, and the expertise of leaders and engineers, workers create a consensual standard that they teach to the system by writing job descriptions. The system then teaches these standards back to workers, who, then, by further analysis, consultation, and consensus, make additional improvements. Continual reiteration of this disciplined process of analysis, standardization, re-analysis, refinement, and restandardization creates an intensely structured system of continuous improvement. And the salient characteristic of this bureaucracy is learning, not coercion. (Adler, 1993: 104)

The NUMMI plant is now a famous example of how the 'worst plant in the world' (according to one manager) was transformed into one of the best. It demonstrates the value of worker empowerment and feedback, as close to the process as possible. This is a method which the Japanese have used for decades, with devastating effect on their competitors. How can these principles be integrated with the process design techniques of this book?

In the list of analysis checks in Table 5.5, two types of feedback are noted. The first, 'information feedback', provides data on the process, which can then be fed back to the process as an input. Examples include production rates, variations in production

[*]One of the most popular, the Gunning Fog Index, provides a rating of readability based on overall sentence length and the number of words per sentence that contain more than one syllable.

quality, etc. The second type of feedback is process improvement, where the effect of a process is monitored and used to improve the process itself. This is done through changes to the authority for the process, or the process definition.

Appendix 2, with a QPL chart of the Malcolm Baldrige Award criteria, has many examples of process improvement feedback, as shown by a loop from the process directly to its authority. Figure 7.5 is an excerpt and shows several feedback loops for Category 7 (Customer Focus and Satisfaction). The two processes provide self-feedback to improve their own processes and service standards. They also receive feedback from the company-level analysis process and provide feedback both to customers and to the rest of the organization.

Feedback loops are essential for a well-designed process. Ideally, feedback should be provided close to the process, so that the information is direct and can be used by the process owner to make improvements frequently. Ownership of the feedback process should be the same as the process itself, to ensure that there are no layers of bureaucracy to be crossed. If there is a worry that the process owner will not be objective and realistic in soliciting and interpreting feedback, then an independent and qualified reviewer can also be included to assist in evaluating feedback and in implementing process improvement.

If the example in Figure 7.5 were to be applied to a customer service process, then the first step for feedback would be to identify the owners of the process. In this case, it is 'customer relations'. They would ensure that they were gathering feedback for two specific purposes:

- improvements to their processes, methods and measurement scales
- improvements to service standards.

They would also interact with company-wide processes to provide feedback on performance from customers.

A golden rule for designing processes

Design is essentially a creative activity and can never be fully defined or even explained. For process design, however, a simple rule sums up the essence of design: coherence within diversity. The designer needs to provide for the diversity of many different requirements, both internal and external to the process. Yet a coherent set of rules and steps must also be provided for, to give sufficient guidance and to empower staff to complete the necessary operations in the most straightforward way.

In process redesign, this principle is often disregarded, as new processes are added, but obsolete processes are not removed or simplified. Indeed, much of the effort of BPR consists of simplifying and modifying processes until they are coherent and straightforward, yet also provide for the many variations which the process needs to handle and the sub-cultures within the organization.

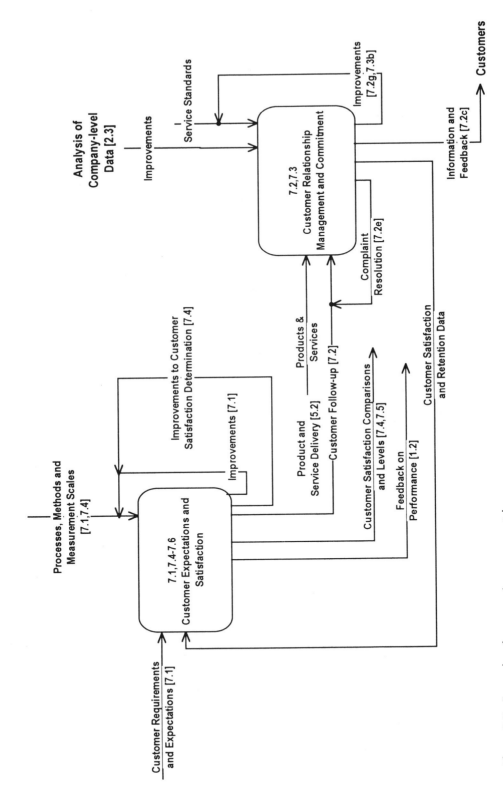

Figure 7.5 Example of process improvement loops

7.4   A CHECKLIST FOR DYNAMIC SYSTEMS

Chapters 5 and 6 give rules for static systems—in other words, the rules which processes and process descriptions need to obey at a particular moment in time. It is as if we were to take a photograph of a street scene, and use rules to determine whether it was of the world as we know it. If people were strolling up the sides of buildings, we would be right in assuming that something was odd!

But what about movements in the photograph? People and cars are moving down the street; a boy is throwing a ball. With the rules for dynamic processes, we now move into the equivalent of films and television. Are people and cars moving backwards? Is the ball falling upwards? Are pedestrians walking faster than cars (assuming it's not rush hour)? All of these phenomena are undetectable in photographs, but when we look at a film, it is obvious that something is wrong. This is the difference between a dynamic rule and a static rule.

The lists of checks for static errors can be expanded for dynamic errors as well. Unfortunately, dynamic checks do not lend themselves to the neat descriptions given in Chapters 5 and 6. Therefore, these rules will be provided in the form of checklists, which can, however, still be used to check that process descriptions are well formed and will support stable dynamic processes. They also provide a starting point for BPR: examining existing processes to discover areas of significant improvement.

The checks are grouped into the four types of changes discussed in the last section and detailed below.

Changes in input and output

Input capacity: Can the process deal with its inputs quickly enough so that it does not get jammed?
Adaptable input capacity: Can the process accommodate small variations in the volume of input without needing to change the process?
Output capacity: Can the process produce outputs quickly enough to supply other processes in the supply chain?
Adaptable output capacity: Can the process accommodate small variations in the volume of output without needing to change the process itself?

Changes in time

Synchronization: When two processes need to work together to produce a result, have they been designed to be activated at the same time or by another signal?
Parallel working: Can steps which currently are done sequentially be changed to work in parallel?
Imbalanced information: Does a process produce outputs faster than they can be consumed by another process or placed into planned storage?

Internal changes

Baselining a process: Before a process is changed, is it well enough understood so that the effects of change are clear and that it will be possible to measure those effects?
Feedback loops: For all major processes, are clear feedback loops provided, so that information about changes are fed back and used to 'tune' the process?
Production improvements: Could changes to the process be made, to:

- reduce the cycle time
- cut down the distance which materials or information need to travel
- decrease the number of steps
- reduce the cost of production
- decrease the lead time for modifications or new products
- or other improvements which would improve efficiency or competitiveness?

Inspection improvements: Can the process be redesigned to minimize the number of inspection steps or improve their effectiveness? Alternatively, can inspection be reduced or eliminated by incorporating it into production steps?
Avoiding redundancy: Can the process be redesigned to eliminate unnecessary duplication? Is there any unnecessary copying or storage of information? Are the same operations being carried out by more than one process?

Imposed changes

Process adaptation: Is the process sufficiently adaptable and flexible so that it can be rapidly changed if external conditions change (say a fall in orders)?
Empowerment: Does the authority (or authorities) for a process empower the process owners/roles, by giving them the necessary flexibility and sanction to adapt processes to changing conditions?
Red tape: Is the complexity index as near 1.0 as possible (so that there is neither too much red tape nor too little guidance on how to carry out tasks)?

7.5   RE-ENGINEERING PROCESSES

It should be borne in mind that there is nothing more difficult to arrange, more doubtful of success, and more dangerous to carry through than initiating changes in a state's constitution. The innovator makes enemies of all those who prospered under the old order, and only lukewarm support is forthcoming from those who would prosper under the new.

Machiavelli, 1975: 51

The pace of change has reached an amazing speed. Spurred on by a combination of factors—an increasingly open and competitive world economy, the availability of cheap and good communications, and a greater emphasis on quality and customer satisfaction—individuals and organizations need to change at a killer pace. Techniques for controlling and facilitating this are called change management, while techniques for redesigning the processes needed for change are grouped as business process re-engineering (BPR). This section concludes the chapter by pulling together some common strands from QPL relevant to some major issues in this subject.

Interestingly, BPR has strong historical connections with quality. It is a management philosophy based on total quality and just-in-time principles. It places emphasis on elimination of waste, inefficient processes and unnecessary information, but also positively, on empowerment, teamworking and better communications. Like total quality management, its purpose is one of improvement in all processes, but unlike it, the concentration is on radical redesign of business processes, making maximum use of new technologies and a well-trained and motivated workforce.

To achieve a radical redesign of processes, we need to ask some very hard questions about the organization, its goals and its means for achieving them. We also need to examine existing processes at all levels, to determine where significant redesign will provide benefits. While some of this depends on intuition and creativity, rigorous analysis is also required. QPL assists this by providing a structured and consistent notation for process descriptions. It also provides a basis of hard questioning of existing practices, through its checks and analysis techniques.

Thus, QPL provides a foundation for examining business processes in depth. The following sections provide some guidance on using the techniques in this book for BPR.

Principles of process redesign

Organizations need to change for a variety of reasons. Externally, they are subject to constant changes to their competitive environment, requiring continuous re-evaluation of their processes. Internally, changes in technology and culture produce an additional pressure to keep things in a state of flux. There are many differences between the new, process-oriented organization and the traditional one, as shown in Table 7.2.

This table emphasizes the harder, systems aspects of business redesign. However, they will not work unless a supporting culture is also in place. As Table 7.2 illustrates some differences between traditional and the newer, process-oriented organization, we can also compare static cultures with dynamic cultures (Table 7.3).

Many resources need to be harnessed to achieve such massive changes of emphasis, not least of which is process design or redesign. Throughout, the goal is the continual improvement of the organization and its operations, achieved by simplifying and clarifying processes.

Some QPL techniques are particularly useful for this:

● simplifying instructions, yet ensuring they are well specified, by aiming for a complexity index of 1.0 (see earlier in this chapter under 'Good design practice')
● removing unnecessary process steps (see checklist in Section 7.4 under 'Internal changes—Production improvements')
● using process hierarchies to reduce complexity (see Chapter 4)

Table 7.2 Differences between traditional and process-oriented organizations

	Traditional organization	Process-oriented organization
Business focus	Internal functions	Customer
Customer contact	Division into specialists	Single point, backed by computer technology
Organization structure	Functional and hierarchical	Multi-skilled teams
Managerial role	Control	Facilitation and leadership
Materials handling	Buffer stocks	Just-in-time production
Performance measures	Functional performance	Customer satisfaction
Information and systems	Functional and technical requirements	Customer satisfaction and internal communications

Table 7.3 Differences between static and dynamic cultures

	Static culture	Dynamic culture
Values	Predictability Clarity Specialized skills Finishing things	Versatility Room for expansion Ability to learn new skills Always room for improvement
Emphasis	By the rules Hierarchical power structures Functions	Philosophy, mission and values Informal networks and teams Processes
What success means	Good enough The way things always ought to be	Always aim higher *Too* much success breeds complacency
Typical slogans	'Right first time' 'Do it right, then move on' 'Do each step as specified'	'Learn from mistakes' 'Concurrent engineering' 'Procedures are needed but are only starting points for good work'

- maximum use of inherited authorities, to reduce duplication of instructions and to ensure that policies and procedures are in harmony (see Chapter 4 and Section 7.3)
- ensuring that processes are well formed, by utilizing the rules and checklists in this chapter and in Chapters 5 and 6.

These and other QPL techniques provide an effective set of processes for an organization. They can be used in conjunction with other, non-process-oriented methods to help the organization to prosper in difficult times and to fulfil the objectives of its staff and other stakeholders.

Benchmarking

No matter how hard it looks at itself, an organization can never tell how good it is without looking at others as well. There is no limit to the amount of creativity which humans will apply to problems, and chances are that a competitor has at least a few better ideas. The technique of tracking what other, similar organizations are doing is called benchmarking. In benchmarking, the best industry practices are brought out, analysed and, where appropriate, adapted to one's own organization. Even if the practices are not transferable to one's own organization, they provide an indication of what it is possible to achieve, a kind of Olympic gold medal to aim for.

While we aim to know as much as possible about the processes and behaviour of competitors, this information may not be readily available. In that case, indirect benchmarking is of use. We can gather aggregate data about organizations, such as their turnover, turnover per employee, volume of sales per member of sales staff, defect rate of shipped product, etc. While this information does not provide any detail about the actual processes, it does provide an indication of what the 'best in class' are capable of doing and what others could do with the right processes, resources and people.

There are some problems with this traditional view of benchmarking. First, it is extremely difficult to obtain such information, as competitors tend to regard it as highly valuable—not surprising, since you wouldn't be interested in it otherwise! Secondly, it is not usually easy to find the causes of a competitor's better performance. Even if most of their processes are well known, it is usually hard to pinpoint exactly what gives them a competitive edge. With Sony, is it their reputation for innovation, or superior marketing processes? With Braun shavers, is it a better process for manufacturing, or is it their striking design? Or is it a bit of both? Finally, processes are not the complete picture. The best organizations evolve their processes over many years. They cannot be copied without also imposing their underlying culture.

In QPL, process benchmarking can be used rather differently. It is based on the template introduced in Chapter 6. The template is a model of a process, without the details and cultural influences of a specific organization. It also embodies the best practices and goals of a process. Any organization can achieve compliance with a template process and thus establish that it is working toward its desired objectives.

The Malcolm Baldrige template in Appendix 2 provides an example. While the checklists on which it is based are a set of criteria for deciding who will win this prestige award, the equivalent process template also provides a benchmark for an organization aiming for quality in all its processes. It does this by showing 12 key processes essential for quality, along with connections between them and feedback loops which are used for continuous improvement.

Each company using this template will apply it in a different manner. A company providing ball bearings will carry out very different analysis of information than a restaurant chain, but the connections with other key processes and the feedback loops will be the same. Used this way, the Baldrige criteria obtain a far greater significance than the award itself, which is awarded to only a handful of companies each year. They become a combined benchmark upon which any organization can gauge itself and derive a path for improvement.

Quality and process improvement

The Baldrige template illustrates the importance of feedback loops and their use for improvement of processes. It also illustrates an approach for quality improvement, summarized in three steps:

(1) Break down the process into well-understood steps, with a process owner for each of them.
(2) Provide a means of measuring the significant results of the process.
(3) Use the measurements to improve the process, through its authority.

What is measured in step 2 depends on the process and its value to the organization—typically, cycle time, distance moved, variations in output quality and rework rate are used to measure the process and provide feedback for its improvement.

This approach facilitates working in small quality circles or QITs (quality improvement teams). The process step defines the scope of the measurement and of the activities which can be improved, which focuses the team on local and tractable problems. The unit which carries out the measurement and performs the analysis is that responsible for the process step (or which reports to the process owner, when that is an individual responsibility). After analysis and development of process redesign, the local team can implement the changes, possibly with the help of specialist staff. As they are also responsible for executing the process step, it will then be easy for them to monitor the redesigned process. This will help them determine if the desired improvements have come about and to make adjustments wherever problems arise.

In more complex situations, this principle of small local QITs can be extended to groups of processes, using process hierarchies. However, to be effective, the lines of communications between processes must be clear to all concerned.

As a simple example, take a restaurant in a shopping mall. Normally, demand is fairly even, with peaks on weekends, and the rota of staff reflects this. However, during sales in the mall, the demand increases sharply with the greater number of shoppers, and the normal rotas are not sufficient to meet this demand; there will be a long wait to get served. In this case, the serving team is unable to do its job well; on analysis, staff will determine that the cause is not a problem in their own process, but arises from increased demand. Therefore, the problem is referred to the staff manager, who revises the rotas to reflect the increased demand during sales. In this case, the people noting the problem (the serving staff) are not able to solve it themselves, but by clear communication with another process owner, they are able to work out a satisfactory solution, which can then be fine-tuned over succeeding sales periods.

Modelling change in QPL

The mechanism for handling change in QPL can be described in terms of a series of stages extending from the existing process to the desired process. An evolutionary approach is used, since organizations are rarely able to carry out radical changes with just a single change: they have existing customers to serve, and staff without the new skills which will be required. Change is also a process, which needs to be carried out in a succession of significant, but less extreme changes. A common template model links and controls the stages of change.

Earlier examples have treated the template as a process model of a regulation, standard or other document which must be complied with. It has also been treated as a benchmark for an organization, which would provide objectives and allow it to measure its progress toward improved processes.

An alternative use of the template is to produce a common model of otherwise diverse practices in a large organization. By extracting the parts which are common to all, the organization can ensure that a minimum set of practices are enforced, thus providing an assurance of compatibility where it is required. For example, many large manufacturing companies in Europe, including automobiles and computers, have plants in many countries. Each of them follows different procedures, depending upon national cultures and laws. However, because production needs to be shifted around the plants, a common set of practices is also required. This is provided by a template model which specifies the minimum set of common practices. However, it does not impose uniformity on the individual plants, since they are free to follow their own practices, as long as they comply with the common set.

The QPL approach provides some other models as well. The foundation model is the model of the existing practices and procedures followed by the organization, while the target model is the model of what the organization would like to become at an identifiable horizon. While the foundation model is not compliant with the template model, the target model always will be.

These three models provide the beginning, direction and end to the change that the organization wishes to accomplish. However, to provide support and markers along the way, two further types of model are needed:

- *Baseline model*: A stage in going from the foundation model to the target model, where achievement of this stage is capable of measurement.
- *Transition model*: A process model for going from one baseline to another.

Figure 7.6 illustrates the use of these models for change management.

When an organization re-engineers its processes, it always starts with an understanding of its processes, in the form of the foundation model. It then constructs a generic template model appropriate for its business or role—this may be a general-purpose model, like ISO 9001 or the Malcolm Baldrige criteria, or a more industry-specific model like the US Food and Drug Administration's Current of Good Manufacturing Practices (FDA, 1989). Finally, it prepares a vision of where it would like to be in the future, in the form of the target model.

We need to remember that organizations cannot change overnight—people need retraining, long-standing cultures need to be transformed and new technology needs to be implemented. Therefore, the organization develops a plan for managing the change and for evolving to the target. The baseline models provide recognizable stages for the plan, while the transition models describe the processes needed to move from one baseline to another. For example, a typical transition model will contain processes for organizational development, such as training, restructuring of functions and workgroups, revisions to marketing strategy and modifications of mission statements.

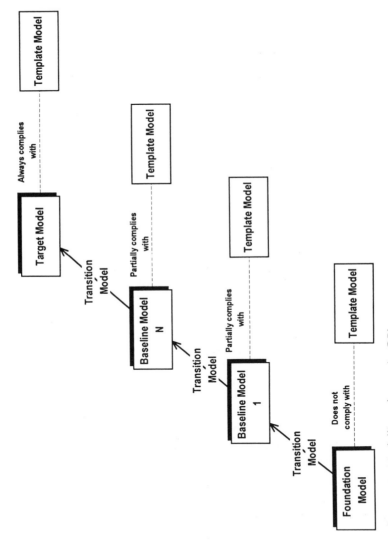

Figure 7.6 Modelling change in QPL

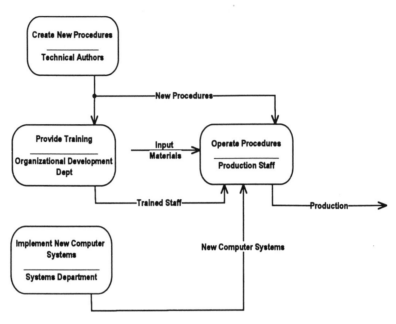

Figure 7.7 Example of a transition model

The case studies of Chapters 5 and 6 illustrate the process of change in QPL. The case study provided two QPL models, the first being the foundation model for the ABC purchasing procedures, before they have been reviewed. Afterwards this process was re-engineered, as shown in the later QPL diagram; this is a baseline model and is a stage in improving the effectiveness of the purchasing function.

In Chapter 6, this baseline process was checked for compliance with part of ISO 9001, and some violations were listed in Table 6.2. The next baseline for this process would address these violations, before another compliance check is made and a new baseline produced.

As the organization evolves through the baseline models, it needs to provide for additional staff, training, new technology and changed documentation. These are provided through transition models. An example of a generic transition model is provided in Figure 7.7.

7.6 SUMMARY OF THE QPL APPROACH TO CHANGE

The QPL approach to change in organizations is summarised by the following points:

● Four types of change are relevant to processes:
  – changes in the quantities of input and output
  – changes in time, mainly the time needed by a process to complete a cycle (i.e. to transform a unit of input into a unit of output)

- internal changes, such as the use of feedback loops for process improvement and other changes to the process
- imposed changes in the external environment, such as a change in the conditions of trading or the need to expand output.

● See the checklists for each of the four types in Section 7.4. This chapter also suggests basic checks on a process description to confirm that it is well formed and that it is stable.

● The principle of *process balance* states that a process or group of processes is balanced when a change to one of its elements can be countered by a change in another element. This basic design principle ensures that processes are robust and capable of withstanding the changes imposed by a tough business climate.

● *Flow process analysis* is a complementary technique for analysing and improving processes on the shop floor. It is particularly useful for analysing inefficiencies connected with layout, transportation delays, storage areas and other common industrial problems.

● QPL provides two measures of complexity to assist in refining and improving processes. The *complexity* is an absolute measure, while the *complexity index* measures the complexity of a process relative to an ideal value. High values of this index indicate that the process description is poorly structured, with much repetition, while low values indicate that not enough information has been provided about the process and that it is underspecified.

● QPL supports BPR with a series of models. The *template model*, which was introduced in Chapter 6, can be used for *process benchmarking*, and also provides a gauge on the progress made toward process improvement goals. Other models are provided for the current and future processes, as the organization changes its processes and culture. The *transition model* is the model of change itself, along with the resources required to achieve the change.

Putting it together

An ounce of practice is worth a pound of preaching.

Traditional proverb

OVERVIEW

This chapter highlights the practical issues involved in process design and implementation. It begins with the values expressed by the QPL approach and applies them to the people side of processes: empowerment, teamwork, consultation and customer service.

Guidelines for the practical use of the QPL approach consolidate material in earlier chapters. The emphasis is on a working partnership between the process owner and the process designer, i.e. between those with the knowledge and skills about their job, and those with the specialist knowledge and experience of process management and organization. The former contribute their detailed knowledge about how things work and what is feasible, and the latter provide structure and suggestions for improvement. Three scenarios provide examples: the new organization, the existing organization without documented processes, and the organization undergoing significant change.

QPL techniques are never used in isolation and need to be integrated with other techniques and methods used by organizations. A brief commentary outlines how QPL complements several common techniques.

No modern organization can function effectively without the use of computers, communications and other recent technology, which also support the QPL approach. Uses include tools to create QPL diagrams, automation of processes, teleworking and other applications using computer networks.

Finally, the most basic question of all: where do I go from here? This provides a summary of the use of QPL and some guidance on getting started with quality process modelling in your organization.

8.1 INTRODUCTION

The previous chapters provide a comprehensive view of process modelling and its application to business and quality management. They are based on a notation for representing processes—the quality process language (QPL). The QPL notation is used to structure processes and organizations, to investigate faults and weaknesses in processes and to describe compliance with regulations. The QPL approach provides a powerful framework for designing and managing change in an organization.

But we have not yet discussed the side of quality process modelling that applies to people, and there are also some practical issues associated with the application of these principles:

● How will the use of QPL affect important people-based issues like empowerment, ownership, teamwork and customer service?

● What do we need to do when using QPL techniques in a real organization, where people aren't trained in the sort of framework which it covers?

● How do I use QPL to reflect existing procedures of an organization or to re-engineer them?

● How can we utilize QPL in a way which respects and reflects existing methods in an organization?

● What is the best way to employ computers and other modern technology when using the QPL approach?

This chapter provides some answers to these questions. They will be enough to start you down the path which QPL provides; as you go down this path, you will discover the remaining answers for yourself.

These are the 'messy' problems encountered in implementing process-based solutions. Whereas the rest of the book deals with problems and their solutions logically, this chapter looks at them pragmatically. It shows how to tailor the logical framework of QPL to the real situations of companies and other organizations. It also deals with the effect of these principles on what really counts: people. There are four main areas of interest:

How people are affected by the QPL framework: Processes ultimately depend on people: how well they teach and how well they learn, with what interest they implement processes, and with what enthusiasm they improve processes. There is a danger that the systematic framework of QPL will be applied in a way which ignores the human issues. This would be counter-productive and not make use of the significant potential for improvement which this framework offers. This chapter, under the heading 'Is process modelling good for your health?', provides some practical suggestions for applying QPL in a way which supports and empowers the people working in the organization.

How to apply the QPL framework and principles in real situations: The application of QPL techniques will be made in real situations and will require much adaptation of the techniques, as well as some compromise on occasion. The greatest problem is how to use the sophistication and power of QPL without losing communication with the people who need to implement the solutions. This chapter provides specific guidance on how to fit QPL techniques into existing frameworks and how to apply them as a facilitator, while supporting the staff in an organization.

How the QPL techniques can be adapted to or supplement existing methods: Many organizations have an established set of techniques for modelling and analysing their processes, and it would be expensive to rewrite them to make use of QPL. In fact, there is no need, as QPL techniques can be used with and add value to any other process modelling technique, including flow charting. This chapter shows how to supplement established methods of business and process modelling with the additional analysis tools which QPL offers.

How to automate QPL techniques: Computers are part of many organizational processes now, and it would be foolish to ignore their use in a process-oriented approach such as QPL. The section entitled 'Automating QPL' gives advice on how to utilize computers when working with QPL. In particular, it shows how to use computers to create and update QPL diagrams, which is necessary for all but the most trivial process descriptions. Secondly, there is a tendency to use process description as a first step toward automation of business processes, through such approaches as workflow and team/group work. This section provides some practical guidance on how to make use of QPL to describe the processes, which can then be automated.

The principles of this book work for all sizes and types of organization. They have been applied successfully on many types of enterprise, including a small voluntary organization, a management consultancy, a small computer company and one of the largest manufacturing companies in the world. The QPL principles work because they are based on a simple but complete approach to organizations. This chapter illustrates this on a range of different enterprises.

8.2 IS PROCESS MODELLING GOOD FOR YOUR HEALTH?

Das eigentliche Studium der Menschheit ist der Mensch.
[The proper study of mankind is people.].
Johann Wolfgang von Goethe, Elective Affinities

Like it or not, approaches to process description and improvement do not have a good reputation. From the early part of the twentieth century, industrial engineers have been studying work processes and devising 'improvements', ranging from the layout of factories to the detailed descriptions of the movements workers should use to carry out assembly line operations.

There is also a great deal of debate about regulation issues, with a strong view that compliance with regulations costs companies and consumers a fortune in the costs associated with red tape. In this view, documenting organizational procedures leads to bureaucracy and fossilization of existing practices, inhibiting the changes which an organization needs to make to stay competitive. These viewpoints hold that people are restricted by documented procedures, with their creativity stifled by analysis of processes and subsequent dictates of management.

QPL techniques present a positive approach which can correct these abuses of process management. They provide a framework for an approach to processes where the emphasis is on people—those who carry responsibility for the processes, and those who use the products of the process. A set of five statements expresses the values which underlay QPL and its use in describing and improving working practices and organizations.

(1) The goal of QPL is to provide the simplest and most compact description of actual processes in an organization.

(2)   QPL provides a framework for regulation, where the regulations to be complied with can be expressed simply and where members of the organization know precisely what they need to do. Furthermore, this framework enables the organization to do only what is required by the regulation and no more, thus allowing it greater creativity and freedom of action.

(3)   With its structuring techniques, QPL provides a language for scoping processes and assigning responsibility to them. Once this is done, the process owner can be given greater autonomy and responsibility for the operations which constitute the process. This is the essence of empowerment, providing the maximum power for employees at the most local level, while also providing accountability for their activities and decisions.

(4)   This structuring also enables process owners to measure the results of processes and to use this feedback to make improvements continuously.

(5)   QPL's guidelines for analysing and improving processes provide a structured set of questions which designers can use to optimize processes and produce the most creative set of working practices.

The last value statement may jar the traditionalist: surely it cannot be better for a worker to be asked to work harder and more efficiently? Why should any group of workers actually choose to work under a system which asks more of them: not only to work more efficiently, but even to continuously assess and improve their work? The answer lies in empowerment.

Empowerment

Work is valuable and rewarding only when it provides a basic level of satisfaction to employees. Three ingredients are essential to satisfaction at work and are at the heart of empowerment:

● a sense of achievement in what is accomplished
● a sense of control over the means of production
● a pace of work which is appropriate for both the worker and what is produced.

QPL provides the conditions for all three of these. It provides for the production of quality products and services and for monitoring that this is the case. By increasing the control of process owners, which ultimately extends to all employees, it provides greater empowerment and a knowledge that the process is under the control of those who carry it out. Finally, with process analysis we can determine a pace for carrying out the process which suits not only the process owners but the owners of the other processes which interact with it.

   This is supported by research done by various psychologists concerned with optimal experience. This approach to human activity, which was pioneered by M. Csikszentmihalyi (1990) at the University of Chicago asserts that a number of conditions characterize enjoyable, satisfying work, even of the most trivial nature:

(1)   The task is one we are capable of completing and where we are allowed full control over our actions.

(2)   We are able to concentrate entirely on the work in hand.

(3) It has goals which are clear, although not necessarily defined in detail.

(4) It provides immediate feedback.

(5) It gives us a feeling of deep but effortless involvement that removes from consciousness the worries and frustrations of everyday life. We are also much less aware of time, and long tasks may appear to take only a short time.

(6) While we are actually doing the task our sense of self disappears, only to return with added strength when the task is finished.

All these conditions are satisfied by the use of QPL. By scoping processes carefully, we ensure that goals are clear, that process owners have full control over their tasks and that they can concentrate on them. The balance of authority with ownership also ensures that the process owner is capable of completing tasks successfully and provides for deep yet effortless involvement in the process. The use of feedback loops and quality improvement provides feedback and an enhanced sense of self-worth when tasks are completed.

Consultation

Since consultation is such an important part of empowerment, it is easy to overlook it as a component in its own right and to ignore the value which it brings an organization. Consider four essential contributions which it makes:

(1) Consultation is a major part of effective feedback. Before making major changes or implementing process redesign, it is essential to obtain the views of those who will be affected. Otherwise, we take the risk of ignoring important information about processes which only those close to them will know about.

(2) As QPL structuring brings out, organizations are organisms, with all parts mutually dependent. A change to any part will have unexpected effects on all the other bits. We can avoid these problems entirely by calling consultation meetings with the groups affected and then using their comments to make alterations to the proposed changes.

(3) For process empowerment to work, the process owner needs to be consulted about everything which could affect the results. At an extreme, when the people involved in a process feel that the key decisions are made distantly and without consulting them, their natural tendency is to lose interest in the process, treating their work as mere routine. Genuine process ownership is impossible in these circumstances, and the level of responsibility in the workplace will be minimal. At the opposite end, consultation enhances the self-worth of workers and increases their sense of responsibility for their work.

(4) In modern organizational development, we accept that participant buy-in is an essential prerequisite to implementing a new process. This principle says simply that staff will take an interest in a process only when they have a stake in it. That stake can come from many different orientations—profit sharing and bonuses are financial ways of providing it, but there are others which do not involve financial reward. One of the best ways is to involve staff in all stages of decision-making, and this naturally involves consultation as one of its elements. Later in this chapter we provide further information on how to involve staff in process description and design.

Teamwork

These days, one hears more and more about teamwork; ironically, as enterprises become more international in scope and viewpoint, the emphasis is shifting to small, multifunctional teams. At the least, organizations are reducing their degree of hierarchy and layers of management; more radically, they are experimenting with concepts such as rotation of tasks and of leadership within workgroups. New communications technologies such as workflow and groupware enable teams to be spread over many sites or even continents.

How does QPL support teamworking? First, the clear delineation of tasks and of process ownership in QPL makes it easier to allocate responsibilities and to provide training. Its support for feedback makes it easier for team members to work together, to improve their own processes and to identify genuine problems in the interface with other teams and processes. For example, by clarifying the exact processes and responsibilities, QPL makes it easier to pinpoint the causes of problems and to put them right.

If your organization is thinking of moving from a hierarchy structure to one based on teamworking, you should first carry out a QPL study of the existing processes, which of course will reflect the current structure. Some considerable effort will then be needed to design a new organization based on teams, with a greater sense of responsibility and autonomy than in the old organization. In carrying this out, the new teams must be strongly represented in the redesign process, and you should check that the new structure provides clear scope to processes and clear communication between teams. It will also be necessary to provide training of the teams after redesign is complete, as new responsibilities and methods of communication will be required.

Customer service and support

We have all learned the importance of customer relationships and the key rule that in the end, an enterprise only survives and prospers if its customers are satisfied. Total quality has also taught us to value our fellow employees in treating them as internal customers. What can QPL teach us about nurturing these all-important relationships?

First, who are the customers? These days, organizations tend to distinguish between core processes and support processes, with the former directly adding value to goods or services produced for the ultimate consumer. The latter provide necessary support to those core processes but do not in themselves add value. In this viewpoint, the external customers are those who will consume the end-product, while the internal customers are those in the value chain of core processes.

QPL supports this by facilitating identification of core processes. In simple terms, the core processes are those on a direct input—output path from the source—an order from the customer—to the destination, the external customer. Each of their process owners is an internal customer. The support processes are represented by the lines of inherited authority. The QPL diagram for ISO 9001 (Appendix 2) illustrates this. From the diagram, we can readily identify core processes, such as design ('design control'), production ('process control'), shipment ('control of delivered product') and servicing. Support processes relate to them through inherited authority and include provision of the quality system, verification, inspection and testing, and traceability.

QPL also supports customer support by identifying soft communications, not just hard information and materials flow. These soft areas include non-explicit information, such as that revealed in conversations with the customer—Winograd and Flores (1987) provide many fascinating insights into the nature of conversations and their relationship to processes. Soft areas also include confirmations, such as when we confirm an order with the customer, or the customer confirms that our understanding of the requirement is correct. Many of the failure mode errors discussed in Chapter 5 fall in this category. For example, information feedback checks for feedback from the customer, to ensure that the result of a process was satisfactory. The reception check ensures that information sent to a customer was actually received and understood correctly.

8.3 GUIDELINES

By this point you have probably asked yourself how easy it is to apply the QPL approach in real situations. You may have asked questions such as whether it can be taught to workgroups so that they can use QPL techniques to improve their own processes. Or perhaps you have wondered how to use QPL for a new organization, where no existing procedures exist to be documented. This section provides several suggestions for applying the QPL approach to four situations:

● on the shop floor
● in new organizations
● in existing organizations and working practices
● for re-engineering existing processes.

Using QPL and process design on the shop floor

Modern methods of organization emphasize the importance of ownership. This principle asserts that people and their workgroups are most productive when they take responsibility for the processes within their control. In turn, this requires a sense of owning a process—that they feel that they have had a share in the creation of the process and have an influence on how it is modified or otherwise improved.

QPL provides a common language for documenting and discussing processes on the shop floor. It is not necessary for all workers to spare the time and effort required to learn the complete set of QPL techniques. Fortunately, they can still use QPL effectively, with a combination of simplified process modelling techniques and the use of especially trained staff.

In this approach, all members of a workgroup should learn the basic techniques of process mapping—how to identify a process, describe how process steps are sequenced, and identify the information which links processes. Some structuring can also be introduced, especially that of process hierarchies. Finally, we can also teach the general principles of authorities and their inheritance, since examples are everywhere

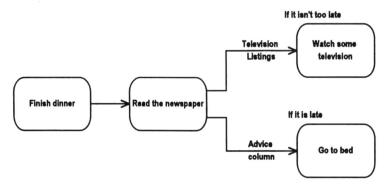

Figure 8.1 Example of simplified QPL notation

in the workplace—in fact, whenever policies or regulations are reflected in actual procedures. These are the basic principles of QPL, and they are all that is required to provide a model of most processes.

Figure 8.1 shows an example of a simplified QPL notation which could be used. In it we have done away with the distinction between changed and unchanged output and ignored control and ownership. If these elements are important, we can always annotate the chart, as shown in the figure.

While the workgroup uses this simplified notation for its own process analysis and improvement, process designers also have an important role to play. With an in-depth knowledge of processes and their characteristics, gained from QPL principles, they work in a partnership with the workgroup. While the latter has a knowledge of how processes work and what people do within them, the designer provides insights and raises key questions, which in turn lead to insights by the group—that wonderful cry of 'I never saw it that way before!' Working together, the process designer and the workgroup identify vulnerable areas and determine significant improvements.

The following sections, which illustrate three different situations of process design and implementation, provide examples of how the process designer, working as a facilitator and problem-solving expert, can assist workgroups to improve their processes.

Cooperation between workgroups and process designers: an example

It is essential that workgroups do their own process description and analysis, but a facilitator can work with them as a specialist using additional QPL techniques. The case study of NUMMI (Adler, 1993) quoted in Chapter 7, provides an example of cooperation between workgroups and process designers:

In NUMMI's view, the primary purpose and responsibility of the management hierarchy is to support the production teams with problem-solving expertise.

At NUMMI, in radical contrast to GM-Fremont, team members themselves hold the stopwatch. They learn the techniques of work analysis, description and improvement. This change in the design and implementation of standardized work has far reaching implications for worker motivation and self-esteem, for the balance of power between workers and management, and for the capacity of the company to innovate, learn and remember.

The job design process itself is relatively simple. Team members begin by timing one another with stopwatches, looking for the safest, most efficient way to do each task at a sustainable pace. They pick the best performance, break it down into its fundamental parts, then explore ways of improving each element. The team then takes the resulting analyses, compares them with those of the other shift at the same work station, and writes the detailed specifications that become the standard work definition for everyone on both teams. ...

Standardized work also has the overall benefit of giving control of each job to the people who know it best. It empowers the work force. Not surprisingly, NUMMI discovered that workers bought into the process quite readily. As one manager put it, 'They understood the technique because it had been done *to* them for years, and they like the idea because now they had a chance to do it for themselves.

... at NUMMI, middle management layers are layers of expertise, not of rights to command, and if middle managers have authority, it is the authority of experience, mastery, and the capacity to coach.

(Adler, 1993)

Creating new organizations and processes

At a greenfield site, without the history, inertia and established bureaucracy of an existing organization, we have an extraordinary freedom to create an optimized set of processes. But it is extremely rare to create a substantial organization totally from scratch. More commonly, we are likely to encounter a re-organization, or the establishment of a new team, department or office. While we are free to design new rules, processes and procedures, there also is a history to take into account.

If we are working on a new establishment within an existing organization, we also have the advantage of some framework for the new processes. In particular, we can utilize existing practices to form a set of templates which the new processes need to comply with. There are many ways to get started in such a situation. To name a few:

Brainstorming: Work with representatives from the organization to highlight the key processes and problem areas, to facilitate process description and structuring.

Interviewing/outlining: Interview one or more leaders or representatives to obtain an outline description of the key/core processes for the organization, which can then be used as a basis for further detail. Alternatively, ask them to write down such a description.

Process mapping: Working with a group, chart the basic process steps and flow of information. Display them on the walls to encourage suggestions and refinement.

Rich pictures: In a workshop, get key team members to create pictures of their activities and how roles in the organization interact. Rich Pictures is part of the soft systems approach to describing and analysing systems, pioneered by Peter Checkland at the University of Lancaster in the United Kingdom (Checkland, 1981).

Benchmarking: Utilize a model of a similar organization and modify it to suit the new organization.

Strawman: Create a rough and idealized model of the envisaged organization. Then obtain comment and suggestions from members, to refine it and add detail.

In almost all the above techniques, the facilitator takes an active role in producing process descriptions. He or she encourages the others to describe the proposed activities and produces working documentation of what is agreed. A simple picture is the best way to do this at a meeting. A simplified QPL diagram or a flow chart are often the most understandable pictures to use, although the existing culture will dictate the best type of picture. There are only two rules to follow:

- Be sure to make the process steps as clear as possible, with a clear picture of the conditions and information flow between steps.
- Don't put too much information on one chart or page (try to deal with limited complexity).

The process chart is then discussed with the group, who will be able to see more clearly how their proposed processes will operate and how they will interact with the rest of the organization and other parties. For the moment, compliance issues should be avoided unless compliance with a regulation is essential for the success of the organization.

Following the initial meetings, the facilitator and key members of the group iterate, producing new versions of the process chart as understanding of the processes evolves in the group's collective mind. Whenever possible, the facilitator should try to get people to write commentaries on the charts, which could then form the basis for the written procedures later. As more detailed processes are revealed, they should also be described and commentaries provided by members of the group.

As the process description approaches completion, compliance issues need to be addressed. Chapter 6 explains how to spot compliance violations and how to incorporate compliance into the process.

After the final process description is ready, it is an excellent foundation for the written procedures. There is the added benefit that key members of the organization really understand how it works. These can be retained for further benefits by incorporating the flow charts or other process mappings into the written procedures. The combination of the picture approach of these mappings with textual descriptions provides a thorough, yet understandable, set of instructions for all staff. Figure 8.2 provides an example of such an annotated flow chart, based on the case study example in Chapter 5. This example was also used in Figure 3.7 to illustrate the use of flow charts in procedures and work instructions.

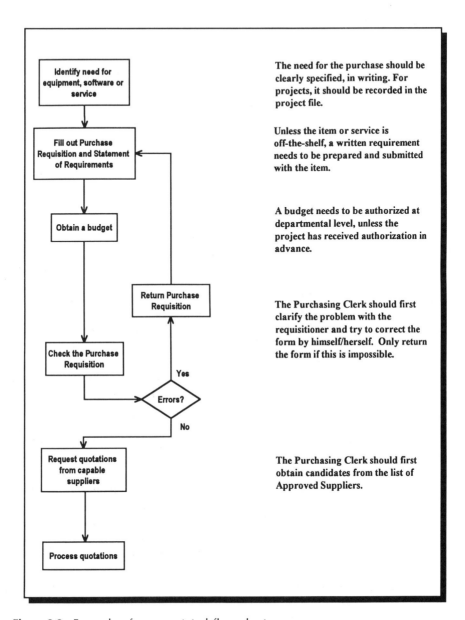

Figure 8.2 Example of an annotated flow chart

Documenting processes

With existing processes, we do not have the freedom to design an 'optimal' process, but in compensation there are many ways to approach the problem. Use whichever is most suitable to your organization or client. If much is written down already, the 'highlighting pen' technique is very effective. This approach uses a different colour of highlighting pen for each major element of QPL; each colour is then applied to the words in the document, to classify it by type. This technique gives a rapid understanding of the processes involved in the document and is a powerful basis for creating a QPL diagram, since the elements of QPL have already been identified on the document. Figure 8.3 shows an example of text from ISO 9001 (1987), annotated with the elements of QPL (different types of outline denote the different colours).

If printed documentation doesn't already exist, there are various options. You can carry out interviews and document the results, or ask key people to write down descriptions of what they do. Then you can analyse the results, using the highlighting pen technique just illustrated. Alternatively, you can work with the key people and chart the processes directly (see the suggestions under 'Consultation' earlier in this chapter). After there is consensus on the actual processes, the diagrams can then either be photographed, or copied to a computer with flow charting or process modelling software (see Section 8.4).

Unlike greenfield work, the process analyst needs to be careful to capture what people actually do. Remember that there are three types of processes going on at any time in an organization: What people *say* they do; what they would *like* to do; and what they *actually* do! Only the last can form the basis of a process model for the current situation, although the other two should be recorded also, as they provide valuable information for improving the processes.

There are other techniques as well, depending on the existing culture and feeling of comfort with putting things into words. But whatever technique is used to extract the information, be sure to chart the processes afterwards. You need a process map (such as a QPL diagram) to apply the techniques in this book, and even process owners will find it much easier to understand and critique their own processes if they can see it in the form of a picture or roadmap.

As with greenfield processes, the designer or analyst works in collaboration with the team, providing comments and interjecting with observations where appropriate. But there probably won't be as much trial and error as before, since the processes are already in use. The exception, of course, is when the organization wishes to move on to re-engineer its processes, when several versions of possible designs will be produced. The next section provides an illustration of this.

At the end of this exercise, when the processes are understood, you can produce written procedures in almost any form. Again, provide them as diagrams if possible; this is easier for staff to follow and orients them around the steps needed to do their job.

Chapter 3 contains many examples of how to document the processes in an organization.

Re-engineering processes

When the goal is to re-engineer processes, then the above techniques need to be combined. First, document and understand existing processes. Then, visualize how they should be changed. In doing this, two techniques are especially useful: benchmarking, to understand best practice in the relevant industry or sector, and obtain lessons which could be useful for process improvement; and measurement, to understand the causes and magnitude of problems with existing processes, so effort is

4.2   Quality System

The supplier shall establish and maintain a documented quality system as a means of ensuring that product conforms to specified requirements. This shall include:

a) the preparation of documented quality system procedures and instructions in accordance with the requirements of this International Standard

b) the effective implementation of the documented quality system procedures and instructions

. . .

Key: ⬚   Process

⬚   Process owner (role)

⬚   Information Item

⬚   Authority

The supplier shall establish and maintain a documented quality system as a

means of ensuring that product conforms to specified requirements. This shall

include:

a) the preparation of documented quality system procedures and instructions in

accordance with the requirements of this International Standard

b) the effective implementation of the documented quality system procedures and

instructions

. . .

Figure 8.3   Use of the highlighting pen to annotate documents for QPL

focused where it is most required. These also provide base measurements to gauge future improvements.

The creative leaps required by BPR do not take place in a vacuum or without deep and critical analysis of what exists. They usually follow a period of intensive questioning and argument about what is wrong or weak about the existing situation, and how it can be improved. QPL assists this in two ways. First, it provides a common language for describing and structuring processes; this aspect in itself is a powerful tool, as it avoids the many arguments that people have in deciding what 'is really going on'. Secondly, the analysis techniques described in previous chapters provide an extensive list of questions which can jar people into radical leaps of creativity—it is like seeing the obvious, for the first time.

Almost any of the analysis checks provides an example of their use in re-engineering processes. A straightforward one is that of process balance, described in Chapter 7. Among other things, this rule asserts that the authority for a process must be balanced by the capability of the owner of the process, who must have sufficient training or other ability to carry it out. In a workshop, the participants can take each major process in turn, and ask:

- Has an authority been specified for the process?
- Has an owner been assigned to the process?
- Does the owner have sufficient understanding and resources to carry out the process according to its authority?

They can look at other aspects of process balance to stimulate a creative discussion. Suppose that there were a sudden doubling in orders—could the processes cope? This provides a valuable insight into the current processes and their weak points. Even if the imagined situation never materializes, an inability to cope with it indicates areas of process weakness and points to an area where re-engineering is required.

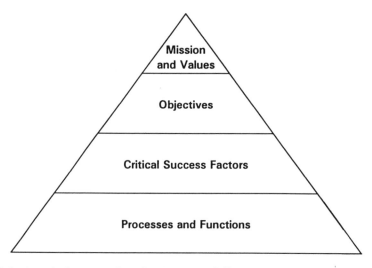

Figure 8.4 A typical approach to business modelling

Business modelling

In business modelling, we seek to understand not only the process but also the values, objectives and culture of the organization. When working with large organizations, it is a major challenge to combine all these elements into a single model of the organization, where influences and changes to one component will have an effect on another. Figure 8.4 shows a typical approach used in business modelling.

This model provides four levels within an organization; they are not hierarchical, in that they do not correspond to a neat partition of emphasis. The mission and values of the organization are everyone's concern, not just that of the chief executive or CEO. Each level in this model corresponds to a number of concepts in QPL:

Mission/values: These are the highest-level statement of why the organization is there and what distinguishes it from its competitors. They are the guiding principles for the entire organization. They correspond to QPL's high-level authorities and serve as templates for the organization's structure and its processes.

Objectives: At the next level, the organization lists its objectives over a defined period of time. These must be compatible with the mission and values of the previous level. In QPL, objectives correspond to two elements:

● outputs, i.e. the end result of the core processes of the organization
● measurable information items, such as cycle times, customer satisfaction and lead times, which also indicate feedback loops that need to be set up.

As objectives are still at a very high level, they correspond to outputs and measures at the aggregate level, representing the performance of the organization as a whole, rather than a specific function, department or process.

Critical success factors: Critical success factors (CSFs) reflect the activities which are required to achieve the objectives. They correspond to stable and higher-level processes which must be operating efficiently and effectively in order to produce the outputs and measurements which constitute the objectives. For example, an objective could be to increase turnover by 30 percent in five years: this is very high level. The CSFs to achieve this could include:

● reduced time to design and market new products
● improved after-sales service
● improved product quality
● better and more targeted advertising
● increased production capacity.

Each of these is an attribute of one or more processes of the organization. Collectively, their achievement will be required to achieve the specified growth target.

> *Processes/functions*: Finally we get to the full range of processes. Their structure, interfaces and information flows determine the required functions and hierarchies. QPL structuring facilitates the design of an organization structure which is compatible with its processes. Process analysis techniques facilitate the optimization of processes.

Typically, a business model consists of various levels, like the four just described. For the organization to remain coherent and viable, it must ensure that the four levels are consistent and support each other. Here, QPL techniques are at their most powerful. Using the three structuring principles described in Chapter 4—sequence, hierarchy and classes—we can organize the information into a form where it is easier to check for compatibility. Normally, inheritance checks reveal any inconsistencies in mission and values, since these are normally reflected in the authorities for all lower-level processes. Since objectives consists of outputs and measures, compatibility is checked by aggregating selected measures of information items of lower level processes. Finally, since CSFs are attributes of higher-level processes, the dynamic rules of Chapter 7 can be used to check that their lower-level components are compatible and work together efficiently.

8.4   AUTOMATING QPL

Drawing QPL diagrams and other process models

When you implement a QPL approach, you will soon discover that the diagrams can be difficult to draw by hand. This is not a fault in the notation—QPL uses only simple symbols, commonly available on plastic flow charting templates, and even a relatively large chart can be drawn quickly. If anything, it is easier to draw QPL charts than flow charts, since its use of structuring permits a very compact representation of processes. The problem, then, is not in drawing a QPL chart, but the way in which we obtain and document the information. This involves frequent iterations, making it very difficult to maintain hand-drawn charts.

Why do we need to draw QPL charts iteratively, instead of getting all the information 'right first time'? Simply because the documenting process itself is iterative. People are unable to describe everything they do at once, and we need to make a drawing of what they have told us before they remember these 'hidden' aspects of the process. Thus, when preparing a process description, we use existing information to develop a first draft of the process map; this provides a basis for discussion with those involved in the process, which in turn leads to another version of the process map; and so on. It is not uncommon to produce a dozen or more versions of a process before it accurately represents what actually happens.

Even with processes documented already, we need to do a considerable amount of structuring and supplemental questioning before a stable and accurate QPL diagram is produced. With BPR, this iterative development is reinforced by the need to consider various trial redesigns, each of which has its own process model.

Fortunately, the iterative development of process models is well-catered for by software packages commonly available. All the process models in this book were produced with one of them (Micrografx Inc.'s ABC FlowCharter®). Use of a computer-based system enabled illustrations to be produced quickly and then revised with relatively little effort. Features such as automatic drawing of lines between process boxes and entry of text mean that such programs can make production of such a diagram ten times or more faster than drawing it by hand. Finally, the availability of laptop and other small computers means that the process designer can take drawing tools to the site, rather than needing to take notes and then return to the office for drawing the diagrams.

There are other packages available directly for process mapping. Some of them also provide limited process analysis. Most of them cover a sub-set of the techniques in this book and can be useful in speeding up drawing, updating and analysing process diagrams. With the increasing power of computers and interest in process modelling and engineering, the availability of reasonably priced tools is bound to increase.

Process enactment

The second aspect of automation involves the enactment of processes on computers. With the increased power and sophistication of small computers, we can automate many processes that traditionall needed to be done manually. This is having a striking effect on the traditional, functionally based organization, where it is no longer necessary to have specialists dealing with individual aspects of an operation. A few years ago, it was necessary to have up to 20 specialists to process an insurance application; because of the communication delays involved in sending forms from one post to another, this could take several weeks to complete the processing. These days, insurance companies are placing knowledge of how to process such applications into the computer, making use of expert systems and other 'intelligent' techniques (Born, 1985). These permit the processing to be handled by a single operator, and reduces the processing time from weeks to hours or minutes. They have the added advantage of assigning a single operator to an application, thus making it much simpler to answer queries: the caller needs to speak only to a single operator, rather than to several specialists.

QPL provides a basis for such process enactment, with its notation for describing processes and their operators. As we have seen in previous chapters, we can form a complete model of any process with QPL. In addition, its analysis checks enable us to inspect the completeness and effectiveness of the model, before beginning the expensive process of translating it into a computer system. In fact, the original motivation for the QPL notation arose from an automated quality system which the author designed and developed in the late 1980s (Born, 1992). This involved the modelling of a complete quality and management system for a software company, and its translation into a set of rules which operated the computer system. QPL was developed, as no adequate existing language or notation could be found for describing the full range of management and quality procedures used by the organization.

The general subject of process enactment is attracting great interest, as organizations seek to improve their service to customers and to streamline their operations. It is called by other names, including workflow, groupware, teamworking and document image processing systems. While a description of these techniques is beyond the scope of this book, they will become an increasingly common method for doing business. The graphical notation of QPL supports these techniques and with its other features provides a complete foundation for their development.

8.5   WHERE DO I GO FROM HERE?

> Motorist: 'How do I get to Chicago from here?'
> Farmer: 'If you want to go to Chicago ... I wouldn't start from here.'
>
> *Traditional 'joke'*

Fortunately, this old, bad joke does not apply to QPL. QPL techniques can be applied to just about any situation, with any existing way of documenting processes. It even is effective when the information about processes is stored in people's heads! As shown earlier, a printed document can be turned into a QPL process model just by using coloured highlighting pens to identify the key QPL components (see Figure 8.3). With an automated charting tool, it is very easy to turn this annotated text into a full-powered QPL model. Or we can interview people when nothing is written down, and then annotate the notes which we produce afterwards.

In an existing culture

If flow charting or other form of process modelling has already taken place, we have the choice of translating them into QPL diagrams or of using the QPL techniques with these existing notations. The appropriate technique will depend on the situation and the need to communicate with others. The general rule is to use the QPL notation if those involved have been trained in its use. When they have not been trained, then its notation and key QPL concepts can be translated into a notation they feel comfortable with.

This book has provided a number of approaches to modelling processes. For example,

- Chapter 3 provides a seven-step procedure for writing procedures and work instructions
- Chapter 6 includes a design cycle for implementing compliance in an organization
- Chapter 7 provides a series of models for BPR.

While these procedures and steps are useful for modelling processes and implementing change, they need to be tailored to each organization. If it already has a methodology for modelling, or a preferred notation, then it is preferable to use that. Better yet, try to introduce some of the QPL-recommended practices, to encourage improvements to their existing methods. But the rule always is to communicate with the practitioners in their own language.

If the organization does not have an existing investment in a means of modelling processes, then of course it is best to introduce QPL and all its concepts as soon as possible. But however it is introduced—formally, or as an underlying approach—QPL will have a marked influence where it is used.

The QPL-transformed culture

Whether or not there is an existing culture, use of the QPL approach will have a major effect on the processes of any organization. All too often, people in an organization know that there are weaknesses in its processes, without being able to state the problems clearly. It is even more difficult to provide solutions coherently. The QPL approach empowers people, by giving them the power to make explicit what they already know, to discover the inherent structure of their activities and to create a new approach to their work.

How do we recognize a QPL-transformed culture? Here are some suggestions:

● All parts of the organization talk a common language, which breaks down departmental barriers, removes ambiguities and accelerates the improvement process.
● There is more emphasis on common goals and better coordination of staff doing different roles.
● There is an enhanced focus on processes and the core activities of the enterprise. Processes are re-engineered more quickly because they are better understood.
● Less time is spent educating staff about quality and checking procedures for compliance.

The techniques in this book have been used to model and improve processes on organizations of all sizes and complexities, with very different cultures. In many cases, the organizations were not aware of the full QPL notation, simply because it was unnecessary. In all cases, the QPL techniques were applied in a form which enabled the process owners to understand their own processes better and to discover improvements for themselves. The QPL facilitator played an essential role in this, by helping them to formulate their processes effectively. This involved:

● a language for expressing processes and information
● techniques for structuring their activities into descriptions which could be managed and discussed in groups
● a critical analysis of existing and proposed practices, to focus their attention on the most important problems and feasible solutions.

The QPL approach facilitates each of these tasks, even if expressed in a form different from the formal QPL notation.

While each use of QPL is different, we should measure the success of an assignment by our ability to express and clarify processes and how they can be improved. For those involved in implementing the processes—the process owners—success will be measured by greater clarity of how the processes work, achievement of process objectives and an enhanced sense of control and harmony in everyday work.

APPENDIX 1
Summary of the QPL notation and techniques

CONTENTS OF APPENDIX 1

OVERVIEW

This book is based on the QPL approach to modelling and analysing processes. The various chapters have described aspects of this approach in figures, tables and lists. This appendix brings some of them together for a quick review and summary of the principles. The figures and tables are given their original numbers for ease of cross-referencing.

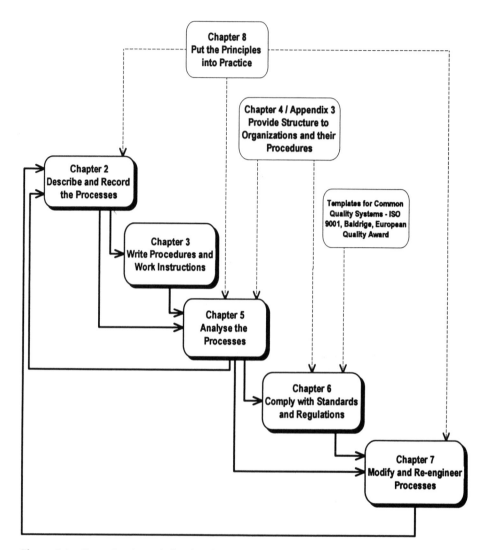

Figure 1.1 Organization of this book

THE VALUES EXPRESSED BY QPL

1) The goal of QPL is to provide the simplest and most compact description of actual processes in an organization.

2) QPL provides a framework for regulation, where the regulations to be complied with can be expressed simply and where members of the organization know precisely what they need to do. Furthermore, this framework enables the organization to do only what is required by the regulation and no more, thus allowing it greater creativity and freedom of action.

3) With its structuring techniques, QPL provides a language for scoping processes and assigning responsibility to them. Once this is done, the process owner can be given greater autonomy and responsibility for the operations which constitute the process. This is the essence of empowerment, providing the maximum power for employees at the most local level, while also providing accountability for their activities and decisions.

4) This structuring also enables process owners to measure the results of processes and to use this feedback to make improvements continuously.

5) QPL's guidelines for analysing and improving processes provide a structured set of questions which designers can use to optimize processes and produce the most creative set of working practices.

THE OBJECTIVES OF THE QPL APPROACH

1) A systematic method is required to integrate process management and quality management.

2) The method should support the controlled and documented design of all organizational processes.

3) The method should be applicable to:
   a) all aspects of quality management involving procedures and compliance with standards and regulations
   b) provision of good communications with other systems within the organization.

4) The method should provide a framework for monitoring effectiveness and efficiency of all processes and for using the results to improve them.

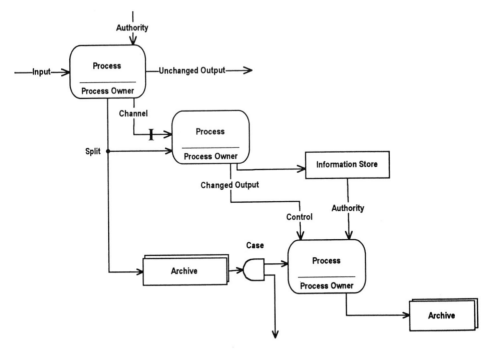

Figure 2.19 Summary of the QPL notation

LIST OF SUGGESTED STEPS FOR WRITING PROCEDURES

1.   Provide a description of the document to be produced—the statement of requirements.
2.   Collect and document all activities and information.
3.   Annotate the written description with the elements of QPL.
4.   Draw QPL diagrams.
4.1 Analyse the information by working top-down.
4.2 Identify the five QPL elements.
4.3 Draw QPL diagrams which represent the information collected.
4.4 Identify weaknesses or missing elements.
5.   Verify the contents of the QPL diagrams.
6.   Write the procedure, using the QPL diagrams.
6.1 Restructure the QPL diagrams into a form suitable for the audience.
6.2 Structure the steps into a nested hierarchy.
6.3 Write the procedure.
6.4 Verify that the procedure reflects the QPL diagram accurately.
6.5 Check the readability and usability of the procedure.
7.   Review and revise the procedure.

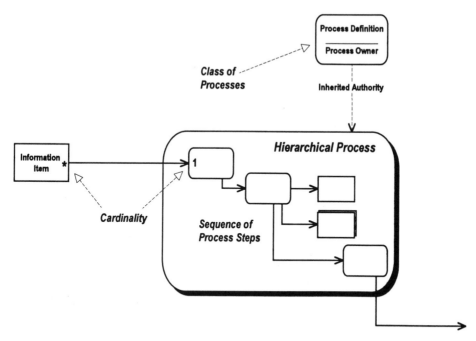

Figure 4.4 QPL structuring notation

STEPS FOR STRUCTURING INSTRUCTIONAL DOCUMENTS

1) Start with known facts about the organization's structure, then expand into process and information descriptions using QPL.

2) If the resulting process/QPL description clashes with the organization's structure, modify the QPL diagrams to provide a compatible structure.

3) Check that the relationships between processes make full use of the structuring principles of hierarchy, classification and sequence. Abstract the aspects of processes which are general, and define them as 'generic' processes. Define the specific processes which will inherit characteristics from the generic processes. Iterate back to step (2), if necessary.

4) Determine where the information on the QPL diagrams fits into the three types of document: standard/directive, general procedure or work instruction.

5) Write the three levels of documents, verifying them regularly against the QPL diagrams.

6) After the documents are completed, validate them with the actual users to determine if they match expectations and are both readable and usable.

QPL ANALYSIS CHECKS

Table 5.1 The ten types of incompleteness error

Type of error	Description
Information errors	
(a) Unused information	A process generates an information item which is never used by a process step or sent to a destination. (A source is a provider of information external to the process.)
(b) Uncreated information	An information item is used by a process step but is never generated or provided by a source. (A source is a provider of information external to the process.)
(c) Unused source	A source exists on the diagram but does not produce any information items.
(d) Unused destination	A destination exists on the diagram but does not receive any information items.
Process errors	
(e) Unconnected process	A process is not connected to any sources, destinations or other processes.
(f) Hostile process	A process has no inputs or control.
(g) Infertile process	A process produces no outputs.
(h) Broken path	There is no possible path of information between a related source and a destination.
(i) Missing authority	No authority is shown for a process.
(j) Missing ownership	No process owner (role) is shown for a process.

The eight types of inconsistency error

Table 5.2 The eight types of inconsistency error

	Type of error	Description
(a)	Misprocessed information	An information item is processed inconsistently with its type (channel, information store or archive).
(b)	Misused information	An information item is used inconsistently with its class.
(c)	Inconsistent information	A process uses an information item in a way which is incompatible with its content.
(d)	Absent input	A process requires information which none of its inputs can provide.
(e)	Absent output	A process provides information which none of its outputs can take.
(f)	Incompatible information	An information item is split and, after one or more of the threads is transformed by a subsequent process step, rejoined. This will make them incompatible.
(g)	Authority mismatch	A process is inconsistent with, or has a different scope from, its authority.
(h)	Interface error	The input or output for a process does not link with the equivalent input or output for an adjoining process.

Types of hierarchical incompatibility error

Table 5.3 Types of hierarchical incompatibility error

	Type of error	Description
(a)	Hierarchical mismatch	There is a mismatch between the input or output of a process and one of its sub-processes.
(b)	Hierarchical incompleteness	When a process is broken down into its component sub-processes, the parts do not match the full process.

Types of inheritance incompatibility error

Table 5.4 Types of inheritance incompatibility error

Error of type		Description
(a)	Inheritance mismatch	A child process is incompatible with the parent process, when it handles information items which are members of a class handled by the parent.
(b)	Cardinality* mismatch	The cardinality of a child process is incompatible with that of a parent process.

*Cardinality is described in Appendix 3.

The ten types of failure mode error

Table 5.5 The ten types of failure mode error

Type of error		Description
(a)	Information validation omission	There are no checks to catch incorrect or incomplete information items.
(b)	Process validation omission	There is no mechanism for catching or correcting an incorrectly applied process.
(c)	Reception omission	There is no mechanism for checking that an information item is received by a process after being sent by another process.
(d)	Transmission omission	There is no mechanism for checking that an information item required by a process has been sent by another process.
(e)	Information feedback omission	Information on the effect of a process is not returned to it as an input.
(f)	Process improvement omission	Information on the effect of a process is not returned to it as an authority.
(g)	Non-activated process	A process can never be activated (e.g. one of its inputs will never exist).
(h)	Process redundancy	An unnecessary process step is included (i.e. the results of the overall process would be identical without the step).
(i)	Information redundancy	Some of the information content of an information item is never used by any process.
(j)	Process exception	A process is not designed to handle a possible situation within its scope.

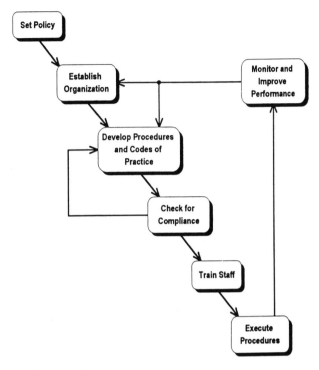

Figure 6.1 Steps for compliance

SUMMARY OF THE QPL APPROACH TO COMPLIANCE

- Compliance is the development and checking of a process to ensure that it does not contradict a standard or set of regulations.
- A template is the process model of the regulation, standard or other document which must be complied with.
- Compliance is established on a QPL diagram by connecting one process to another process, as an authority.
- A template is connected to on operational process by connecting each of its sub-processes to the applicable sub-processes of the latter. As before, they are connected as authorities.
- Compliance auditing checks that an operational process meets all the requirements of the template process. This reduces to two checks:
  - that the operational process contains no direct contradictions of the template process (hierarchical compatibility)
  - that class membership of the operational process is compatible with that of the template process (inheritance compatibility).
- The compliance audit is carried out using QPL's standard analysis checks, after the template has been connected to the operational process.
- Process design is the creative act of creating workable processes which comply with external and internal requirements for an organization.

Table 6.1   Common compliance violations

Description	Error types	Correction
General violations		
Incomplete process—the scope of the standard or regulation is not dealt with completely.	Authority mismatch Hierarchical incompleteness Broken path	Add additional sub-processes or otherwise increase the scope of the operational process.
Inconsistent process—sub-processes in the operational process use information in different ways (i.e. the operational process is inconsistent in its inter-pretation of the template).	Inheritance mismatch	Reinterpret the template to achieve consistency, or redefine the sub-processes to achieve consistency in applying the template.
Non-comprehensive process—there are certain feasible conditions or types of information which cannot be handled by the process.	Inheritance mismatch	Widen the scope of the operational process.
Process violations		
The details of the process contradict those of the template.	Authority mismatch Inheritance mismatch	Redefine the operational process to ensure agreement with the template.
Information violations		
Information items in the template are incorrectly represented by the process (e.g. the template states that a form should contain a parti-cular item, but the operational process omits this item).	Inheritance mismatch	Correct the operational process.
An information item in the template is of the wrong type (e.g. an archive in the template is represented in the operational process as an information store).	Inheritance mismatch Misprocessed information	Correct the representation of the information item and modify sub-processes, if necessary.
Authority violations		
An authority in the process is missing, unclear or inexplicit.	Authority mismatch	Add an explicit authority where required.

continued

Table 6.1 (*continued*)

Description	Error types	Correction
The authority for the process contradicts that of the template.	Authority mismatch	Re-examine the connections from the template to the sub-processes. Then modify the authority in the process to provide compatibility with the template.
An authority for the process has a lower scope than that of the template (an authority for a sub-process does not have sufficient scope to cover the requirements of the template).	Authority mismatch	Widen the scope of the authority within the operational process.
Ownership violations		
Definition of an owner in the process conflicts with that of the template.	Inheritance mismatch (Possibly) missing ownership	Redefine the process owner in the operational process, or make the owner more explicit.
Control violations		
The conditions for executing the process or one of its sub-processes conflict with those in the template.	Inheritance mismatch	Redefine the condition in the operational process, or make it more explicit.

Complexity and complexity index formulas

$$\text{Complexity} = \Sigma(\text{Process steps} \times \text{Number of authorities for each step})$$

$$\text{Complexity index} = \frac{\text{Complexity}}{\text{Total number of process steps}}$$

Analysis checklist for dynamic systems

Changes in input and output

1.1 Input capacity: Can the process deal with its inputs quickly enough so that it does not get jammed?

1.2 Adaptable input capacity: Can the process accommodate small variations in the volume of input without needing to change the process?

1.3 Output capacity: Can the process produce outputs quickly enough to supply other processes in the supply chain?

1.4 Adaptable output capacity: Can the process accommodate small variations in the volume of output without needing to change the process itself?

Changes in time

2.1 Synchronization: When two processes need to work together to produce a result, have they been designed to be activated at the same time or by another signal?

2.2 Parallel working: Can steps which currently are done sequentially be changed to work in parallel?

2.3 Imbalanced information: Does a process produce outputs faster than they can be consumed by another process or placed into planned storage?

Internal changes

3.1 Baselining a process: Before a process is changed, is it well-enough understood so that the effects of change are clear and that it will be possible to measure those effects?

3.2 Feedback loops: For all major processes, are clear feedback loops provided, so that information about changes are fed back and used to 'tune' the process?

3.3 Production improvements: Could changes to the process be made, to:

- reduce the cycle time
- cut down the distance which materials or information need to travel
- decrease the number of steps
- reduce the cost of production
- decrease the lead time for modifications or new products
- or other improvements which would improve efficiency or competitiveness?

3.4 Inspection improvements: Can the process be re-designed to minimize the number of inspection steps or improve their effectiveness? Alternatively, can inspection be reduced or eliminated by incorporating it into production steps?

continued

Analysis checklist *continued*

> 3.5 Avoiding redundancy: Can the process be re-designed to eliminate unnecessary duplication? Is there any unnecessary copying or storage of information? Are the same operations being carried out by more than one process?
>
> *Imposed changes*
>
> 4.1 Process adaptation: Is the process sufficiently adaptable and flexible so that it can be rapidly changed if external conditions change (say a fall in orders)?
> 4.2 Empowerment: Does the authority (or authorities) for a process empower the process owners/roles, by giving them the necessary flexibility and sanction to adapt processes to changing conditions?.
> 4.3 Red tape: Is the complexity index as near 1.0 as possible (so that there is neither too much red tape nor too little guidance on how to carry out tasks)?

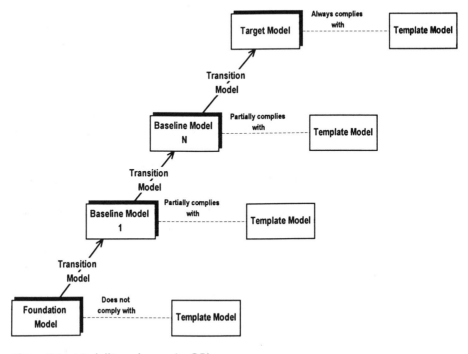

Figure 7.6 Modelling change in QPL

APPENDIX 2
QPL charts for ISO 9001, the Malcolm Baldrige Award and the European Quality Award

This appendix provides high-level templates for three widely accepted quality models: ISO 9001, the Malcolm Baldrige Award and the European Quality Award. In addition to a QPL diagram, some process descriptions are also provided. These assist organizations to tailor the template to their own processes and also provide a textual equivalent of the QPL notation.

The diagrams for each template are shown only at the highest level, i.e. core processes and main information links. These are sufficient for most organizations in checking their alignment with one or more of the quality models, but the diagrams can be expanded into much greater detail if that is required, using the framework of these high-level diagrams.

The templates may appear very complicated at first, since a large number of high-level processes and information items are provided. In practice, however, only a part of the diagram, or a sub-set of its content, will be used for a specific purpose. An example of this is provided in Chapter 6, where a sub-set of the ISO 9001 template is used for compliance checking.

These templates are interpretations of the models, in that they extract general processes and information items from the lists and examples given in the texts. They also provide connections between processes, using information items, where the quality models leave this open to interpretation. Users may wish to reinterpret the models for specific situations or contexts.

Each of the templates is available on disk or as a large printed chart. Further details can be obtained by contacting the author at the address given in the Preface.

QPL CHART FOR ISO 9001

International quality standard ISO 9001 (ISO 9001, 1994), also known as European Standard EN 29001 and British Standard BS 5750 – Part 1, is a widely accepted model for quality systems in use throughout the world. There are two other equivalent standards, ISO 9002 and ISO 9003, which have less scope and tend to be sub-sets of ISO 9001. The QPL diagram can easily be modified to cover them by deleting certain process boxes and information items.

The chart includes modifications in the 1994 revision. The revision marks will also assist those who are moving from the 1987 version of the standard to its revised form. Paragraph numbers are consistent with both the 1987 and 1994 versions.

Processes

A—Define quality policy (4.1.1)

Inputs: this process has no inputs and is activated when the organization decides to adopt ISO 9001.

Outputs: the quality policy for the organization.

Authorities:

- the set of ISO 9001 requirements
- customer needs
- organizational goals and expectations.

As this has no inputs and provides an input for several other cornerstone processes, it needs to be carried out early in creating a quality system.

B—Establish quality organization (4.1.2, 4.1.3)

Inputs:

- the previous version of the quality system (if any)
- results of internal quality audits.

Outputs:

- the reviewed quality system
- identification of staff for establishing and maintaining the quality system (process C) and for 'Inspection and testing' (process L)
- the management representative
- verification requirements
- verification resources and personnel.

Authorities:

- ISO 9001 requirements
- the quality policy of the organization.

Like process A—Define quality policy, this process should be carried out early in developing a quality system.

C—Establish and maintain quality system (4.2)

This is one of the key processes in the template for ISO 9001 and it has several inputs, outputs and authorities.

Inputs: the inputs are product quality records, which are provided by several other processes.

Outputs: the instructions and procedures for the organization, namely:

- quality manual, quality plan and documented work instructions
- required procedures for other processes of ISO 9001
- the quality system for the organization.

Authorities:

- the requirements of ISO 9001 itself
- the quality policy set by process A—Define quality policy.

Ownership for this process is provided by process B—Establish quality organizations, in the form of identified staff, the management representative and verification resources and personnel.

D—Verification

This is a generic process, used by four other processes in the template:

- H—Review contract
- I—Design control
- J—Purchased product conformance
- L—Inspection and testing.

In designing parts of the organization's processes for these four parts of the template, the designer must also ensure that the requirements of this process are satisfied.

Inputs:

- statistical techniques
- verification requirements
- products
- documents.

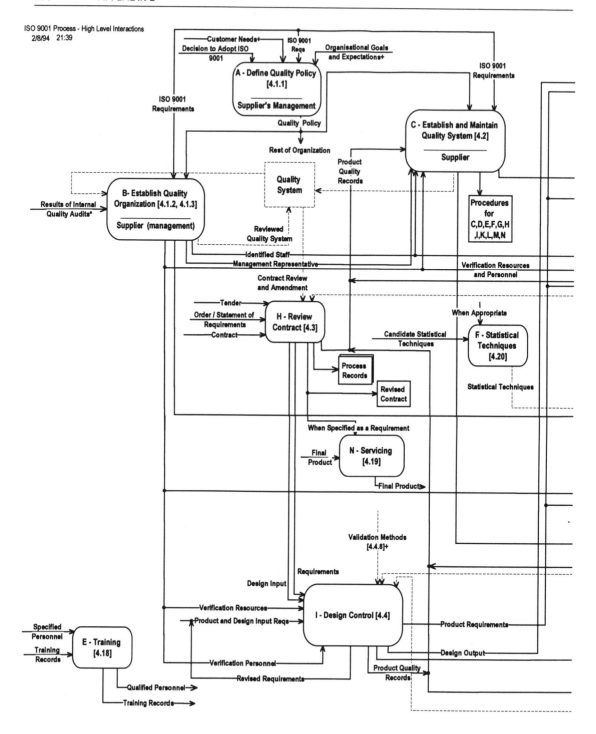

ISO 9001 Process - High Level Interactions
2/8/94   21:39

Figure A2.1   ISO 9001 process—high-level interactions. © Gary Born 1994

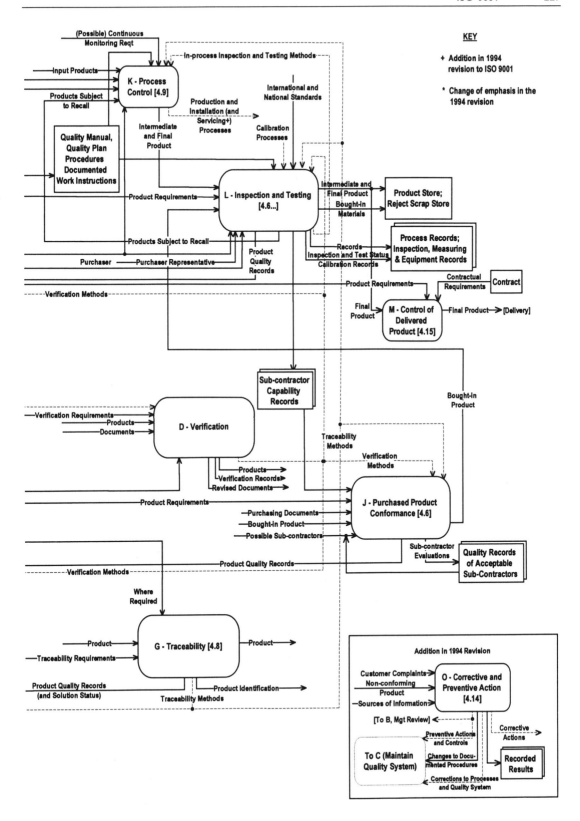

+ Addition in 1994
  revision to ISO 9001

* Change of emphasis in the
  1994 revision

Outputs:

- the verified product
- verification records
- documents revised as a result of verification activities.

E—Training (4.18)

This process is implicit throughout the template and therefore is not directly connected to any of the other processes.

Inputs:

- personnel doing specific assigned tasks (as required by this section)
- training records.

Outputs:

- qualified personnel
- training records.

In complying with this paragraph of the standard, the designer must examine all activities within the organization's total process to determine if there is a training requirement. If so, then this part of the template applies to the activity.

F—Statistical techniques (4.20)

This process is applicable only if appropriate, i.e. if it is needed to verify 'the acceptability of process capability and product characteristics'.

Inputs: possible statistical techniques, which this process will evaluate for applicability.

Outputs: the selected statistical techniques.

G—Traceability (4.8)

This is a generic process, used by four other processes in the template:

- I—Design control
- J—Purchased product conformance
- K—Process control
- L—Inspection and testing.

In designing the organization's processes for these parts of the template, the designer must also ensure that the requirements of this process are satisfied.

Inputs:

- the product subject to traceability
- requirements for traceability.

Outputs:

- the product subject to traceability (unchanged by this process)
- identification of the product
- product quality records.

This process is applicable only where 'traceability is a specified requirement'.

H—*Review contract (4.3)*

This process is subject to the requirements of process D—Verification.

Inputs:

- the tender documents
- the order or requirements in the tender
- the contract.

Outputs:

- design input
- the requirements (after revision by this process)
- process records
- the revised contract
- product quality records.

I—*Design control (4.4)*

This process is subject to the requirements of process D—Verification and (if applicable) to those of process G—Traceability.

Inputs:

- design input
- the requirements (after review of the contract)
- product and design input requirements
- verification resources.

Outputs:

- product requirements (unchanged by this process)
- design input
- traceability requirements for the remainder of the process

- product quality records
- revised product and design input requirements.

This process is the main differentiator between ISO 9001 and the other two standards in the ISO 9000 series for quality systems (along with Servicing, paragraph 4.19). While the standard does not define 'design', BS 5750, Part 4 (BSI, 1990) provides guidance on applicability of this paragraph: 'The supplier's design function should be capable of taking the customer's needs and translating these, in a systematic and controlled way, into a specification which defines a product or service.'

J—Purchased product conformance (4.6)

The requirements of this process apply to any product which is purchased and is to be used in producing the product or service covered by the overall quality system.

This process is subject to the requirements of process D—Verification, and, if applicable, to those of process G—Traceability.

Inputs:

- bought-in product
- sub-contractor capability records
- product requirements
- purchasing documents
- possible sub-contractors (required in selection of suppliers for bought-in product).

Outputs:

- bought-in product (unchanged by this process)
- sub-contractor evaluations
- product quality records.

K—Process control (4.9)

The requirements of this process apply to any post-design production or installation process.

Inputs:

- input products
- design output
- product requirements
- products subject to recall (only if the continuous monitoring requirement applies).

Outputs:

- intermediate or final product
- documentation for production, installation and servicing processes.

Authorities: this process is subject to the requirements of process D—Verification and (if applicable) to those of process G—Traceability. The other authorities for this process are:

- a possible continuous monitoring requirement, in which case the process is applied continuously
- the quality plan or documented work instructions.

L—Inspection and testing (4.6 ...)

The requirements of this process apply to all inspection and testing activities, from that of bought-in product, through intermediate inspection, to final product testing before delivery to the customer.

Inputs:

- bought-in, intermediate or final product
- product requirements.

Outputs:

- intermediate or final product (which is unchanged by the process)
- bought-in materials (which are unchanged by the process)
- inspection and testing records
- calibration records
- updated sub-contractor capability records
- product quality records
- products subject to recall (only if a continuous monitoring requirement applies).

Authorities: this process is subject to the requirements of process D—Verification and (if applicable) to those of process G—Traceability. The other authorities for this process are:

- international and national standards
- the quality plan or documented work instructions
- general calibration processes.

M—Control of delivered product (4.15)

The requirements of this process apply to four sub-processes:

- handling
- storage
- packaging
- delivery.

Inputs: the only input to this process is that of the final product.

Outputs: the only output from this process is that of the final product (unchanged).

No changed outputs are produced because this process is responsible only for delivering the product in a form unchanged from its production.

Authorities: that of the product and contractual requirements.

N—Servicing (4.19)

The requirements of this process are applicable only when specified in the contract (see process H—Review contract). It applies to all post-delivery activities (see process M—Control of delivered products).

Inputs: the only input to this process is the final product.

Outputs: the only output from this process is the final product, as modified by servicing.

Authorities: this process has no authorities other than ISO 9001 itself.

O—Corrective and preventive action (4.14)

The 1994 version has changed significantly from the 1987 version (where it was called just 'Corrective action').

Inputs:

- customer complaints
- non-conforming product
- sources of information.

Outputs:

- corrective actions
- recorded results (an archive)
- preventive actions and controls
- changes to documented procedures
- corrections to processes and the quality system.

The last three are sent to process C—Maintain quality system. The list of preventive actions is also sent to process B—Establish quality organization.

Information items

These items are specifically listed on the process template and are key documents and records for the ISO 9001 process.

Procedures for ...

These are the 'documented procedures' which ISO 9001 specifies shall be produced for several of its sub-processes. Their production has been collected into a single process (C—Establish and maintain quality system), although the actual production of these documents may be distributed in other processes.

Process records; inspection, measuring and equipment records

These records, which in QPL are specified as archives, are required by the inspection and testing sub-process.

Product store; reject scrap store

This is an information store required by the inspection and testing sub-process and used to hold materials and products after testing, but before they are:

● returned to the supplier
● scrapped or reworked
● re-graded for alternative applications
● delivered to the customer.

Quality manual, quality plan and documented work instructions

This information store is used as an authority by two sub-processes in the template, 'Process control' (K) and 'Inspection and testing' (L).

Quality system

This is the overall system produced and maintained by the organization and subject to the requirements of the ISO 9001 process template. It is produced by the 'Establish and maintain quality system' process (C). The 'Establish quality organization' process (B) is responsible for reviewing it.

QPL CHART FOR THE MALCOLM BALDRIGE QUALITY AWARD

This section provides a high-level template for the Malcolm Baldrige Award (Baldrige, 1994), which is widely used in the USA as a model of a quality system. In addition to the QPL diagram, some guidance notes are also provided. These assist organizations to tailor the template to their own processes and also provide a textual equivalent of the QPL notation.

As shown in Chapter 6, the template can be used to check that the parts of an organization's procedures are compatible with its approach and also can assist in designing or redesigning its processes.

To assist in relating the template to the text of the *Application Guidelines*, 1994, paragraph numbers have been attached to all processes and most information items. While the details of individual paragraphs vary from year to year, the seven main sections of the Baldrige criteria tend to remain the same. Number in brackets [ ] refer to section numbers in the 1994 Examination Criteria.

Processes

1—Leadership processes

Inputs:

- feedback on performance [1.2]
- reviews of performance [5.2].

Outputs:

- actions to assist sub-standard units
- customer focus and quality values [1.1]
- requirements for managers and supervisors [1.2].

Authorities: public responsibilities.

2.2—Competitive comparisons and benchmarking

Inputs:

- benchmark data
- evaluation results

Outputs:

- analysis of benchmarks and comparisons
- field and benchmark data
- improvements to needs and criteria
- improvements to processes
- stretch targets.

Authorities:

- needs and criteria
- processes (descriptions).

2.3—Analysis of company-level data

Inputs:

- analysis of benchmarks and comparisons
- quality and performance data.

Outputs:

- improved products and services
- improvements to customer relationship management and commitment [7.2 and 7.3]
- quality and operational data and results (relationship to financial performance).

Authorities: none.

3.1a, 3.1b—Development of strategies and business plans

Inputs:

- customer satisfaction comparisons and levels [7.4, 7.5]
- quality and operational data and results (relationship to financial performance).

Outputs:

- business plans
- company strategies and plans.

Authorities:

- customer focus and quality values [1.1]
- evaluation results
- requirements for managers and supervisors [1.2].

3.1c—Deployment of plans

Inputs: performance.

Outputs:

- process descriptions and practices
- resource requirements
- results
- work unit plans.

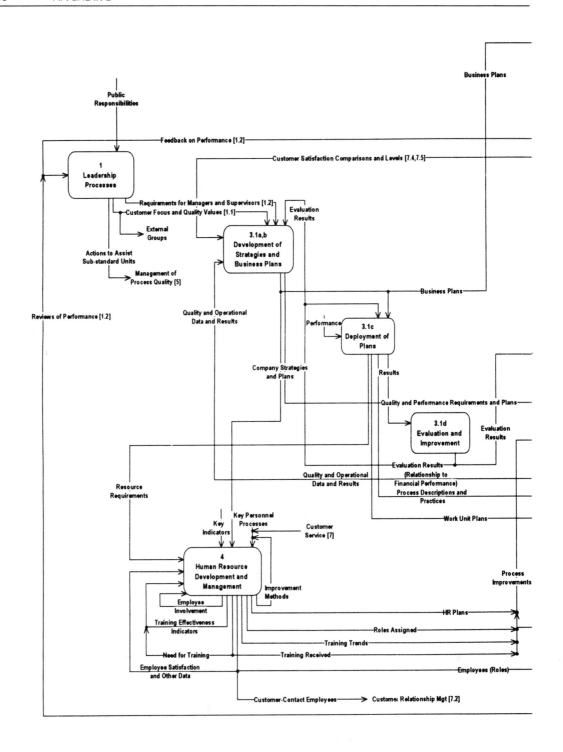

Figure A2.2 Malcolm Baldrige process—high-level interactions. © Gary Born 1994

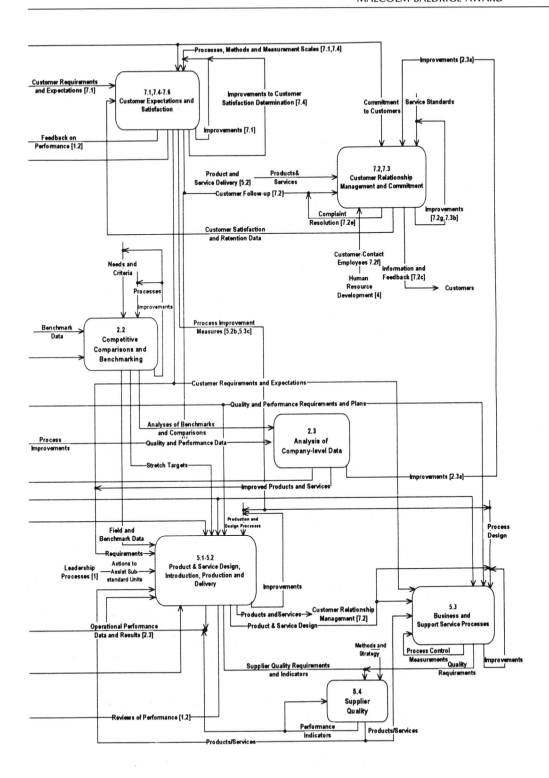

Processes, Methods and Measurement Scales [7.1,7.4]

Improvements [2.3a]

Customer Requirements
and Expectations [7.1]

**7.1,7.4-7.6
Customer Expectations and
Satisfaction**

Improvements to Customer
Satisfaction Determination [7.4]

Commitment
to Customers

Service Standards

Improvements [7.1]

Feedback on
Performance [1.2]

**7.2,7.3
Customer Relationship
Management and Commitment**

Product and
Service Delivery [5.2]

Products &
Services

Customer Follow-up [7.2]

Improvements
[7.2g,7.3b]

Complaint
Resolution [7.2e]

Customer Satisfaction
and Retention Data

Customer-Contact
Employees 7.2f

Information and
Feedback [7.2c]

Needs and
Criteria

Human
Resource
Development [4]

Customers

Processes

Improvements

Benchmark
Data

**2.2
Competitive
Comparisons and
Benchmarking**

Prrocess Improvement
Measures [5.2b,5.3c]

Customer Requirements and Expectations

Quality and Performance Requirements and Plans

Analyses of Benchmarks
and Comparisons

**2.3
Analysis of
Company-level Data**

Process
Improvements

Quality and Performance Data

Stretch Targets

Improvements [2.3a]

Improved Products and Services

Production and
Design Processes

Process
Design

Field and
Benchmark Data

Requirements

Actions to
Assist Sub-
standard Units

Leadership
Processes [1]

**5.1-5.2
Product & Service Design,
Introduction, Production and
Delivery**

Improvements

**5.3
Business and
Support Service Processes**

Products and Services

Customer Relationship
Management [7.2]

Product & Service Design

Operational Performance
Data and Results [2.3]

Methods and
Strategy

Process Control
Measurements

Quality
Requirements

Improvements

Supplier Quality Requirements
and Indicators

**5.4
Supplier
Quality**

Reviews of Performance [1.2]

Performance
Indicators

Products/Services

Products/Services

Authorities:

- business plans
- evaluation results.

3.1d—Evaluation and improvement

Inputs: results of deploying business and other plans

Outputs: evaluation results

Authorities: none.

4—Human resource development and management

Inputs:

- employee involvement
- employee satisfaction and other data
- need for training
- resource requirements
- training effectiveness indicators.

Outputs:

- customer-contact employees [7.2]
- employee involvement
- employee satisfaction and other data
- employees and roles assigned
- human resource plans
- methods for improving training
- need for training
- training effectiveness indicators
- training received
- training trends.

Authorities:

- company strategies and plans
- key indicators (for human resource development and management)
- key personnel processes.

5.1–5.2—Product and service design, introduction, production and delivery

Inputs:

- actions to assist sub-standard units

- field and benchmark data
- products and services
- operational performance data and results [2.3]
- requirements and expectations (customers and internal).

Outputs:

- improvements to production and design processes
- operational performance data and results [2.3]
- products and service design
- products and services
- reviews of performance [1.2]
- supplier quality requirements and indicators.

Authorities:

- process descriptions and practices
- production and design processes
- quality and performance requirements and plans
- stretch targets
- work unit plans.

Process owners: employees (roles).

5.3—Business and support service processes

Inputs:

- customer requirements and expectations [7.1]
- process control measurements
- product and service design
- products and services.

Outputs:

- improvements to process design
- process control measurements
- quality requirements.

Authorities:

- process descriptions and practices
- process design methods
- quality and performance requirements and plans.

5.4—Supplier quality

Inputs: performance indicators.

Outputs:

- performance indicators
- products and services.

Authorities:

- methods and strategy for supplier quality
- quality requirements and indicators for suppliers.

7.1, 7.4–7.6—Customer expectations and satisfaction

Inputs:

- customer requirements and expectations [7.1]
- customer satisfaction and retention data.

Outputs:

- customer follow-up [7.2]
- customer requirements and expectations
- customer satisfaction comparisons and levels [7.4, 7.5]
- feedback on performance [1.2]
- improvements to processes, methods and measurement scales [7.1, 7.4]
- process improvement measures [5.2b, 5.3c]
- quality and performance data.

Authorities:

- business plans
- processes, methods and measurement scales [7.1, 7.4].

7.2, 7.3—Customer relationship management and commitment

Inputs:

- customer follow-up [7.2]
- products and services [5.2].

Outputs:

- complaint resolution [7.2e]
- customer satisfaction and retention data
- information and feedback [7.2c]
- improvements to service standards.

Authorities:

- commitment to customers
- improvements to customer relationship management and commitment [2.3a]
- service standards.

Process owners: customer contact employees [4].

Information items

The template does not provide any specific categories of information items. All information items in this model are used as simple input, output and authorities. No generic processes are used as authorities.

QPL CHART FOR THE EUROPEAN QUALITY AWARD

This section provides a high–level template for the European Quality Award (EFQM, 1993), which is gaining recognition in Europe and elsewhere as a useful guideline for a total quality organization. In addition to the QPL diagram, some guidance notes are also provided. These assist organizations to tailor the template to their own processes and also provide a textual equivalent of the QPL notation.

As shown in Chapter 6, the template can be used to check that the parts of an organization's procedures are compatible with its approach and also can assist in designing or redesigning its processes.

Unlike the other two quality models in this appendix, the European Quality Award specifies a high–level graphical model, with nine elements (see Figure A2.3):

(1) leadership
(2) people management
(3) policy and strategy
(4) resources
(5) processes
(6) people satisfaction
(7) customer satisfaction
(8) impact on society
(9) business results.

When converted into QPL form, the first five are represented as groups of processes, and these occupy most of the template. Each of the five groups is broken down into sub-processes which follow exactly the EQA sub-divisions.

'People satisfaction' and 'customer satisfaction' are treated as information items in the template, while 'impact on society' is treated partially as a process and partially as information items. 'Business results' are represented in a single process box in the template.

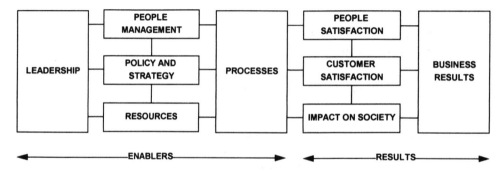

Figure A2.3 The high-level model for the European Quality Award

Processes

1—Leadership

Each process within this section is 'owned' by the managers in the organization.

1a—Take positive steps for visible involvement in TQM

Outputs:

- accessibility to staff
- commitment to total quality.

1b—Take positive steps toward a total quality culture

Inputs:

- progress in total quality—composed of:
    - measures of customer satisfaction
    - people satisfaction
    - the impact on society of the organization
- awareness of total quality.

Outputs: commitment to achieving total quality.

Authorities: commitment to total quality.

1c—Provide recognition and appreciation:

Inputs:

- internal individuals
- external individuals
- teams.

Outputs: internal and external recognition.

1d—Support total quality with appropriate resources and assistance

Inputs: progress in total quality (see 1b).

Outputs: resources, used by the processes in section 4.

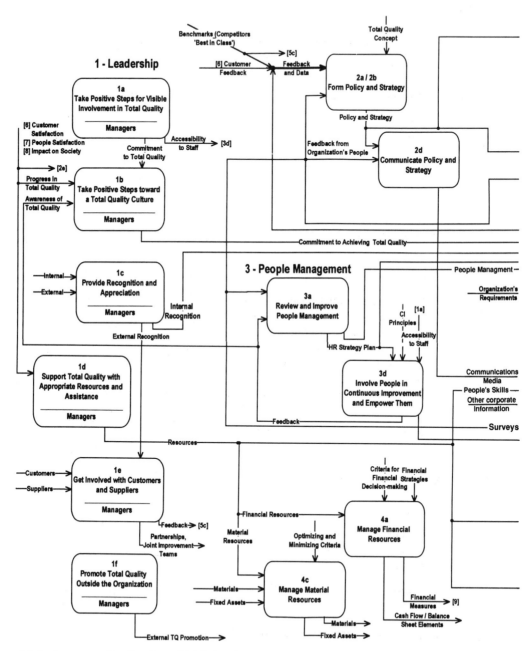

Figure A2.4 European Quality Award high level interactions processes. © Gary Born 1994

2 - Policy and Strategy

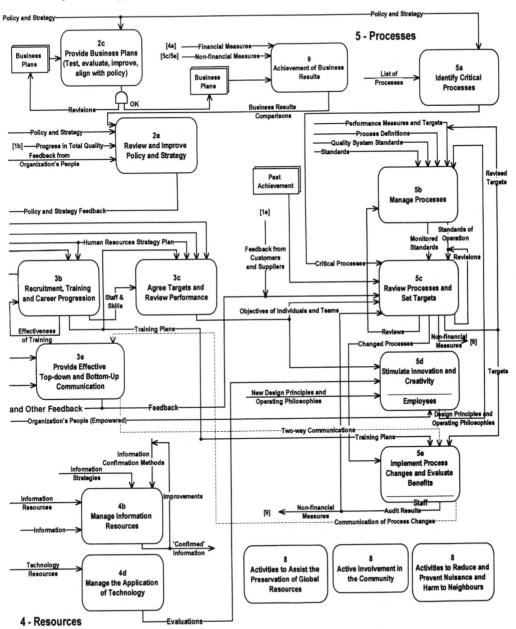

5 - Processes

4 - Resources

1e—Get involved with customers and suppliers

   Inputs:

   ● customers
   ● suppliers.

   Outputs:

   ● feedback to 5c (Review processes and set targets)
   ● partnerships and joint improvement teams.

   Authorities: 'external recognition' (which was an output from 1c).

1f—Promote total quality outside the organization

   Outputs: external total quality promotion.

2 Policy and strategy

2a/2b—Form policy and strategy

   Inputs:

   ● feedback and data (based on benchmark and competitor data, customer feedback and policy and strategy feedback)
   ● feedback from the organization's people.

   Outputs: policy and strategy for the organization.

   Authorities: the total quality concept.

2c—Provide business plans (test, evaluate, improve, align with policy)

   Inputs: business plans.

   Outputs:

   ● the business plans themselves
   ● revisions to the business plans.

   Authorities: the organization's policy and strategy.

2d—Communicate policy and strategy

> *Inputs*:
>
> - the organization's policy and strategy
> - feedback from the organization's people.
>
> *Outputs*: communication of policy and strategy through the organization.

2e—Review and improve policy and strategy

> *Inputs*:
>
> - comparisons of business results
> - policy and strategy
> - progress in total quality
> - feedback from the organization's people.
>
> *Outputs*: feedback on policy and strategy.

3 People management

3a—Review and improve people management

> *Inputs*: feedback and other data from the organization's people.
>
> *Outputs*:
>
> - human resources strategy plan
> - people management policies and practices.

3b—Recruitment, training and career progression

> *Inputs*:
>
> - organization's requirements for staff and skills
> - personnel resources
> - knowledge of the skills of people
> - feedback on the effectiveness of training.

Outputs:

- measures of the effectiveness of training
- training plans
- staff and their skills.

Authorities:

- people management policies and practices
- human resources strategy plan.

3c—Agree targets and review performance

Inputs: staff and their skills.

Outputs: objectives of individuals and teams.

Authorities:

- training plans
- human resources strategy plan
- internal recognition of staff
- management's commitment to achieving total quality.

3d—Involve people in continuous improvement and empower them

Inputs: none.

Outputs:

- feedback to review
- improve people management and empowerment of the organization's people.

Authorities:

- human resources strategy plan
- continuous improvement principles
- accessibility to staff.

3e—Provide effective top-down and bottom-up communication

Inputs:

- communications on policy and strategy of the organization
- other corporate information.

Outputs: feedback from the organization's people.

Authorities: communication of process changes.

4 Resources

4a—Manage financial resources

Inputs: financial resources.

Outputs:

- financial measures
- cash flow and balance sheet elements.

Authorities:

- criteria for financial decision-making
- organization's financial strategies.

4b—Manage information resources

Inputs: information resources and information.

Outputs:

- improvements to methods for confirming information (see *Authorities*)
- confirmed information itself.

Authorities:

- information strategies for the organization
- methods for confirming information (assuring its 'validity, integrity, security and scope').

4c—Manage material resources

Inputs:

- material resources
- materials
- fixed assets.

Outputs:

- materials
- fixed assets.

Authorities:

- criteria for optimizing material inventories
- minimizing material waste.

4d—Manage the application of technology

> *Inputs*: technology resources.

> *Outputs*: evaluations of alternative and emerging technologies.

5 Process management

5a—Identify critical processes

> *Inputs*: list of candidate critical processes.

> *Outputs*: critical processes of the organization.

> *Authorities*: policy and strategy of the organization.

5b—Manage processes

> *Inputs*: reviews of the organization's processes in operation.

> *Outputs*:

- monitored standards
- standards of operation.

> *Authorities*:

- standards of the organization
- quality system standards
- process definitions
- performance measures and targets
- design principles and operating philosophies.

5c—Review processes and set targets

> *Inputs*:
>
> - critical processes (identified in 5a)
> - past achievement
> - benchmarking data
> - feedback from the organization's people, customers and suppliers
> - objectives of individuals and teams
> - process audit results.
>
> *Outputs*:
>
> - process reviews
> - change processes
> - non-financial measures
> - revised targets for improvement
> - revisions to standards of operation.
>
> *Authorities*: output from 5b:
>
> - monitored standards
> - standards of operation.

5d—Stimulate innovation and creativity

> *Inputs*:
>
> - objectives of individuals and teams
> - technology evaluations
> - new design principles and operating philosophies.
>
> *Outputs*: design principles and operating philosophies which will be utilized.
>
> The process is owned by the empowered people of the organization whose 'creative talents ... are brought to bear'.

5e—Implement process changes and evaluate benefits

> *Inputs*: the changed processes from 5c.
>
> *Outputs*:
>
> - results of auditing changed processes
> - communication of process changes.

Authorities:

- training plans (from 3c)
- two-way communications (from 3e)
- targets for improvement (from 5c).

6 Customer satisfaction

This is represented by an information item in the QPL chart.

7 People satisfaction

This is represented by an information item in the QPL chart.

8 Impact on society

Processes in this section do not have information items which can readily be expressed in a QPL chart. Therefore, they are placed on the template with no inputs or outputs.

- Active involvement in the community
- Activities to assist the preservation of global resources
- Activities to reduce and prevent nuisance and harm to neighbours.

9 Business results

9 Achievement of business results

Inputs:

- business plans (from 2c)
- financial measures (from 4a)
- non-financial measures (from 5c and 5e).

Outputs: comparisons of business results with planned business performance.

Information items

The template has used general categories of information items, as mentioned in the EQA guidelines. Specific examples of information items, as mentioned in the guidelines, have been avoided except when they have a general significance.

All information items in this model are used as simple input, output and authorities. No generic processes are used as authorities.

APPENDIX 3
Principles of structuring

The structuring principles of QPL are derived from the principles of object-oriented analysis and design. This discipline dates to the 1960s, but it did not achieve prominence until the 1980s, and it is growing in status and popularity in the 1990s. Schlaer and Mellor (1988), Coad and Yourdon (1990) and Booch (1991) provide accessible approaches to this subject. This appendix provides additional detail for the QPL structuring principles, which are summarized in Chapter 4.

THE THREE METHODS OF ORGANIZATION

There are only three methods of organization:

- hierarchies and assemblies—breaking the whole into its parts
- classification and commonality—determining what things have in common
- sequence and causality—determining the order of things, in time and space.

These are the three basic methods of logical organization. The following sections describe each in more detail, along with some examples.

There is also a fourth method of logical organization: deduction (for example, 'Based on the following pieces of evidence, and the fact that b follows from a, we can conclude that ...'). This is not a genuine method of *structuring* objects, however, but a useful way of presenting conclusions, and one which usually combines the three 'classical' methods. Even so, it is rarely useful as a means of expression in procedures and work instructions, as these deal only with what to do rather than the logical reasoning behind them. For a detailed discussion of deduction and the other three structuring principles, see Minto (1991).

Hierarchy (assembly)

The hierarchy is the form of structure most easy to understand, as we encounter it from birth. Families are composed of their members: grandparents, mother, father, aunts, uncles, and children. Each is a distinct 'unit', and they can be grouped together in many ways: the nuclear family (parents and children) or the extended family (parents, grandparents, aunts, uncles and children, for example). The components of the structure are individual and distinct, and this makes it easier to group them into different structures.

We can also group units geographically. For example, in the United States, the largest unit is the USA itself. The next unit is the region, followed by the state, then the county, and finally the city, town or village. In terms of an organization chart, this hierarchy can be illustrated as shown in Figure A3.1.

Structuring by hierarchy is very popular in business and service organizations. Two examples are the functional hierarchy (see Figure A3.2) and the staff hierarchy (see Figure A3.3).

The above examples concentrate on hierarchies of things or people, but processes can also be structured in hierarchies. They can be structured in much the same way. Take the following examples:

Personnel processes: Appointing and managing staff is composed of three processes (see Example 1, Chapter 3):

- appoint officers
- compile performance reports
- appoint staff.

Purchasing process: Selecting a supplier is composed of three processes (see Example 2, Chapter 3):

- prepare list of candidate suppliers
- telephone candidate suppliers
- evaluate the candidates.

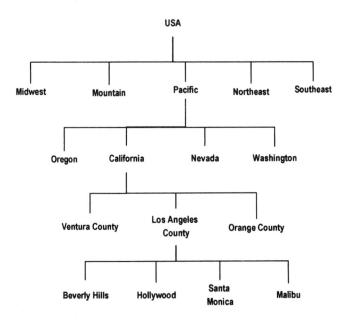

Figure A3.1 An example of a hierarchy structure

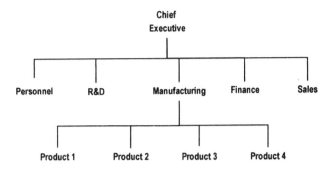

Figure A3.2 An example of a functional hierarchy

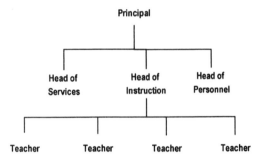

Figure A3.3 An example of a staff hierarchy

Each process can be broken down into further hierarchical processes. For example, 'Evaluate the candidates' can be broken into:

- reject non-compliant bids
- rank bids by price
- rank bids by quality
- select best value for money.

Manufacturing process: Manufacturing a component is composed of the following six steps:

- receive raw materials
- inspect materials
- build the component
- inspect the component
- store the component
- deliver the component.

In each example, the sub-processes are discrete processes, and the sum of all the sub-processes is the main process itself. This provides a very useful property of hierarchical processes: encapsulation. The main process encapsulates, or hides, the details of the sub-processes which constitute it. Formally, encapsulation is defined as the hiding of all of the details of a process which do not contribute to its description (adapted from

Booch's definition, in Booch, 1991). In terms of structuring and simplifying our understanding of processes, encapsulation is invaluable, as it permits us to view only the level of detail required at any particular moment. If we are interested only in the information needed for and produced by selecting a supplier, then it is not necessary to understand or even to list the internal processing of this information. Conversely, if we are studying a single sub-process, then it is unnecessary to understand the other sub-processes which constitute the main process, or the main process itself.

Encapsulation is also valuable for supporting the customer—supplier relationship, at the heart of many total quality approaches. In QPL, each process has a role or responsibility associated with it, and that person (or other unit) acts as either a customer or supplier, depending on whether the relationship with another process is that of input or output. Through encapsulation, several other roles (for the sub-processes) can be incorporated within the main process, without a confusion arising about who is the actual supplier or customer. In the manufacturing example given above, the customer for input materials, and the supplier of the component, is the manufacturing function responsible for the main process. Those responsible for sub-processes—the receiving staff, inspectors, assembly staff, storeroom staff and delivery staff—contribute to the main process, of course, but do not take responsibility for the whole. They are freed to take customer and supplier responsibilities only for their own processes.

The property of encapsulation is one of the most useful tools we have for describing processes compactly but also coherently. It enables the writer of procedures to describe only the level of detail required for a specific element of the hierarchy, rather than all the other processes either at the same level or which constitute the process.

Classification (commonality)

The hierarchical structure is extremely useful for grouping distinct physical units into various levels. However, it is not always sufficient for structuring real things, because in practice, categories often overlap. Business hierarchies often are not an adequate model, as people have more than one role: a person may be a member of the purchasing department, yet also have accounting responsibilities, and report to the accounting manager.

Increasingly, organizations are seeking to avoid structures where people or even departments are locked into single functions, and moving to more adaptable structures where the whole process, rather than individual functions, is the primary objective. To do this, it is necessary to view both individuals and departments as multi-skilled units, possessing many skills and capable of performing a range of functions, who can adapt quickly when the process requires innovation or there are temporary and short-term changes.

This leads to classification as the next means of providing structure. Classification identifies the common characteristics of different things. Automobiles all have the common characteristics of being vehicles, travelling on roads and self-propelled by an engine. Whatever the make, size or engine type of a car, it will always have those characteristics in common with other cars. Similarly, aeroplanes and airships are both flying machines for obvious reasons, but the former share the common characteristic of being heavier than air, and the latter of being lighter than air.

Classification is allied to the concept of *abstraction*, which is the formal way of defining classification:

> An *abstraction* denotes the essential characteristics of an object that distinguish it from all other kinds of objects and thus provide crisply defined conceptual boundaries, relative to the perspective of the viewer. (Booch, 1991)

As discussed above, the abstraction for a car involves the three essential characteristics of being a vehicle, powered by an engine and travelling on roads, while the essential characteristics of an aeroplane are that it can fly and is heavier than air.

The concept of abstraction leads directly to that of *classes*, defined as: A class is a set of objects which share essential attributes, which distinguish them from other objects.

Classes are used frequently in QPL, dividing all things into two key classes—processes and information—and then classifying information into four categories—information items, conditions, authorities and ownership. In addition, information items can be broken down into three other categories: channels, information stores and archives.

In working with processes, the concepts of class and abstraction are equally useful. In the purchasing example of Chapter 3 (Example 2), the essential characteristics of the class of purchasing processes are:

- they arise from a need for goods or services
- they are the responsibility of the purchasing department
- their authority is derived from the set of purchasing procedures
- they result in the acquisition of goods or services and in the update of purchasing records.

All processes which have the above characteristics may be classified as purchasing processes.

ISO 9001, an International Quality Standard, refers to a class of processes known as 'Inspection and testing processes' (section 4.10). It defines three other processes which belong to this class:

- receiving inspection and testing (4.10.2)
- in-process inspection and testing (4.10.3)
- final inspection and testing (4.10.4).

Appendix 2, which contains a QPL version of ISO 9001, shows the usefulness of common membership of this class and other classes.

As noted earlier, categories often overlap. I am a human being, as well as a mammal. I am also a member of the class of residents of England, and of the class of fathers. And so on, through hundreds of different classes to which I belong. For each class of which I am a member, I have the characteristics of that class. This leads to a final definition, that of *inheritance*, defined as 'explicit representation of commonality'. An object inherits all the properties of the classes to which it belongs. As a human being, I inherit the characteristics of walking on my hind legs and speaking words. As a resident of England, I inherit the characteristic of having a home in this island kingdom. As a member of the class of fathers, I inherit the characteristic of having a son or daughter (sons in my case!).

Given the use of the term 'inheritance', it is not surprising that we say that the child inherits characteristics from the parent. For example, the class of human beings is a parent class, while the citizens of the USA is a child class, since they all inherit the characteristics of being human.

Processes also inherit characteristics. All purchasing processes inherit the characteristics described above for such processes. In ISO 9001, cited above, all final inspection and testing processes inherit characteristics such as:

- carried out in accordance with the quality plan or documented procedures
- products are not released until inspection and testing procedures are completed.

Note that a process or other object can inherit from more than one class. If we define the class of domesticated animals, then a pet bird inherits some characteristics from the class of birds, and others from the class of domesticated animals (e.g. 'accustomed to home life and management', from *The Concise Oxford Dictionary*, 1990). The process for goods inward inspection and testing inherits the characteristics of both the class of inspection and testing processes, as well as that of receiving processes.

Classes and inheritance provide an elegant means for writing procedures very concisely. If several processes have common characteristics, we need describe them only once, as a general class. We can then speak of the individual processes as inheriting characteristics from the general process. From that point, our effort in describing the individual processes is adding the characteristics which distinguish them from the others. The result, from the viewpoint of the user of the procedure, is information which is presented simply and compactly, yet is also easily accessible.

Sequence (causality)

Neither hierarchies—which are composed of distinct units, where a higher level is exactly the sum of its parts—nor classes—which group units by their common characteristics, so the whole may be more than the sum of the parts because the units can inherit additional characteristics from parent classes—is suited to structuring things in terms of an order, where one comes before the other. The means of providing this type of structure is the sequence.

There are many everyday examples of sequences:

- Place—stops on a bus or train journey; locations by latitude and longitude; ordering of places by height above sea level.
- Time—diary entries for a date; events in soap operas (except for flashbacks!); order of meals: breakfast, then lunch, then dinner.
- Cause and effect—to get a new job, I must first apply for it, then fill out the application form and finally attend an interview; if a company never makes a profit, it will go out of business; to purchase goods or services, I must first complete a purchase order.

In terms of processes, sequences are easy to understand, as they consist of chains of activities, or sub-processes. We saw some examples of these chains earlier. Selecting a supplier consists of three processes in a sequence: (1) prepare list of candidate suppliers, (2) telephone candidate suppliers, (3) evaluate the candidates. In the personnel process, 'Appointing and managing staff' is composed of three sequential processes: (1) appoint officers, (2) compile performance reports, (3) appoint staff.

The other two types of structuring apply to information as well as to processes. However, this is not the case with sequences, which do not apply to information. This is part of the nature of sequences, where things are always structured by the nature of some activity. Even when it appears that information is sequenced, the underlying reality always reveals processes which are sequenced, forcing the same sequencing on the information. Thus, in archived information, the order of retaining copies is determined by the processes which created the information; the information created by an earlier process precedes that created by a later process. In an earlier example, stops on a train journey were sequenced; again, this is a characteristic of the process of making the journey. Even a sequence which appears to be non-process driven, such as alphabetizing information, ultimately reduces to a set of process-driven rules, such as:

- If the first letter is 'a', place the item in tray 1. Otherwise place it in tray 2.
- For each item in tray 2, move it to tray 3 unless the first letter is 'b'.
- For each item in tray 3, move it to tray 4 unless the first letter is 'c'.
- ... and so forth.

The order of utilizing these rules determines the sequence of the information affected. Even cause and effect relationships ultimately reduce to repeated observations of the effect appearing regularly, following the appearance of the cause. See Hume's *Treatise on Human Nature* (Hume, 1739) for a lucid explanation of this phenomenon.

Structure in organizations—summing up

The three types of structure—hierarchy, classification and sequence—provide all the tools needed to structure instructions. Further, they also provide a concise framework for providing the instructions. In providing documented instructions, we want to encourage flexibility and robustness, yet provide sufficient rigour to ensure their correct execution. We also want to encourage people to work in autonomous or semi-autonomous units, taking responsibility for decisions, yet working to a common set of procedures and rules.

Responsible autonomy is provided through hierarchy (encapsulation), where details of processes are not relevant except to those who carry them out. As long as required operations are within the scope of the encapsulated process, those responsible can carry out their tasks with no interference. However, when the scope *is* violated—say because of a situation which it was not designed to handle—then responsibility automatically passes to a higher-level. Figure A3.4 shows a QPL representation of the scope of an autonomous process.

Flexibility and *robustness* are provided by classification and inheritance, where the inherited process defines only those essential characteristics which ensure that all requirements are met.

Sequences provide for a clear and rigorous description of the flows of information and control through a process, providing further assurance that it is carried out as specified and required.

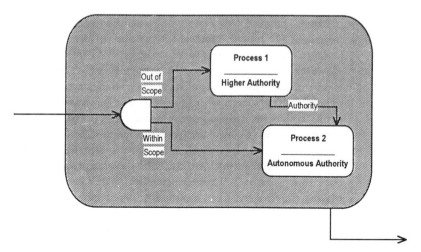

Figure A3.4 Example of autonomous authority in an encapsulated process

CARDINALITY

In drawing simple QPL diagrams, we can assume that each process or information item box on the diagram corresponds to exactly one actual item. This reflects an assumption made for simplicity: that exactly one process produces one information item, and one information item is used as input to one process. Thus, in Figure 3.3—Select a supplier—there is only a single list of candidate suppliers, which provides information into the process 'Telephone suppliers', which in turn produces a single product, the 'List of prices and conditions quoted'.

The restriction that each process or information box represents exactly one item limits our ability to represent processes realistically. In practice, the supplier selection process will produce several individual quotes, which may never be consolidated on to a single list. One way of handling this situation of multiple inputs and outputs is the 'split' symbol (see Chapter 2). This permits information items to be reproduced and used in several processes. However, representing each copy can get messy and hard to follow on a QPL diagram, if items are split several times during a process.

A better way to handle this situation is with the concept of cardinality (for further information see Lenzerini and Santucci, 1983; Coad and Yourdon, 1990; Booch, 1991). This provides a further means of stating a relationship between a process and an information item: in terms of the number of possible occurrences of that item. For example, there may be a zero- or one-to-one relationship: a conditional process produces a product. If the conditions are not met, then there is no occurrence of the process. One-to-many relationships are very common: in the case of purchasing, a single 'Issue a call for tenders' process may result in the issue of dozens of an information item, the 'Call for tenders'.

In QPL, processes are never connected directly to other processes, and information items cannot be connected directly to other information items. This takes the form of a string of alternating processes and information. Many cardinality relationships are possible between processes and information items: a single process may produce many copies of an information item, and many variants of the same information item may be processed by a single process. Conversely, a single information item may be processed by several variants of the same process (for example, a single request for quotation may be processed by several potential bidders). Interestingly, it is *not* possible for many processes to produce a single information item, as they need a mechanism for coordinating their individual products. This mechanism requires a new process, with separate input streams, but a single product as output. Table A3.1 gives a complete list of the cardinality relationships possible in QPL.

In QPL, the following symbols are used to represent cardinality:

[Blank]   Exactly one occurrence
Ø   Exactly zero or one occurrences
*   Zero or more occurrences
+   One or more occurrences

Table A3.1   Possible cardinality relationships in QPL

Processes	Information items		
	Zero or one	One	Many
Zero or one (P-to-I)	Yes (e.g. a conditional process produces a conditional output)	No (all information items must originate with a source)	No
Zero or one (I-to-P)	Yes (if the information item doesn't exist, the process will not be 'triggered')	Yes (an input to a process exists, but the process can be conditional on other inputs, which may not exist)	Yes (same as column 1)
One (P-to-I)	Yes	Yes	Yes (e.g. a process produces many copies of an output for distribution)
One (I-to-P)	Yes (e.g. a process will use an input if available, but executes even if not)	Yes	Yes (e.g. many inputs of the same type are handled by a single process)
Many (P-to-I)	Yes (e.g. conditional output)	No (to produce a single output, the separate processes would need an additional process for synchronization)	Yes (e.g. several identical processes produce several outputs of the same type)
Many (I-to-P)	Yes (multiple bidders may or may not get answers to their queries to an ITT)	Yes (e.g. a single ITT is processed by several bidders)	Yes (e.g. controlled copies of an ITT are processed by several bidders)

Key: Yes: relationship is possible; No: relationship is not possible; P: process; I: information

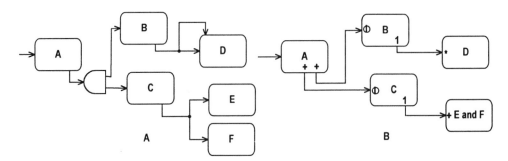

Figure A3.5 Use of cardinality in QPL

While QPL can always represent cardinality explicitly, it often is not necessary if we want only to represent the connections between processes and information. However, it is often preferable to use cardinality, for greater accuracy and more compact process descriptions. For example, it can often be used to replace splits, as well as cases or conditions, when the details are not important. Figure A3.5 shows the same process, A with splits, cases and conditions, and B with these replaced by cardinality. In the full QPL notation, cardinality is assigned to relationships between processes and information items, not between processes directly, as in this diagram. This diagram is only used to illustrate how cardinality can simplify process descriptions.

APPENDIX 4
Quality systems

This appendix provides guidance for those developing or maintaining conventional quality systems. Such systems utilize documentation—and record-based quality assurance and control, including the 'model' for the ISO 9000 series of quality standards (ISO 9001, 1994; ISO 9002, 1994; ISO 9003, 1994). These systems are complementary to more 'holistic' approaches, such as total quality management, just-in-time or business process re-engineering.

This appendix introduces the documentation which is part of or relevant to quality systems, such as standards, procedures and requirements. It describes some attributes of such documentation, the qualities which the QPL approach concentrates on, and it introduces some of the processes needed to produce and maintain quality system documentation. It also provides guidelines for modelling quality information and processes with QPL. Information includes quality system documentation, while processes concentrate on typical quality 'support' processes, such as configuration management and traceability. The appendix concludes with a QPL model of a quality feedback loop and a summary of how QPL models quality management elements.

TYPES OF QUALITY DOCUMENTATION

Standards and regulations

Standards and regulations provide either a regulatory framework or act as a voluntary code of practice by which manufacturers undertake to guarantee a specification or are enabled to interchange components. For example, communications standards—agreed worldwide by the telecommunications providers and manufacturers—provide a common framework and protocol for all electronic communication. Regulatory standards, such as for financial services, building and safety, set a requirement which must be met if suppliers are to trade and stay within the law. Figure 4.1 shows two examples of standards and regulations.

4.16 Control of quality records

The supplier shall establish and maintain documented procedures for identification, collection, indexing, access, filing, storage, maintenance and disposition of quality records.

Quality records shall be maintained to demonstrate conformance to specified requirements and the effective operation of the quality system. Pertinent quality records from the subcontractor shall be an element of these data.

All quality records shall be legible and shall be stored and retained in such a way that they are readily retrievable in facilities that provide a suitable environment to prevent damage or deterioration and to prevent loss. Retention times of quality records shall be established and recorded. Where agreed contractually, quality records shall be made available for evaluation by the customer or the customer's representative for an agreed period.

The International Quality Standard ISO 9001 (ISO 9001, 1994)

RECORD KEEPING

7.1.1 All members shall maintain such records as may be necessary to establish at any time that they have complied with the Rules relating to transactions with or on behalf of clients, including movements on or in client accounts and safe custody of clients' property. All members shall maintain such other records as may be necessary to demonstrate compliance with all other requirements of these Rules. Such records shall be maintained for at least seven years after the date on which the relevant transaction is effected or the relevant power or authority is terminated.

FIMBRA (Financial Intermediaries, Managers and Brokers Regulatory Association) Rules (FIMBRA, 1987)

Figure A4.1 Examples of standards and regulations

In the modern world, organizations are subject to hundreds of such regulations and standards. For a manufacturer within the European Union, this may involve compliance with Internationally Agreed Standards, EU directives, national laws and regulations and local ordinances!

Procedures and instructions

The organization's procedures and instructions ensure compliance with relevant standards and regulations. They are also a mechanism for implementing its individual objectives and policies. As a general rule, they should be written so that compliance is obvious or easy to check. Most importantly, they must be written so that staff can understand them easily, understand their individual responsibilities and know how to handle all situations that may arise. They must be practical and economical—too many such documents will easily bring an organization to its knees. To quote one quality manager: 'We have so many procedures, the system would come to a halt if staff actually followed them!'

More positively, procedures and instructions have a tremendous potential for improving the quality of organizations. They are the framework for their activities, and they provide the definitive reference for improving those activities. If they are ineffective, then they also provide a reference point by which quality improvement groups can analyse the deficiencies of the current system and propose specific improvements. Because they are written down, they provide the visibility and openness that are at the heart of a modern organization's working practices. Figure A4.2 shows an example of a procedure which complies with the ISO quality standard in Figure A4.1.

Contracts and requirements

At the next level, the organization agrees contracts and requirements with suppliers and customers. These are legally binding documents which regulate the specific product or service to be provided. Compliant with wider standards and regulations, as well as with the procedures of the supplier, they provide the detail of how quality is to be measured in fulfilling an order or providing a service.

The *contract* provides the specific legal framework for work to be undertaken. While contracts vary widely in different countries and for different industries, they tend to

---

The quality records shall provide the following information:

- Degree of achievement of the quality objectives.

- Level of customer satisfaction and dissatisfaction with the service.

- Results of the quality system for review and improvement of the service.

- Analysis to identify quality trends.

- Corrective action and its effectiveness.

- Appropriate sub-contractors' performance.

Figure A4.2 Example of a procedure which complies with ISO 9001 (4.16)

cover issues such as communication (such as meetings and faxes) between customer and supplier, acceptance procedures, payment terms and disputes procedures.

The *requirement* provides the technical specification for the product or service to be provided. It lists technical details which must be met for acceptance. It may also describe how acceptance tests are to be carried out. In unusual cases, it may also define some of the procedures for designing or building a product. A requirement may be quite short—perhaps only a few pages of texts, or a few drawings—or may extend over thousands of pages, as in the case of government procurement of computer systems.

Designs and (finished) product descriptions

The requirement statement is the external description of what is to be delivered; the designs and product description are the internal descriptions. They are used within the organization to document details of the product or service to be supplied, and the processes used to produce it.

A typical production process is shown in the flow chart in Figure A4.3. After interpreting the requirement, the company designs a product to meet the requirement, as well as the manufacturing processes it will need. Those designs are recorded as documents which will form an essential part of the quality documentation set for that product. Later, after the product is produced, further documents describe it and its characteristics. Some of this description may be developed after tests or trials of the product are conducted. Finally, this description is compared with the original designs to determine the quality of the results. If they do not agree, there is a problem with product quality, which can be resolved only by altering the product to match the design, or by altering the design itself.

Data and reports

Collection of data, and reports which summarize them, are an essential part of quality improvement. To quote the Guidelines for the Malcolm Baldrige Quality Award:

> Meeting quality improvement goals of the company requires that actions in setting, controlling, and changing systems and processes be based upon reliable information, data, and analysis. Facts and data needed for quality assessment and quality improvement are of many types, including: customer, product and service performance, operations, market, competitive comparisons, supplier, and employee-related. (Baldrige, 1991)

A good quality system will incorporate data collection mechanisms, as well as the means for organizing, storing and analysing this information. It will also provide a mechanism for using the results of the analysis to improve its processes, resulting in improved quality.

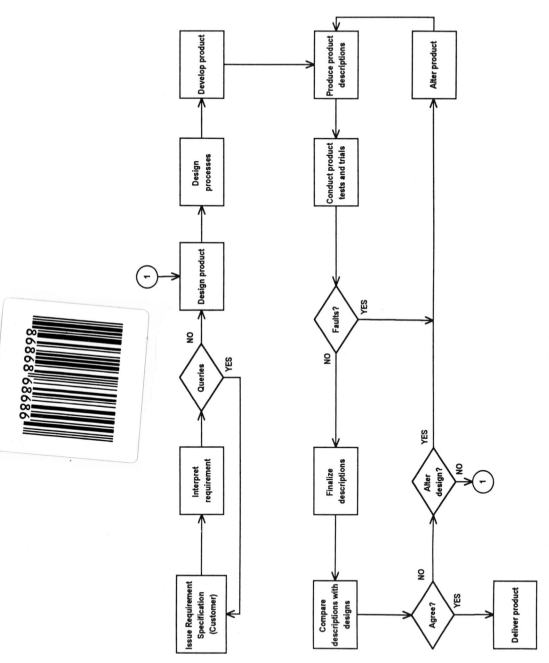

Figure A4.3 Flow chart of a typical production and checking process

ATTRIBUTES OF QUALITY DOCUMENTATION

What characteristics are possessed by good documentation for quality? The answers will have an effect far beyond the documents themselves, as the quality of these documents affects not only the quality system but all activities within the organization. Paying attention to the five attributes discussed below contributes to a management system which delivers the results, respects its staff and allows for continuous improvement in all its activities and products.

Clarity and comprehension—suitable for the reader

Organizational documentation is designed for one principal audience: the staff who must administer and carry out the procedures and instructions which they document. This goal can be achieved only if the documentation is written with the active reader in mind. Such documentation always has one essential characteristic: it provides information *to be used*. That is, staff read the documentation not for enjoyment and not for mere learning: they read it only to be able to carry out the instructions that they contain, or to check that someone else is carrying them out correctly.

This obliges the designers and writers of such documentation to consider carefully the needs and behaviour of the audience. Do they have the background information to be able to absorb this information at this point in the procedure? Will they retain sufficient interest at this point to keep up the required concentration? Is there super-fluous information—more information than is just required for them to carry out their jobs effectively? Can information in the procedure be found and extracted quickly, and is it unambiguous in its interpretation?

Correctness

Is the information accurate and consistent? Is it suitable to the problem dealt with in the document?

Quality documentation—particularly procedures and work instructions—will be used as the basis for all other activities and documentation within the organization. The quality of that organization depends on them. If those basic documents are themselves inaccurate, so that they produce mistakes or are not trusted by staff, then the basis of quality crumbles.

Checking the correctness of procedures is a fundamental task for quality management—Chapter 5 provides a framework for this.

Structure of the documentation set

Large organizations may have hundreds, even thousands of procedures. Understanding them, and being able to obtain information readily, can be a huge problem. For example, suppose a manager needs to order an item of equipment needed to fill an order. The required procedures could easily extend over many volumes—for example, the manuals for purchasing, contracts (since a contract may have to be let), accounting (since the manager's budget will be debited to purchase the equipment), invoicing (if the customer can be charged directly for the cost of the equipment), transport, goods inward, and so on.

Structure—hierarchy, classification and sequence—is the essential means for making documentation accessible. Chapters 3 and 4 and Appendix 3 provide guidelines for structuring processes and documentation.

Compliance with standards and regulations

The quality system for an organization must be compliant with the external standards and regulations applicable to its business. The quality documentation ensures that this is the case and that it can be demonstrated in case of a query. The latter issue is of increasing importance, as product liability and customer rights assume a greater importance. The consumer has the right to know if a product or service meets the regulatory criteria expected of it. In case of fault, the supplier must be able to demonstrate that the best available practice was followed, and that applicable regulations were complied with. Again, the organization's procedures can do this by demonstrating that they do in fact meet these requirements. If they do not, the organization will have little defence either professionally, or before the law.

Suitability for audit

Accountability is one of the principles on which modern quality systems are built. This enables responsibilities to be undertaken on a basis of trust, with the knowledge that those responsible are accountable to their 'customers' for the decisions they take and actions which result. If quality documentation is visible and straightforward to use, then the great tool for accountability, the audit, becomes available.

In the financial audit a trained accountant examines and reviews the accounts of a company and determines if they are in order. A management or quality audit follows similar principles, but is based on processes and documentation rather than finance. The key questions for such an audit are: 'Do the procedures of the organization comply with standards and regulations? Are they observed within the organization? Have they helped to achieve its desired objectives?'

The starting point for such an audit is the quality documentation set, and it needs to provide the basis for audit. It can do so only if the documentation has the attributes noted above. In addition, the objectives of each procedure must be stated clearly, so that the audit can determine if they are being achieved. Is the purchasing procedure used to procure items quickly, or cost-effectively, or both? What if these objectives conflict? How much paperwork does the procedure require, and is that paperwork actually produced (and filed) in practice? When the procedure is applied are staff utilized in a way that challenges them and keeps them occupied? Do any activities required by the procedure conflict with those required by other procedures?

EFFECTIVE QUALITY DOCUMENTATION

The previous sections describe the documents in a quality system and their attributes. They treat the documents and records involved as static and unchanging. However, in reality they are created by people, used by people (and machines), updated when required and, when they are no longer needed, disposed of. In other words, document-ation is constantly changing, and may be said to go through a life cycle. In certain disciplines, notably systems and software engineering, the concept of a life cycle is well established and is used for the basis for all activities and documentation. The term refers to a clearly defined set of activities and deliverables in a project, starting from the earliest formulation of the requirement to delivery and maintenance of the completed system.

What are the activities which contribute to and make use of quality documentation?

Developing the quality system

As a starting point for a quality system, we must look at the needs of the organization concerned, as well as its staff and customers. Two good starting points are the mission and the philosophy statements. The mission statement is a concise statement of the objectives of the organization: what it produces or the services it provides. It is the *what* of the organization. The philosophy statement is an equally concise statement of the means and methods it will use to achieve those objectives. It is the *how* of the organization, at the highest level. See Figure A4.4 for examples of philosophy statements.

The next step is to review the applicable laws, regulations, codes of practice, and standards which apply to the organization. As we have seen, the procedures to be written must reflect these implicitly by complying with them.

These activities are the foundations for the detailed steps in developing the quality system, namely:

- Determine or describe the organizational structure, and the roles which have responsibilities within the organization

> *Basic business principles*
> To recognize our responsibilities as industrialists, to foster progress, to promote the general welfare of society, and to devote ourselves to the further development of world culture.
> *Employees' creed*
> Progress and development can be realized only through the combined efforts and cooperation of each member of our Company. Each of us, therefore, shall keep this idea constantly in mind as we devote ourselves to the continuous improvement of our Company.

Figure A4.4 Examples of philosophy statements from the Matsushita Electric Company (Pascale and Athos, 1986: 51)

● Determine and describe the activities carried out and the documentation required to describe them.

These two steps are interactive, as the structure and roles depend on the activities and documentation and vice versa. In practice, these two steps are done together; if they are done separately, they will take some time to converge into a coherent quality system.

Documenting the system

When the quality system is partially or fully developed, it needs to be documented. The number of documents—procedures, work instructions, codes of practice, etc.— varies enormously, depending upon the size, complexity and quality requirements of the organization. At the very least, it will have a single quality manual, describing all processes and documentation which may affect quality. For a moderately complex organization, the number increases, from a few dozen to one or two hundred. For the largest organizations—for example, those meeting government procurement conditions, those subject to significant regulatory authority (telecommunications services, oil companies, etc.) or with a wide variety of products and services—the number of such documents will run into the thousands.

Keeping records

If the quality system is well designed, data will be collected 'automatically'; the system will include processes for collecting, storing and updating such data, as well as the repositories for the data. Such data will include that essential for the organization— financial accounts, staff records, purchase records, etc.—but also quality data. These include records of production processes, reject rates and variations in tolerances. After products and services are delivered to customers, the quality data continues to flow, through records of customer complaints, reliability, order repetition rates etc.

Traceability enables us to link these records and to use them effectively. It is an important contributor to quality, but it is also relevant to non-quality issues. For example, if we can collect cost data for each process contributing to production of an item, then we are in the position to introduce new processes, which can maintain or improve quality yet reduce the cost.

Improving the system and keeping it up to date

One of the basic principles of good quality management is that of continuous improvement: that we must continually monitor performance to improve quality. This occurs at various levels and frequencies. At a local and frequent level, many Japanese companies have daily meetings of work groups. They review the previous day's problems and take actions to resolve them immediately. At a less frequent level, quality records and metrics must be examined regularly for opportunities to improve processes and communication between parts of the organization.

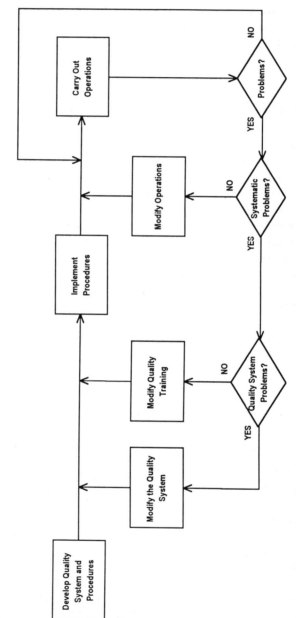

Figure A4.5 Feedback loop for quality improvement—based on the Rooney Loop (Rooney, 1990)

Less frequently still, the wider quality system needs to be examined. Management need to examine the effectiveness of procedures and determine areas for improvement. It may be a problem of training—in which case some of the measures noted above can be used. But it will often require a revision of the procedures themselves. In either case, constant feedback through quality data is required to determine the effectiveness of any changes introduced. Figure A4.5 provides an example of a feedback loop based on these principles of continuous improvement of the quality system.

MODELLING INFORMATION FOR QUALITY MANAGEMENT

Standards and regulations

Standards and regulations are produced by government or transnational bodies and provide a normative framework to which individual organizations' systems must comply. In QPL they are modelled as template or generic processes. Organizations comply with standards and regulations, and in QPL this is modelled by connecting the templates to the relevant sub-processes in the organization, by means of authority relationships. Chapter 6 provides further detail and some examples of connecting such templates to organizational processes.

Note that standards and regulations normally are outside the scope of an organization's own processes, since they cannot change them directly. In terms of encapsulation, this means that the organization's own processes, and their definitions, are within its scope. For example, the creation and update of a procedure is also within that scope. Since standards and regulations are outside the scope, they must be modelled externally to the organization's processes.

Procedures and work instructions

These documents are created by the organization itself and thus they occupy two positions in QPL. On the one hand, as documents, they are *information items*. They are created by processes (such as writing a procedure), and need to be retained, normally as an information store. On the other hand, they also act as *authorities* for the operational processes of the organization. In describing quality systems, this is made explicit by drawing information lines directly from the processes which create and change procedures and work instructions, to the authorities of processes which utilize these documents.

For clarity, it is usually preferable to place the process which creates an authority at a higher level in the hierarchy than that which uses it to control an operational process. This does not imply that authority authorship is more important or critical to the organization than any other process. However, it does reflect the centrality of such processes and the fact that the relationship between authority-creation processes, and operational processes is not two way: the authority directs the operational process, but the operational process does not direct the production of the authority. While there will be feedback into the latter process, it is indirect.

Physical objects and materials

As noted in Chapter 2, QPL does not treat physical objects and materials directly. It models information about these objects. ISO 9001, an International Quality Standard, provides some examples of this approach:

> 4.6.3 Purchasing Data
> Purchasing documents shall contain data clearly describing the product ordered, including, where applicable:
>   a) the type, class, grade or other precise identification
> . . .
> 4.12 Inspection and Test Status
> The inspection and test status of product shall be identified by suitable means, which indicate the conformance or nonconformance of product with regard to inspection and tests performed.

In all cases of quality management, it is sufficient to model information and attributes of physical objects and materials, rather than these items directly.

Documentation

The range of quality system documentation was described earlier in this appendix. Such documentation includes narrative documents, such as reports, letters, memos, designs, manuals and business plans. Records are the other type of documentation in a quality system, and include financial accounts, production records, customer records and quality data.

Since documentation is almost always stored over a period of time, it rarely is classified as a channel, where retention is not relevant. The decision on whether to classify it as an information store or as an archive will depend on the use made of it. For narrative documentation, usually only the latest version is relevant, and then it is classified as an information store. For records, it is usually necessary to store more than the latest version, and thus an archive is the appropriate classification.

For the most part, documentation serves as input and output only. However, it can also act as the other elements of QPL. For example, a business plan when implemented will certainly serve as an authority for many business activities. The business plan may also specify the owners of these activities and their corresponding processes. Records can often provide control information, such as when a customer's record causes a process to be activated (e.g. after a fixed number of routine complaints by a customer, the account manager is required to contact the complainant to determine if the complaints are being dealt with satisfactorily).

MODELLING PROCESSES FOR QUALITY MANAGEMENT

Configuration management and integrity checks

Configuration management consists of dividing a system into its significant parts, called configuration items, and then identifying those items, controlling the release and change of those items and recording and reporting the *status* of those items. It sometimes also includes responsibility for verifying the *integrity*—correctness or suitability—of configuration items.

Configuration management is an important support process for product and service design. Since design is not a straightforward activity—involving cooperation between many parties, and involving many cycles of design and evaluation—various versions of designs will be issued before one is agreed. Configuration management is required to keep track of these versions. Similarly, if the organization produces modifications of a basic design to customize a product, then it requires configuration management to determine which version of the design corresponds to the customized product.

In general, QPL identifies configuration items by noting the scope of processes: for a non-trivial process, the inputs and outputs constitute configuration items. In general, more than one version of a configuration item must be retained, implying that the archive is the most appropriate form of information storage. Support processes are used to control release and change of configuration items, along with recording and reporting on their status.

In QPL, integrity issues are handled by inserting processes where required. For example, a process can verify that an item satisfies specified criteria before it is shipped—an example of final quality control. Special processes may also be inserted to comply with specific requirements, for example, to ensure that the storage environment of goods is within their environmental tolerance limits.

Traceability

Traceability is 'the ability to trace the history, application or location of an item or activity . . . by means of recorded identification' (ISO 8402, 1986). This concept is used extensively in quality systems to ensure that responsibility for decisions can always be traced back to a person, system or document. It is also used to trace the design history of an item, to identify a particular version of a design that produced a particular result.

Suppose that a customer regularly obtains shipments from a supplier, and that a particular shipment is found to have faulty items. Naturally, the customer will want this problem corrected, but it is also in the supplier's interest to determine where the problem occurred, so that any faulty design or processes can be corrected.

If the documentation system is fully traceable, then it will enable the supplier to trace all processes which contributed to that particular batch. If a design activity was also involved, it will also enable it to pinpoint which designs and decisions led to the faulty product. This information can then be used for analysis, to ensure that the design is corrected or any faulty processes improved.

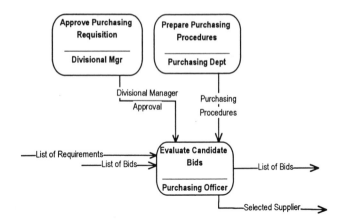

Figure A4.6 Use of the authority link in QPL to connect standards with processes

In QPL, traceability is embodied in the *archive* information type. When an information item is designated as an archive, by implication this item is fully traceable by any process which uses it as input. Thus, the process has access to the history of the information, including all previous versions which are still relevant.

Note that the actual implementation of traceability is a complex issue which is dealt with in designing the details of the processes which implement traceability. For example, processes are required to delete obsolete versions, and this will involve a detailed knowledge of the retention times of such versions.

Development of standards and procedures

The processes of a quality system are recorded in its printed documentation, which act as authorities for the processes within the scope of the quality system. In QPL, this is illustrated by an information line which links the output of standards development with the process which will use that output as its authority (Figure A4.6).

DIAGRAMMING A QUALITY SYSTEM

Figure A4.5 provides a flow chart of a quality system in the form of a quality improvement process. This can be expanded into a QPL diagram, as shown in Figure A4.7.

As expected, the QPL representation has more information. The actions of the flow chart have a direct equivalent in one of the QPL processes. The decision points in the flow chart are represented by the two effectiveness evaluation processes and by the case statement which sorts out recommendations from one of these processes. The authorities of ISO 9000 and the quality system standards and procedures are explicit, as are the connection with sub-processes. Finally, information items—including the standards and procedures, feedback information, and recommendations—are shown explicitly and also recorded for future use.

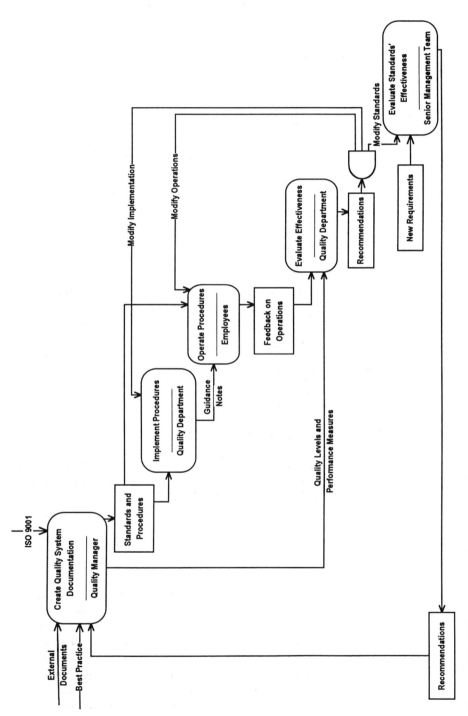

Figure A4.7 QPL representation of a quality improvement process

SUMMARY OF QUALITY MANAGEMENT ELEMENTS IN QPL

Table A4.1 shows the correspondence between QPL elements and common entities in quality systems and management.

Table A4.1 Quality management elements in QPL

Process	Developing quality standards and procedures
	Reviews
	Audits
	Configuration management
Information	Trend data
	Statistical reports
	Audit reports
	Quality feedback
	Quality documentation and records
	Memoranda
	Letters
	Telephone conversations
Process owners	Managers
	Administrators
	Suppliers
	Customers
	Quality management staff
Authorities	Standards
	Procedures
	Work instructions
	Professionals and other experts
Control	Time
	Location
	Numbers of instances
	Thresholds
	Other conditions

References

Adler, Paul S. (1993) Time-and-motion regained. *Harvard Business Review*, January–February.

Baldrige (1994) *Malcolm Baldrige National Quality Award: 1994 Application Guidelines*. US Department of Commerce/National Institute of Standards and Technology.

Bateson, Gregory (1972) *Steps to an Ecology of Mind*. Ballantine Books, New York.

Booch, Grady (1991) *Object-oriented Design with Applications*. Benjamin/Cummings Publishing Company, Redwood City, CA.

Born, Gary (1985) Getting quality into your plans: how the expert systems approach can help. *National Computing Centre DP Circle Annual Meeting*, Birmingham, UK.

Born, Gary (1990) KADS: a methodology for developing large AI systems. *IEEE International Conference on Computer Systems and Software Engineering*, Tel Aviv.

Born, Gary (1992) An expert support system for software quality management. *Proceedings of the 3rd European Conference on Software Quality*, Madrid.

BS 7229 (1989) *British Standard Guide to Quality Systems Auditing*. British Standards Institution, London.

BSI (1990) *Quality Systems, Part 4: Guide to the Use of BS 5750 (ISO 9001, ISO 9002 and ISO 9003)*. BSI Standards, Milton Keynes, UK.

Checkland, P.B. (1981) *Systems Thinking, Systems Practice*. Wiley, Chichester.

Coad, Peter and Yourdon, Edward (1990) *Object-oriented Analysis*. Yourdon Press/Prentice Hall, Englewood Cliffs, N.J.

Crosby, Philip B. (1979) *Quality Is Free*. McGraw-Hill, New York.

Csikszentmihalyi, Mihaly (1990) *Flow: The Psychology of Optimal Experience*. Harper Perennial, New York.

Deming, W. Edwards (1982) *Out of the Crisis*. Cambridge University Press, Cambridge.

Dyer, Connie (1990) On-line quality: Shigeo Shingo's shop floor. *Harvard Business Review*, January–February, p. 73.

EFQM (European Foundation for Quality Management) (1993) *Total Quality Management: The European Model for Self-appraisal—Guidelines for Identifying and Addressing Total Quality Issues*, Brussels.

FDA (1989) *Current Good Manufacturing Practice for Finished Pharmaceuticals* (Part 211), 21 CFR Ch. 1 (4-1-89 Edition). US Food and Drug Administration, Washington.

FIMBRA (Financial Intermediaries, Managers and Brokers Regulatory Association (UK)) (1987) *Rules*. FIMBRA, London.

Financial Times (1991) Big Brother looms into view. 14 May, London.

Flanagan, J.C. (1954) The critical incident technique. *Psychological Bulletin*, 51, pp. 327–58.

Garvin, David A. (1988) *Managing Quality: The Strategic and Competitive Edge*. The Free Press, New York.

Handy, Charles (1989) *The Age of Unreason*. Arrow Books, London.

Harvey-Jones, John (1989) *Making It Happen*. Fontana, London.

Hume, David (1739) *A Treatise of Human Nature* (reprinted in L.A. Selby-Bigge (ed.) (1988) *Hume's Treatise of Human Nature*, Oxford University Press, London).

Ishiwata, Junichi (1991) *IE for the Shop Floor: Productivity Through Process Analysis*. Productivity Press, Cambridge Massachusetts.

ISO 8402 (1986) *ISO 8402: Quality—Vocabulary*. International Organization for Standardization, Geneva.

ISO 9001 (1987) *Quality systems—Model for quality assurance in design, development, production, installation and servicing*, International Organization for Standardization (ISO), Geneva.

ISO 9001 (1994) *Quality systems—Model for quality assurance in design, development, production, installation and servicing*, International Organization for Standardization (ISO), Geneva.

ISO 9002 (1994) *Quality systems—Model for quality assurance in production, installation and servicing*, International Organization for Standardization (ISO), Geneva.

ISO 9003 (1994) *Quality systems—Model for quality assurance in final inspection and test*, International Organization for Standardization (ISO), Geneva.

ISO 9004-2 (1987) *Quality Management and Quality System Elements—Guidelines*. International Organization for Standardization, Geneva.

Kelly G.A. (1955) *The Psychology of Personal Constructs*. Norton, New York.

Lenzerini, M. and Santucci, G. (1983) Cardinality constraints in the entity-relationship model, in *Entity-Relationship Approach to Software Engineering*, ed. C. Davis et al. Elsevier Science.

Machiavelli, Niccolo (1975) *The Prince*. Penguin, Harmondsworth.

Marsh, J. (1988) *Quality Improvement Methods Analysis*. ICL Internal Publication.

Minto, Barbara (1991) *The Pyramid Principle: Logic in Writing and Thinking*. Pitman, London.

Oakland, John S. (1989) *Total Quality Management*. Butterworth Heinemann, Oxford.

Pascale, Richard Tanner and Athos, Anthony G. (1986) *The Art of Japanese Management*. Penguin Books, Harmondsworth.

Price, Frank (1992) The partly failed promises of total quality. *Business Age*, June.

Rooney, M. (1990), Quality management systems for the service sector—meeting the challenge. *Proceedings of the 34th Annual EOQ Conference*, Dublin, pp. 592–604.

Ross, D.T. (1977) Structured analysis (SA): a language for communicating ideas. *IEEE Transactions on Software Engineering*, SE-3(1), 16–34.

Ross, D.T. et al (1979) *Architect's Manual—ICAM Definition Method 'IDEF0'*. Softech Inc. for ICAM Program Office, Wright-Patterson Air Force Base, Ohio.

Scherkenbach, William W. (1986) *The Deming Route to Quality and Productivity*. George Washington University, CEE Press Books, Washington.

Schlaer, Sally and Mellor, Stephen, J. (1988) *Object-oriented Systems Analysis: Modelling the World in Data*. Prentice-Hall, Englewood Cliffs, NJ.

Schumacher, E.F. (1973) *Small is Beautiful*. Abacus Press.

SD-Scicon (1989) *CORE—The Method*. SD-Scicon UK Ltd, Camberley, England.

Sidney E. and Brown M. (1961) *The Skills of Interviewing*. Tavistock Publications, London.

Tebeaux, Elizabeth (1990) *Design of Business Communications*. Macmillan, New York.

TickIT (1992) *The TickIT Guide [Guide to Software QMS Construction using ISO 9001/EN29001/BS5750 Part 1 (1987)]*, Issue 2.0. UK Dept of Trade and Industry, London.

von Hoffman, Nicolas (1991) The rake's progress. *The Independent Magazine* (United Kingdom), No 171, 14 December.

Winograd, Terry and Flores, Fernando (1987) *Understanding Computers and Cognition*. Addison-Wesley, Reading, MA.

Womack, James, P., Jones, Daniel T. and Roos, Daniel (1990) *The Machine that Changed the World*. Rawson Associates, New York.

Wood-Harper A.T., Antill L. and Avison D.E. (1985) *Information Systems Definition: The Multiview Approach*. Blackwell Scientific Publications, Oxford.

Zimmerman Carolyn M. and Campbell John J. (1988) *Fundamentals of Procedure Writing*, 2nd edn. Kogan Page, London.

Glossary

Abstraction   The principle of ignoring those aspects of a subject (process) that are not relevant to the current purpose in order to concentrate more fully on those that are.

Archive   Information which is retained and where previous versions are also needed.

Authority   The description, specification or justification of a process.

Baseline model   A stage in going from the foundation model to the target model, where achievement of this stage is capable of measurement.

Business process re-engineering   The provision of techniques for redesigning the processes needed for change (limited by some to *radical* change).

Cardinality   An attribute of the relationship between a process and an information item, which states how many occurrences of each may exist together.

Case   A QPL element used to categorize an information item into one of two or more types.

Changed output   Output from a process that is created or has been transformed by that process.

Channel   Temporary information (or material) needed only for a limited amount of time and not retained.

Class   A set of objects (processes or information items) which share essential attributes, which distinguish them from other objects.

Complexity index   In QPL, a measurement of the degree to which a process is underspecified or overspecified.

Compliance   The development and checking of a process to ensure that it does not contradict a standard or set of regulations.

Compliance audit   A specific type of review which identifies areas where an organization's processes fail to meet the requirements of a given regulation or other requirement.

Compliance, external   Compliance with a law, regulation or other requirement external to the organization.

Compliance, internal   Compliance with a policy, procedure or other requirement internal to the organization.

Compliance violation   An inconsistency or contradiction between an organization's processes and those to which it must comply, as revealed by a compliance audit or other check.

Configurable   A feature of QPL which enables templates to be connected into operational processes for compliance checking. We say that the template's processes are *configured* when they are all connected to the processes of an organization.

Conformance   The development and checking of products and other concrete objects produced by a process, to ensure that they do not violate a standard or other definition of the product.

Control   The conditions or constraints for activating a process.

Cycle time   The time which a process consumes or requires to convert an item or unit of input into output.

Destination   The person, organization or object which uses the output from a process but which is external to its scope.

Dynamic process analysis   The part of process analysis which deals with changes over time. Examples include changes to inputs and outputs, cycle time for a process, incorporating internal changes into a process and dealing with external changes which affect a process and an organization.

Encapsulation   The process of hiding all the details of a process that do not contribute to its essential characteristics (see *hierarchy*).

Failure mode process analysis   A type of static process analysis, where the process may be correct logically but could be applied incorrectly, resulting in the wrong results or other problems. The name is derived from failure mode and effects analysis (FMEA).

Foundation model   A model of the existing practices and procedures followed by an organization (sometimes called the AS-IS model).

Hierarchy   Division of a whole (process) into its parts, so that the parts are mutually exclusive and, collectively, equate to the whole.

Information (information item)   A description of things in the real world, including printed descriptions and verbal communications.

Information store   Information which is retained, but where only the current version is needed.

Inheritance   Properties or characteristics which one or more processes may receive from a common process definition.

Input   An information item at the point of entry to a process.

Lead time   The time between receipt of an order and the start of the process which fulfils it.

Logical process analysis   A type of static process analysis, where the structure of the process and the flow of information are checked for internal consistency.

Operational process   A process, as documented by a procedure, work instruction or other document, which can be checked for compliance against a template.

Output   An information item at the point of exit from a process.

Persistence   The attribute of information that regulates how long it needs to exist for the processes that require it.

Process   A sequence of steps which transforms information from an initial state (input) to a final state (output).

Process diagram   A representation of processes in terms of process steps and the information or control links between them.

Process owner   The person or other agent responsible for execution of a process.

Process step   A discrete step or series of steps in a process description. In QPL, used interchangeably with *process*.

QPL   Quality Process Language.

Scope   The description of the limit of use of a process: the circumstances under which it is appropriate, and what it requires to carry out its actions.

Sequence   A step-by-step description of a process.

Source   The person, organization or object which provides input to a process but which is external to its scope.

Split   A QPL element used to divide or rejoin paths of information.

Static process analysis   The part of process analysis which deals with aspects which do not change over time.

Target model   A model of an organization's goals for its processes at an identifiable horizon (sometimes called the TO-BE model).

Technical process analysis   A type of process analysis which relies on expert judgement to determine whether the process is correctly described or specified.

Template   The process model of the regulation, standard or other document which must be complied with.

Transition model   A process model for changing an organization's processes from one baseline model to another.

Unchanged output   Output from a process that is identical to an input to that process.

Index